THE AFFECTIONATE EYE

The Affectionate Eye

THE LIFE OF CLAUDE ROGERS

Jenny Pery

Sansom & Company

First published in 1995
by Sansom & Company
an imprint of Redcliffe Press Ltd,
22, Canynge Square, Bristol

ISBN 1 872971 37 7

British Library Cataloguing in Publication Data
A catalogue record for this book is available from
the British Library.

Typeset and printed in Great Britain by
The Longdunn Press, Bristol

CONTENTS

ACKNOWLEDGEMENTS

I should like to thank the people in the following list for their invaluable help in various ways: for spending precious, often hilarious, hours talking to me about Claude Rogers; for providing and checking verbal or written information; for lending, selecting or chasing up illustrations; for reading the manuscript and making useful suggestions; and for general advice, encouragement and support. The list is headed *in absentio* and *ex officio* by Claude Rogers himself, who has been such good company over the past two years, making me think about the nature and purpose of art and making me laugh (not least at his spelling, which I have corrected as it tends to divert attention from his argument). I have derived great benefit from my vicarious acquaintance with an exceptionally generous-hearted and endearing man; and from meeting many of his relatives and friends, in whom those human qualities he valued also abundantly reside. His son Crispin's patient and generous help has been critical to the production of the book. My grateful thanks go, alphabetically, to: Dr Igor Anrep, Mrs Igor Anrep, Mrs Angela Armour-Chelu, John Bangs, Tom Barratt, Professor Quentin Bell, Mrs Quentin Bell, Mrs Beryl Benjamin, Harry Blacker, Mrs Humphrey Brooke, B.A.R. (Sam) Carter, Stephen Chaplin, Sir Jonathan Clarke, Roger Cook, Tom Cross, Christopher Dean, Rita Donagh, Lady Dugdale, Valentine Ellis, Anthony Eyton, Margerie Evans, Carol Fitzgerald, Stanislav Frenkiel, Dr Anna Frenkiel, Dulcie Foo Fat, Terry Frost, Jonathan Fry, Patrick George, Kenneth Gribble, Earl Haig, Marilyn Hallam, Francis Hewlett, Bob High, Martin Higgins, Francis Hoyland, Thelma Hulbert, Mrs Susan Jacobsen, Ian Tregarthen Jenkin, John Jones, Morris Kestelman, Christopher Lane, Professor Bruce Laughton, Suzanne Monelle, Robert Organ, Val Organ, Victor Pasmore, Rosemary Pearce, Christopher Pemberton, Mark Peppe, Lady Proctor, Alan Plummer, Nancy Raphael, Oliver Reynolds, Dr Keith Rogers, Crispin Rogers, Kirsten Rogers, Timothy Rogers, Mark Rogers, David Rogers, Dick Rubinstein, Esther Salaman, Terence Scales, Nancy Sharp, Mary Shields, Philip Sutton, George Sweet, Patrick Symons, Euan Uglow, Paul Vaughan, Julia Weiner, Quentin Williams, John Wonnacott. Without their help this record of the life and work of this hitherto neglected realist painter would never have been written.

Quite an able boy

Round eyes, round glasses, round face, in later life made rounder by an encircling beard; broad shoulders, short sturdy legs, a thickset body encased in hairy tweed, a pungent smell of tobacco – these were the first impressions of the painter Claude Rogers. Further acquaintance revealed a high, drawling voice with 'r's pronounced as 'w's, an earthy and infectious sense of humour, and a warm, approachable and generous personality. He was interested in people and took trouble over them, eventually acquiring an enormous circle of friends and acquaintances. Others have been as widely known, but there can scarcely be another painter of his generation so universally liked.

Claude Rogers was by nature a conciliator, and his art also contains conciliations – of tradition with modernity, of fact with feeling. It is difficult to describe the particular quality of his work. His art is often defined in terms of other people or groups of people – William Coldstream, Victor Pasmore, Camden Town, Euston Road – implying that he was in some way a shadow of other men and movements. Nothing could give a more false impression. Claude Rogers' painting was as solid, positive and identifiable as his own rotund and ebullient person. His training as a painter was a traditional one, but, while never afraid of painting in a traditional manner, he made his own personal experiments in paint and developed a clear identity of his own. His work was never revolutionary, but in its own terms always good. He painted what he saw and experienced, what intrigued and moved him, making his art out of his own life. And he had little doubt that his life was meant for making paintings – painting was as necessary to him as eating or making love. It provided a way of deriving satisfaction from his experiences and of passing on his conclusions, of making what was necessarily transient into something solid and permanent.

It is difficult to theorise about a painter who was self-confessedly anti-theory. Claude Rogers remained all his life suspicious of dogma in art, fearing that too much intellectualisation might blunt his responses, or that he might be hung on the hook of his own theories, which would force his work into rigid formulae. He stuck stubbornly to what he knew and fully understood, and all his comments on his own work and his way of working are straightforward and pragmatic. He has left a remarkably clear and unaffected record of his thoughts. "I like painting very much, that is to say the whole business – the smells, the feel of the brush on canvas and so on. I like painting from things if possible. When I'm working I'm trying to make the painting like and equal to the reality of the thing I'm looking at. If I find myself thinking about the canvas as a picture I now know it is going wrong, and I've noticed that paintings go hopelessly wrong on the rare occasions, probably due to high spirits, when I have thought I could do it. As long as I'm thinking about the thing I am trying to paint, the painting seems to go along alright. Of course, sometimes the result is OK and sometimes it isn't. I have no conscious vocabulary of form or theories of picture-making but I like to try and make all the shapes on the canvas work and fit together like a jigsaw puzzle . . . Most of my pictures are painted directly from nature, and usually from familiar scenes. I don't need something new to excite me . . . I like painting ordinary things such as landscapes, people (portrait and figure subjects), still life and so on, although there is no significant order in this list. In a sense, the factor common to these subjects is that they concern people and people are concerned with them. I prefer arable to wild country . . . I like the effect the farmer has on it without aesthetic intent. I choose for still life things I use and see every day. The arrangement I prefer is casual, the result of chance or use rather than contrivance. People – well, on the whole and by and large I like people. They are interesting and odd so I like to paint them and some of the things they do."[1]

Claude Rogers worked in a determinedly prose style. He distrusted the poetic approach to painting as much as he distrusted the idea of putting 'feeling' into painting. His view was that intense observation and accuracy of depiction would deliver the truth of the matter – if there were feelings to be felt the sensitive onlooker would experience them; any sensationalism or 'cooking-up' of feeling he saw as fake, hypocritical, and working against the purposes of art. He dealt in facts, and the belief that facts are the proper stuff of feeling. He was as suspicious of charm as he was bored by meretricious dullness. Caught between these extremes, and unable or unwilling to label his own sort of painting, his work was, and still is, often overlooked. He belonged to no particular faction: he did what he did, et voilà. He believed that artistic integrity developed gradually through exercise when, before pictures by mature artists, each artist had to decide what is essential and what superficial. He also felt that each artist's 'love interests' made certain things of peculiar value to him or her and influenced the choice of subjects. Claude tried to translate his own experiences and interests into paint, and he struggled for depth of perception.

"My perception of the real and active world which is my environment and contains and holds my interest is incomplete. I only understand and perceive it within the limits of my human faculties. I accept these limits as the boundaries of the kind of painting I want to do, since they can, in my opinion, marry the activity which is my principal interest and preoccupation with my life . . . both with the reality of the canvas as an object and the reality of artistic experience. I have no idea what 'beauty' is or if it is possible to set out to paint 'beauty' or a 'beautiful' object. I get curious or interested about something. Sometimes very faintly but the experience grows as I go on . . . If it happens that the result has something of this quality in it that is a by-product."[2] Claude felt that the job of the modern artist was to pass on a truthful record of his experience, and that these experiences, made visible in paint and filtered through a personality, were in themselves acts of faith. He agreed with Herbert Read that art "is the capacity to allow the personality to express itself in the craftsmanship; some mysterious equivalence between thought and action. The act of putting pencil to paper, brush to canvas, becomes an act of what Croce has called lyrical intuition, and in that act, in the instant, the personality and indeed, the spirituality of the artist is revealed".[3] The artist's personality is expressed in his art, and in the end it is the personality that counts.

On January 24 1907 Rebecca Ida Rogers, the young wife of David de Sola Rogers, gave birth to a boy. Born ten months after her marriage, he was from the start doted on by his mother, for whom he later became the most important male figure of her life. He was born at home, at 28 Sutherland Avenue in London, and was named Claude Maurice Rogers. 'Maurice' was after his paternal grandfather Maurice Cohen Rogers LDS RCS MRCS LRCP, a surgeon/dentist who qualified at Guys Hospital and lived at 30 New Cavendish Street. 'Claude' was a name chosen for personal fancy, and, with its Anglo-French air and painterly associations, served the future painter well in later life.

Claude's father's family were Sephardic Jews. His grandfather, Maurice Cohen Rogers, came originally from Holland. The family name had probably been Rodriguez, anglicised to Rogers on moving to England. Maurice Cohen Rogers became a well-known London dentist, and the author of some books on dentistry, including one entitled *The Teeth as supplied by Nature and preserved by Art*, published in 1864. He married Annette de Sola, the daughter of the Sephardi Hazan (or Minister) David de Sola, and they had three children, James, David and

Rica. David, the middle child, always known as Dick, was born at 30 New Cavendish Street. He remained very close all his life to his elder brother James, four years his senior, although he saw little of his reputedly quarrelsome younger sister. Many years later, in 1937, James wrote to his nephew Keith about his brother Dick. "Poor Dick, it is now seventeen years since he passed on . . . he and I were much closer to each other than most brothers are. I always remained the big brother . . . he was one of the finest fellows ever born, he was generally happy and jolly, very fond of his work in which he was first class, was generally liked and respected by everybody who knew him, and as you know was passionately fond of shooting from a small boy, and was a remarkable revolver shot."[4]

Both James and Dick followed in their father's footsteps and became dentists, doing their training at Charing Cross Hospital and eventually setting up a practice together in Buenos Aires, which had a thriving English community. Dick had already made his home in Buenos Aires when he met and married Rebecca Ida Rubinstein, one of the eight children of Bernard Joseph Rubinstein. Bernard Rubinstein's family were Ashkenazi Jews from Latvia (probably from Mitau which was then part of Greater Russia). The family were driven out of Latvia by the rise of anti-semitism, and eventually came to England with their four children, of whom Bernard was the youngest. Bernard worked as a jeweller, first in Birmingham and then in London, where he bought a house in Maida Vale. In 1863 he married Julia Lazarus, whose mother was of Polish extraction and whose father was of old English Jewish stock from Exeter. There was a Lazarus tomb in the synagogue in Exeter, but it was destroyed during the war. Bernard and Julia had eight children, all born in Maida Vale, and to help keep the large family Julia took in sewing and did embroidery. The Rubinsteins were distant cousins of the nineteenth century Russian pianist Anton Rubinstein and his brother Nicolai, who were founders of the St Petersburg and Moscow Conservatoires. Rebecca Ida (always known as Ida), the sixth child, inherited this musical talent and was pursuing a career as a concert pianist before she married Dick. She was the only girl in her family to marry. One brother, Julius, died young, and the other two, Ernest and Arthur, married and produced children, but four sisters, Katie, Lily, Sybil and Mabel remained spinsters, possibly affected by the dearth of men as a result of the First World War. Ida's marriage to Dick was probably regarded as a social step upwards. His family, being Sephardi, attended the Spanish and Portuguese synagogue, which in those days was considered superior to the Reform synagogue to which the Rubinsteins belonged. Later

Claude was to belong to a social club run by the Spanish and Portuguese synagogue. He was a reluctant attender, pushed by his mother and aunt Lily who felt that he should meet some suitable Jewish boys and girls; he did in fact make friendships there which lasted throughout his life. Dick and Ida were married at Lauderdale Road synagogue in London in March 1906, and after their honeymoon they went out to the Argentine, where Dick's dental practice awaited him.

Dick insisted on his children being born on British soil so that they would have British citizenship. If born in the Argentine, even of British parents, children were deemed Argentinian and the boys eligible for military service there. Ida therefore returned alone to London for Claude's birth in January, taking him back to Buenos Aires at the end of the year. She returned to London for the year in which her second son Keith was born; but apart from this interruption, the first seven years of Claude's childhood were spent in Buenos Aires, in a roomy house with a large garden shaded by fig and pawpaw trees. It seems to have been a happy time, later recalled by Claude in one of his copious notebooks. "We lived in a house built round a patio at San Fernando, a village near Buenos Aires. The back garden sloped down towards the river Tigre. There was a fig tree so fruitful that each year heaps of the rotted fruit lay beneath it giving off an acrid but not unpleasant medicinal odour. Near the railings of the front garden were two impoverished date palms, the fruit hard and fleshless over the pips.

"My mother sometimes took me with her when she went to the shops. In a dim low ceilinged room with wicker hampers and fruit and vegetables arranged around the walls I saw pinned up above me a picture. It was a battle scene. To the left of the foreground, a low hill with a plain beyond, there was a group of horsemen. A figure with outflung arm dominated the group pointing eagerly with a sword. On the plain below, in bright detail, rows and squares of soldiers, horse, foot and guns, were fighting amid drifts of smoke. It was a popular print of an incident during the wars of liberation, the central figure San Martin or perhaps Bolivar."[5]

This picture, seen when Claude was five or six years old, had great significance for him at the time. He claimed to remember it in every detail, but when a student of his, John Jones, returned triumphantly from Buenos Aires bearing what he imagined from Claude's description was the very engraving, showing General San Martin liberating the people from Spanish oppression, it was not as Claude remembered. He may have superimposed several pictures in his memory. He was just beginning to read and his English reading was confined to a very few picture books, among which were *The Child's Life of Wellington*, *The Child's Life of Nelson* and *The Child's Life of Napoleon.* Claude acquired, and never lost, an interest in military history and became something of an expert on the Battle of Waterloo. His father's interest both in making little models and in shooting must have fired his imagination also, and he remembered his father amusing himself by "making trinkets out of dental gold, heavy indian-head cufflinks, detailed and crisp, and small revolvers for watch guard ornaments . . . there were many Bisley trophies in the house. When he had a look at my teeth he gave me a heavy frontier colt to hold, a real gun but with a broken firing pin."[6]

Claude felt that his religious upbringing had been fairly strict, although he himself confessed to never having much feeling for organised religion. Although his family did not keep the Sabbath, they kept Friday nights and observed all the main festivals - Passover, the Day of Atonement - and went to Synagogue, usually arriving late because Claude was reading in the bath. They did not keep a kosher kitchen, but bacon and shellfish were not allowed in the house. Claude later recalled eating a delicious and unfamiliar sandwich at a Slade party and finding that it was filled with ham. He experienced a thrill of orthodox horror followed by exasperation at having been denied this delicacy for nineteen years. He probably knew that it was his mother and aunts' secret delight to go out for a lobster meal.

Claude spent a good deal of his early years with a pencil or crayons in his hand, and there is a family story about him aged 2½ lying flat on his stomach drawing a car and getting into a rage because his mother did not recognise the gear levers. She did, however, encourage him in his efforts and he drew on everything including his school books. Throughout his life his letters were full of amusing drawings, and he was addicted to pictograms, which friends spent hours deciphering.

Early in 1914 Ida and her two sons returned to London to await the birth of another child, a daughter, Beryl. The family was trapped in London by the outbreak of war, and Dick was also effectively trapped in the Argentine. He never again lived en famille with his wife and children. Although when people in the Argentine spoke of 'Home' they always meant England, for Claude this was closely connected with the blue and red Huntley and Palmer biscuit tin which had a building with a tall chimney on the lid. When there was talk of something which happened at home, as when the King died and a new King was to be crowned, as far as Claude was concerned the King lived and the crowning took place in the building shown on the biscuit tin. Argentina was reality for him, and when the family did return to London he found it very cheerless after Frenchified Buenos Aires. "The continuous flat facade of the houses round about Royal Crescent and up and down the hill from Shepherds Bush to Notting Hill Gate was, to my eye, sad and dirty in colour and featureless. The bus conductors unlike out of doors people in the Argentine were unable to understand me [speaking in Spanish]. It turned out that they spoke a sort of English like I did indoors. When I spoke English it was all right. We were at Westgate when war was declared and a seaplane took off. I was sent to Colet Court, St. Paul's preparatory school, and met Michael Reynolds."[7]

Claude spent four years at Colet Court, becoming adept at swimming, and drawing in his school books. He was hauled before the headmaster for fighting with another boy over the ownership of a book, which was finally given to Claude because it was full of his drawings. The other boy received a caning. While at Colet Court Claude also attended Miss Holman's Drawing School of Art for Youngsters, and was certainly encouraged in his efforts by Miss Holman who regularly entered his work for Royal Drawing Society Competitions. He appears to have had some success in these; paintings of his were bought by the Royal Drawing Society, and Claude also gained a distinction in a national drawing competition organised in 1923 by the *Saturday Review*, and judged, among others, by Dr. Tancred Borenius, Professor of History of Art at University College London. Miss Holman also persuaded him to draw from memory, and Claude remembered his feelings about this. "I did not really care for memory drawings but for a short time I did some with an arty woman in a smock who ran a class behind a yellow painted door."[8] Confidential criticisms of his work sent to Claude by R. Ablett, the founder and director of the Royal Drawing Society, included the following, in May 1919: "I have placed the football scene first, as this is apparently done from memory after direct observation. This is the best method of study, preferable to drawing from 'imagination' what one has only seen in pictures, or to copying." In February 1920: "I am very glad to see a strengthening in the figure drawing from more careful observation of attitude and limbs. There is a spirit in the football field scenes and I have mounted two of them on a sheet for exhibition together with one of the scenes of Surrey Dock. They make quite a good looking sheet. Your figures suffer from dumpiness and their legs are apt to be thick and heavy for the bodies . . ." Clearly Mr Ablett had never met the rotund young artist or he would have understood this aberration. He was impressed by the next batch of drawings sent in May 1920, and wrote "the five drawings sent in this month all have good quality in touch, arrangement, liveliness and well observed effects of perspective . . . Will you let us see some more figures next time, the small drawings suggesting figures in action . . . are so promising that I think you should go on observing many figures."[9] By the age of thirteen Claude had experienced conscientious critical appraisal of his work, and it must have helped him to take his drawing and painting seriously.

In 1918 the family moved to Cheltenham to escape the bombing. Claude attended Cheltenham Junior School for Boys. During this year the three children succumbed to the influenza epidemic; Claude recovered enough to be told to read to Keith who was running a high temperature. He chose to read Conan Doyle's *The Speckled Band* and Edgar Allan Poe's *The Pit and the Pendulum*, feeling he was doing Keith a great favour. Keith, however, became acutely aware of the ticking of the grandfather clock in the hall and the dangling bell cord at the head of his bed, and suffered some serious nightmares as a result.

The family were still in Cheltenham for Armistice Day, but returned to London in 1919. Ida had taken a small house in Barrowgate Road, Chiswick, to be near St. Paul's School, which Claude entered in the autumn of 1920. They were joined by Dick who was back from the Argentine to undergo an operation for cancer. Claude remembered little about this reunification with his father, except for one visit with him to the Tate Gallery, where his father solemnly studied a highly coloured painting and turned away with a sigh exclaiming "I don't understand it – I don't understand it at all." Presumably the visit was made with Claude's burgeoning interest in art in mind, and Dick may already have been wrestling with the fact that his elder son's interests were more artistic than medical.

After recovering from his operation Dick returned to Buenos Aires to continue his work. The rest of the family did not go with him, but neither they nor he realised that he was ill with secondary cancer and that they would not see him again. He died in the Argentine in October 1920. A letter from him written to Claude on November 29 1919 survives: "Dear Claude, This is a special letter to you for your thirteenth birthday. It is usual for a father to give his son on that day a long talk about all the things he should do and those he should avoid. I am not going to do that as I am rather a queer sort of father with curious ideas about many of the facts of life and I do not believe that a long lecture from me will do you any good and it would not amuse me to write one. Be a good clean chap both in body and mind and you will be as good as the man next door and better than ninety percent of the folk around you. This birthday is to a yid what the 21st is to a goy and as you were not born in the Far East you are not developed up to that just yet. I hope I shall be in the land of the living when you reach that age . . ."[10] This seems to be characteristic parental ducking of difficult issues; one wonders what Claude must have made of this letter.

After Dick's death Ida, fulfilling a promise that she had made on the eve of her marriage, invited two of her spinster sisters to come and live with her. This arrangement suited her well, as Lily had been something of a mother within her large family circle, and she immediately took the dominant role, running the household and doing all the cooking. Mabel, the youngest sister, attended to the housework. Ida was therefore free to devote her time to her three children, and to minister to all their needs, among which a good and broad education was foremost. Dick's brother James took on the guardianship of the three children at long distance, and money was supplied regularly from the Argentine to support the family and pay the school bills. There was no question of Ida remarrying or taking up her career as a pianist again - she saw it as her duty to concentrate on her children, and at that time it would probably have been considered sinful for her to behave in any other way.

Ida, however, probably had too much time for her children. She became too emotionally involved with their lives, and Claude as the eldest was subject to demands for attention against which he chafed all his life. He found the new household oppressively full of women and was somewhat resentful. For Beryl, the youngest, it seemed quite natural: where other children had a mother and a father, she had a mother and an aunt. Aunt Lily became something of a paterfamilias. She suffered from epilepsy and would sometimes have frightening and embarrassing fits at family mealtimes. The children were bustled out of the room and the episode kept a dark secret. Epilepsy was perceived as some sort of slur on the character, and Ida became very protective of her sister. Lily had strong and not always sensible opinions on how the children should be brought up, often overriding Ida's more reasonable views. She eventually won Claude's affection, however, with a remark guaranteed to endear her to him. None of the children had their own latchkeys. As often happened, Claude had walked home late after a party or a long discussion on art protracted with pots of tea, and had to wait outside the house until someone unlocked the door to take the milk bottles in. He slipped inside and negotiated the stairs, but was spotted by Aunt Lily, whose open bedroom door faced the stairhead. She was lying in bed, not well, and beckoned Claude in. "Just back?" she said. "Don't worry, I shan't tell." She inspected him slowly. "You know," she added softly, "I wish I'd been a bad girl - just once." Lily could be troublesome in other ways, as all the household's affairs passed through her hands. In 1935 Claude, still living and painting at home, wrote to his future wife, "Aunt Lily has drunk my turpentine! I ordered some. It arrived in a wine bottle and Aunt Lily took a swig . . . wicked old woman!"[11]

Dick Rogers' death had left Ida socially and financially insecure. She no longer felt part of his family group, and compared to the de Solas she felt herself a poor relation. She was, and remained, not good with money. Finance came from the Argentine in a mysterious way, and, rightly or wrongly, she came to believe that it did not come from her childless brother-in-law James' purse, but that it derived from investments Dick had made in Argentine Railways. It was a short step from that to believing that perhaps she was not receiving what was due to her by right. James never appeared in England and only made one trip to Europe. He thus loomed all the larger in the family's imagination, and it was with some trepidation that they all went over to Paris in 1928 to meet him and his wife. Ida's confusion and resentment about money and the lack of it, was certainly transmitted to her children, and particularly to Claude, who minded not having the spending power that his friends had. And as the eldest child, Claude was expected to help his mother with her accounts. He dreaded this as his incomprehension equalled hers. Bank statements would come in and if they were in the red Ida would panic and start looking for bills to check. Claude would have to help her and nothing would be found. It was the recipe for great dramatic scenes. Claude in his turn could make scenes when he wanted something. Very often he lusted after some curio from one of the junk shops that he explored with a passion all his life. He would put pressure on his mother to give him the money and she would protest that she did not have it to give. There were frequent rows, but Claude's persistence usually won the day. The day, but not the battle. He never really learned how to handle money and all his life he oscillated between generosity and meanness. He was financially dependent upon his family until he was thirty, and when he married, he virtually transferred this dependency to his wife.

Although Claude's juvenile achievements in art were applauded, there was no particular interest in painting within the family circle, music being the dominant art form. The paintings on the walls were conventional wall decoration, with a pleasant 'school of' Canaletto picture in the dining room, and in the hall a couple of steel engravings of the meeting of Wellington and Blucher at Waterloo and the Death of Nelson, from the paintings in the Houses of Parliament. Claude's addiction to painting was something of a surprise.

Claude's schooldays at St. Paul's were not particularly distinguished, but he clearly enjoyed them and retained an affection for the school, contributing to *The Pauline*, the school magazine, and later organising an exhibition of contemporary painters at the school. When the old buildings in West Kensington were demolished in 1969, Claude seems to have been stricken with nostalgia and he made drawings of them from the old Fives court; he took photographs and, going down to the locked site on Saturdays and Sundays with a flask of coffee, he painted a picture of them in the process of demolition: "My painting looks v. odd . . . almost divided in two – one half you see the innards of the building, the other half something like its old self."[12] Claude was good at history, especially when it concerned military matters, and at one stage it was suggested that he might try for a history scholarship to Oxford. But academically he appears to have been idle. His school reports testify to "quite an able boy, who just fails to do himself proper justice through lack of seriousness". His French teacher complained that "his work for me is valueless, the result of lack of interest", and his chemistry teacher despaired. "He seems to have lost interest, altogether too casual and easy going . . . He does not seem to realise that a slight knowledge of chemistry may prove useful even to an artist!"[13] Claude was stronger in extra-curricular activities. He joined the OTC and it was clear then that he would never make a soldier. His brother Keith shared a bell-tent with him and most early mornings were spent pulling up floorboards in the hunt for Claude's cap or bits of his uniform. He enjoyed sport, however, playing usefully as a rugby second row forward. His love of sport remained throughout his life, and he painted several football paintings. He even illustrated a rugby football textbook for the coach at St. Paul's, published in 1926. The drawings in this book, while necessarily diagrammatic, are essentially Claude – chunky, detailed, the contour line forcefully describing the form, and the action and internal forces in the figures thoroughly understood. At St. Paul's, art became Claude's overriding interest and he won prizes in the school's John Watson Competition for art in 1921, 1922, 1923, 1924 and 1925. At that time academic excellence was regarded as paramount. The High Master was a noted Latin scholar and the school was famous for its Latin and Greek teaching. Art was seen as a form of punishment similar to detention. Claude, however, revelled in this form of detention, and was lucky enough to be taught by two outstanding teachers, the brothers John and Paul Holden. Claude remembered their advice. "A remark by Mr Holden soon after I got to St. Paul's opened my eyes and stuck in my mind. I was trying to do a watercolour in the grounds and asked him how I was to do the sky. I expected a recipe, I suppose . . . 'I should go and have a look at it first and go on looking before you do anything, huh?' he said. So then I realised I had not really been looking at all and I know this surprised and interested me a lot."[14] It was the right remark at the right time. Writing in *The Pauline* on the occasion of John Holden's retirement, Claude recalled the brothers' teaching methods. "Mastery of the medium employed was aimed at, but it had to be an individual mastery. Each pupil was encouraged to develop his own method, to discover the medium afresh from the point of view of his own pictorial problem and, above all, to be selective. It is easy to learn tricks and easy to acquire them. But although this method will produce a steady stream of competent pupils, it will not produce artists; indeed, it will kill latent talent. During the time Mr Holden was teaching at St. Paul's, the school was peculiarly rich in pupils who are now accepted painters. To name four only: Duncan Grant, Eric Kennington, Paul Nash and John Armstrong. And it is worth noting that none of these is content with the flashiness of academic tricks. They have all struggled towards truly individual expression."[15] From Claude's own later development one can deduce how important an influence the emphasis on careful observation and the avoidance of slickness in the work was to prove.

Claude's prizewinning paintings, usually in watercolour, received perceptive reviews in the school magazine. In 1923, "C M Rogers has followed the well-meant advice he was given last year, that he should work with more care and concentration. His honest studies of form and structure in boats and barges are good in themselves, and show fruit in his watercolour of *The Lower Pool* which has the added charm of pleasant colour." In 1924, "By steady and consistent progress, C M Rogers has risen to first place. He shows, as he has never yet done, an appreciation of the subtlety of colour, while light and atmosphere are skilfully rendered in his seaside drawings. His *Southwark Bridge* is marred by faulty perspective in the bases of the bridge piers, but he shows emphatic power of both colour and design in his striking subject of a galleon bound westward-ho towards the setting sun." In 1925, his final year at school, Claude again took first prize, and his work was again publicly and seriously reviewed. "His work, full of promise, is marked by sound design and by the use of simple and reticent colour. In a spacious landscape, with shadows flung over wide fields, there is the right feeling of unity between earth and sky, and the difficulty of suggesting a sense of recession over miles of flattish country is triumphantly overcome."[16]

Despite his practical efforts in art at school, Claude knew very little about modern art and hardly ever visited a gallery, though he recalled the excitement of handling some real drawings by John Sell Cotman which the elder of the two Holden brothers took him to see. He also remembered a tea party in the vast studio, somewhere near Swiss Cottage, of the marine painter William Lionel Wyllie RA, his mother drinking tea with ladies in elaborate hats and Mr Wyllie as bored as he was. When Wyllie discovered that Claude was interested in drawing, he showed him the process of his method in every detail. "How first of all it was necessary to discover the time of day and the state of tide and wind at the time of action. How he then consulted his sketchbooks, kept from his earliest days and containing notes on every conceivable state of wind and tide and sky effect. These I saw – charming little watercolour drawings done from a boat, with Constable-like notes on the back. Then, he explained, he went to the Maritime Museum and consulted the plans of the ships engaged. By perspective, from elevation and plan, each ship was set up on the canvas; and he showed me a canvas on which this was being done. I was thrilled. Looking back I see that apart from his kindness and enthusiasm, it was his enormous professionalism that I liked."[17]

Despite his relative ignorance about art, Claude put pressure on his mother to allow him to be a painter. He knew only that painting was what he liked doing more than anything else. The family were horrified, as the eldest son of a widow was expected to enter a safe profession and to help provide financially for her and his siblings. Before he died Claude's father, perhaps realising that his son would not wish to practice dentistry in Argentina, had written suggesting a career as a chartered accountant. He certainly did not know his son. Claude's financial sense was minimal, and his determination to paint overriding. The family spectre, often raised, of artists starving in garrets was no deterrent, and Claude riposted that it was his own life and he would be happy to starve if only he could paint. Finally it was the painter Gerald Moira, then head of Edinburgh College of Art, who performed the role of *deus ex machina*. He saw some of Claude's work at the annual exhibition at St. Paul's, where his sons were also pupils, and he wrote to Mrs Rogers that he was strongly of the opinion that C M Rogers should go to the Slade. With this letter he enclosed a note to Professor Tonks. Moira must have followed Claude's subsequent career with some interest, because he wrote to him after his 1954 exhibition, and Claude wrote a graceful reply, offering to show him around the Slade and adding: "It was entirely through you that my mother and my guardian let me become a painter – and certainly but for you I should have gone elsewhere than the Slade . . . At the age of eighteen, with an uncle nursing my late father's practice and waiting for me to qualify and join him, and with no real precedent in the family for a career in the arts, the pressure was such – and my conviction of a vocation in painting so uncertain – that, but for you, I should at the very least have spent many years in medicine before, if ever, I took the plunge and tried to paint."[18]

Despite the battles over painting, home life had plenty of warmth and humour. Claude's younger cousin Dick Rubinstein (named after Claude's father) recalled with amusement his visits to the Rogers household, much more fun if Claude or Keith were there than just the elderly aunts. "I remember Claude taking my school cap and jamming it on his unruly hair and getting Keith to play 'prefect' and give him a ticking off. With a cap on his head he had a great look of William, whose books were popular at the time. My family usually went to Chiswick for the Passover festival and either my father or Claude would officiate at the Passover night supper at which I would always have to recite the questions about 'why is this night different from other nights?' – the role of the youngest present. Claude came to us when we stayed at a bungalow on the Thames at Shepperton. He was a strong swimmer and always fun to be with. He gave my Pa a watercolour painted when he was about fourteen. It was of a freighter being loaded in London Docks and the ship was beautifully done."[19]

Family holidays – all holidays – were painting trips for Claude, and painting had become a way of analysing his experiences. Fifteen years later he experienced one of those moments when the present gives an insight into the past, and he understood the power that looking at the visual world had over him and his desire to paint it. He was staying with Graham Bell at Helen Anrep's house near Ipswich, Rodwell House, Baylham. They were playing a game which involved everyone describing their first remembered picture. Claude remembered the battle scene from the Buenos Aires shop and made a further discovery, solving the puzzle of an earlier experience that had occurred when on holiday with his family at Felixstowe in 1924. As usual when on holiday he had been painting watercolours, and had produced a number of pictures of the beach and bathing huts. One day he tired of drawing the gables of beach huts and followed the seafront to the north. "Presently the view opened out to the west. Leaving the road I took to the fields and was soon brought to a standstill by inexplicable and powerful emotions connected in some way with the view confronting me. The Woodbridge estuary opened out, a flat landscape receding to the distance, diversified by clumps of trees, the lines of hedges, the geometry of different coloured crops and the glint of serpentine waters. The slight hillside upon which I sat overlooked the scene. To my left, and slightly below my level, so that their tops made a low irregular mass just above the horizon, there was a plantation of trees. The scene seemed oddly familiar and moving. I looked at it with an indescribable anxiety and awareness, and with a heightening of perception . . . The connection between the given design of the scene and the composition of the San Martin battle scene never occurred to me . . . It was only later, in the particular circumstances of my conversation with Graham that the connection was made. Nevertheless, for the rest of that holiday at Felixstowe I got permission to set off day after day with my box of watercolours and some sandwiches to that scene. I suppose I must have made a dozen or so attempts to paint that view. The results never satisfied me. Perhaps unaware I wanted to transform hedges and plantations and rectilinear crops into the opposing lines of battle. Confronted with the stubborn facts of the landscape I discovered instead the East Anglian sky and light and painfully tried to set down, with what accuracy I could, that diversified, beautiful and natural design."[20]

During his last year at St. Paul's, Claude more or less persuaded his mother to allow him to go to art school. Moira's letter had impressed her, and she suggested that Claude might go to the Slade for a trial year. He attended evening classes at Heatherley's Art School and built up a portfolio of work. Despite his determination to be a painter, he had some understanding of his family's doubts about his chosen career. "Art was suspect as a means of earning a livelihood, and of questionable respectability. Some echoes of past scandals may have persisted, from Epstein controversies and even, perhaps, from the rumpus caused by the post-impressionist exhibitions before the war. The credibility of art was low, modern art had alarming implications, moral as well as aesthetic, and by the pre-war generation was often identified with bolshevism, a feared and horrid word. Stephen Spender's father regarded modern art as a 'huge, obscene, blasphemous practical joke' . . . Raymond Coxon, writing about the problems of those days from a less comfortable background, says that 'one of the additional burdens of the student, often heroically attempted, was his duty . . . to educate, or convert, or liberalise his parents'."[21] It was probably easier for a daughter to get into art school than for a son, the prospect arousing less family opposition. Nevertheless, Claude's family were persuaded to let him try his luck, and he entered the Slade in October 1925.

NOTES

1, 2 Claude Rogers Papers, Tate Gallery Archive.
3 Read, Herbert, *Art Now*, Faber and Faber, 1933.
4 Claude Rogers letters, collection Mr Crispin Rogers.
5, 6, 7, 8, 9 Claude Rogers Papers, Tate Gallery Archive.
10 Claude Rogers letters, collection Mr Crispin Rogers.
11 Claude Rogers Papers, Tate Gallery Archive.
12 Claude Rogers, letter to Dr Keith Rogers, November 24 1969.
13, 14 Claude Rogers Papers, Tate Gallery Archive.
15 Claude Rogers, *The Pauline*, 1934 p. 172.
16 Hardie, Martin, *The Pauline*, 1923 p. 129, 1924 p. 133, 1925 p. 125.
17, 18 Claude Rogers Papers, Tate Gallery Archive.
19 Rubinstein, Dick, letter to J Pery, November 10 1992.
20 Claude Rogers Papers, Tate Gallery Archive.
21 Claude Rogers unpublished memoir version I, collection Mr Crispin Rogers.

Not a line out of place

The Slade School of Art, part of University College London, had an awesome reputation. In the 1920s it was presided over by the redoubtable Henry Tonks, Slade Professor since 1918, and the previous professor's assistant since 1892. Tonks, the son of a Solihull foundry owner, had originally trained as a doctor, and his medical knowledge supported his teaching of drawing. His paintings were less sculptural, mainly elegant conversation pieces built up in touches of paint. His reputation as a teacher was formidable, and he had complete control over his students at the Slade. He was quite frank about his admission policy. He always accepted talent and had an eye for spotting it. He filled the remainder of the intake with well brought up young women from good backgrounds who might be expected to marry well and become patrons for the cream of his students. Not, as Claude recalled ruefully, that the sexes were always free to meet. The antique room was used by both sexes, but when drawing or painting from the life model, men and women worked in separate rooms. This was common practice not only at the Slade, but also at the Royal College of Art, the Central School of Art and in other art schools, and the separation of the sexes persisted well into the 1950s.

Most students at the Slade relied on their parents for their fees and allowances, although a few had grants from enlightened local authorities. Some had talent scholarships, and the scholarship boys tended to keep to themselves. Another coterie within the school was The Eton Boys. There were always a few Etonians and Harrovians at the Slade, and Claude remembered his friend John Dodgson, a student before the First World War and an old Etonian, being greeted on his first day there by a magnificent and slightly older student who pushed his way through the crowded hall and proferred his hand with the remark 'Thank God, John, someone to lunch with at last!'[1]

One of the first people Claude encountered during his initial week at the Slade was Michael Reynolds, who had been at Colet Court with him. Reynolds, tall and lanky, was the son of Frank Reynolds, an illustrator for *Punch* magazine. In his unpublished autobiography, Reynolds recalled their reunion. "Suddenly I spotted a familiar face, that of a boy about my own age – a good-humoured face, ruddy-cheeked and blue-chinned, with big, expectant brown eyes. The body beneath it was short and exuberantly fleshed, the legs stoutly astraddle. I had not seen him for six or seven years, but there was no mistaking him. He recognised me simultaneously and came forward to greet me with a beaming smile. We even remembered each other's names. His was Claude Rogers."[2] While at Colet Court the two had shared a taste for war games played with toy soldiers and for reading books on battles. Both did drawings of military subjects. But what Reynolds chiefly remembered about Claude at preparatory school was "his spirited resistance to an unpopular master – an old clergyman with a stubby grey beard, who had been an army chaplain in the Matabele war. When any boy in his class incurred his displeasure – and he was easily displeased – he would stand over the offender's desk and buffet him about the ears with clenched fists. I myself endured this treatment on several occasions. Claude endured it only once: the second time he punched the old brute in the stomach. There was a great row about it afterwards. Claude was exonerated by the authorities. The master was not sacked but from that time forward he was less free with his fists."[3]

The two students became firm friends and quickly formed a sort of painting partnership. At the end of their first week at the Slade they made a plan to go sketching together in Kensington Gardens. It was Claude's idea, accepted by Reynolds with some misgivings. "Claude . . . had done a lot of landscape in watercolour and had become very dextrous. My experience in this field had been comparatively slight; it had sufficed, however, to give me a distaste . . . for the discomfort and anxiety of working out of doors. The weather today gave point to this feeling. There had been heavy falls of snow during the night, and it was perishing cold.

"It all looked lovely – like a painting by Breughel, as Claude put it. He was bubbling with enthusiasm – at first. But as we ate our sandwiches, standing on the steps of the Albert Memorial, it began to snow again; the wind grew sharper, and even Claude's ardour gradually cooled. We stayed at the Memorial long enough for a cursory inspection of the sculpture. . . . Then, without having attempted any sketching, we made off along Kensington Gore and Exhibition Road, and kept on until we reached the shelter of that other monument to the Prince Consort's work, the Victoria and Albert Museum.

"Here I felt on safer ground. I took Claude to the Reading Room – where he had never been before – and at his suggestion we got out an illustrated book on Piero della Francesca. We had heard of him for the first time earlier in the week, during a lecture by the Slade's art historian, Professor Tancred Borenius. We were both deeply impressed by the reproductions in the book, particularly those of the frescoes at Arezzo . . . but Claude was more vociferous about them than I. A series of details from the two Arezzo battlepieces suggested comparisons with Uccello's *Rout of San Romano* which had long been one of my favourite pictures in the National Gallery. When Claude insisted that the Pieros were better, I denied it indignantly. The argument became so heated that one of the library staff found it necessary to ask us to lower our voices . . .

"Still disputing, we walked from the Museum - the snow had meanwhile stopped - to the King's Road, Chelsea, where an exhibition of drawings by Augustus John was being held at the Chenil Gallery. I think it must have been a private view - perhaps we had wangled an invitation through the Slade. At any rate, the gallery was crowded with people, including John himself. He was then in his late forties, grey-bearded, but still very handsome and active-looking. I remember noting with awe the formidable spread of his shoulders. Claude and I found ourselves in agreement again about the splendour of the drawings; Claude again expressed his approval more emphatically than I.

"There were scores, if not hundreds, of drawings, some hanging on the walls in whitewood frames, others, mounted but unframed, piled up or scattered about on tables. Claude, stepping back the better to admire a wall exhibit, sat down heavily on one of these tables, making it rock and squeak. The drawings, to the best of my recollection were undamaged; but John turned his head and gave us a baleful look out of his yellow, lionlike eyes - a look that frightened me more than it frightened my friend. I doubt if Claude was even aware of it.

"We rounded off the day at his home in Chiswick, where his mother gave us a supper that included pieces of cold fried fish - something I was unprepared for and did not greatly relish. It was not until later that I learned . . . that it was a Jewish delicacy.

"Mrs Rogers . . . fussed over Claude, who was better able to take care of himself than most young men, in a way that must sometimes have embarrassed him . . . As a goy I was at first, I daresay, viewed with some suspicion by them and by Mrs Rogers; but they soon got used to me, and as time went on they grew - or so I flatter myself - quite fond of me. I certainly became fond of them."[4]

It must have been difficult for the Rogers family coming to terms with the new circle of friends in which Claude was moving. Few of his new friends were Jewish, and this part of his life began to claim less of his attention. At the Slade he gradually abandoned his religious observance and adopted the liberal, agnostic approach of most of his fellows. His contemporaries there included William Coldstream, Geoffrey Tibble, Rodrigo Moynihan, Michael Salaman, Thomas Carr, Anthony Devas, Rupert Shephard, Clive Branson (killed in the Spanish Civil War), Anthony Gross, Robert Medley, Richard Eurich, Robin Darwin, Tristram Hillier, Humphrey Slater, Jesse Cast, Edgar Hubert, Osbert Lancaster, C E Hamilton Dicker (who later entered the church), William Townsend ("a beautiful draughtsman who one day nonchalantly scaled the Slade facade to disappear over the parapet") and Avery Colebrook (who later became a photographer). Among the girls were Ruth Salaman, for whom Claude early on formed a passionate and unrequited attachment, Mary Potter, Helen Lessore and Ithell Colquhoun, Nommie Durrell, Eleanor Bellingham Smith, Nicolette Macnamara, Nancy Sharp and Elsie Few. William Coldstream stood out from his colleagues as the funniest of them all, and Claude appreciated, with reservations, his zest and curiosity about people. He recalled his unique brand of humour wryly. Coldstream "seized on the conversation twisting it about, spinning absurdity out of absurdity until we were helpless with laughter. Once started his invention ran beyond all control. People were tossed about like puppets, battered into ridiculous situations, comically done up. It was painfully funny, not deliberately spiteful and none of it meant to be hurtful but leaving the faintest aftertaste, if only the occasional thought 'How many times has he done this to me?' "[5]

Coldstream met Claude during his second term at the Slade, having only recently arrived. During a rest in the men's life room a "brisk young man, alert and lively looking in a somewhat arty looking suit of rough green tweed and well polished shoes entered. He had bright eyes, a mobile mouth, and large, sinewy, capable hands, in one of which he held a pipe."[6] He came over to where Claude was leaning against the wall smoking his pipe and asked for a fill of tobacco. This was the beginning of a firm friendship that was to last throughout Claude's life. The friendship was to prove a mixed blessing for Claude; while Coldstream undeniably helped him in many ways, he overshadowed him and occasionally cramped his style.

Coldstream, as the youngest child of a doctor, came from a background not dissimilar to Claude's. Because there were doubts about his health he had been taken away from school and studied at home with tutors. He seemed much more assured and more knowledgeable about art than the rest of the students, and was full of idiosyncratic stories. He maintained that he had been able to supplement his income at need while at school by swallowing a worm in a lettuce leaf or by retailing information on sex culled from his father's medical library.

Another contemporary was Justin Pieris Daranujagala, a Singhalese student, who was responsible for introducing Claude to the work of Picasso, Matisse and Cézanne. Having seen their paintings in Paris, he had become enraptured by them, hissing their names to Claude while working in the life room. Claude knew nothing about them, but he caught Pieris' excitement. He consulted Coldstream. Coldstream produced two smudgy black-and-white reproductions by Cézanne. Claude found he could make nothing of them. With Coldstream he searched the Tate Gallery. The modern rooms had recently been opened, and there they found a Matisse painting of the windscreen of a car, a converging road and poplars. They failed to find the only Picasso in the collection, an early painting of a bunch of flowers. But they did find Cézanne's 1880 self portrait. This small picture struck Claude with all the force of revelation. Here was painting that was lucid and clear, and in which the forms were described in terms of colour. "The image looked more real - more like things looked to me in nature than any painting I had ever seen. How to express this flat, solid, colourful, chunky, light-enveloped look surely I could presently achieve . . ."[7] This was the sort of painting that Claude himself would have liked to do, and it became for him a threshold from which to start.

Teaching at the Slade was based entirely on drawing and painting from casts or from the life models. The only outside work required was the annual summer composition. Students spent a probationary period in the antique room working from casts until they received, with emotion, Professor Tonks' permission to move into the life rooms. It was the end of a golden era under Tonks' professorship (he retired in 1930, the year after Claude left). Drawing was understood as the representation of three dimensional objects on a flat surface, and was based on carving away from the nearest part of the form, as in sculpture. Painting was essentially impressionist, concentrating on the way light, and its product, colour, infuses space. Strong colour was frowned upon and a fine sense of tone was cultivated. At the end of each day all the palette scrapings would be collected together in a bucket, which students could use if they were short of paint. This practice gave rise to the term 'Slade mud' for describing the typical colours of Slade paintings. Tonks sought to teach accuracy in judging the direction of a line, and completeness of statement, no bodies without legs or legs without feet. A big cartoon of Tonks made for one of the Slade dances carried the inscription 'Not a line out of place, not a torse without a face'. Tonks was an excellent teacher, lucid when explaining a concept and impressive in his standards. He had his blank spots, however, and could not tolerate Cézanne. As Claude remembered, "beyond the Impressionists Tonks constructed a kind of ha-ha. On the further side of it, in thick grass as it were, terrible beasts could be glimpsed thrashing around. Van Gogh and Picasso for instance, and the arch-enemy Cézanne."[8] Claude wrote "I can never remember Tonks actually thundering out against Cézanne, or painters such as Picasso and Matisse, but we knew they were barred . . . If one had asked the Professor about them it would have been with unease as if one had asked for information about some intimacy of sex. I am not sure that I would not have felt safer asking about sex."[9] A dislike of Cézanne's work was shared by Sickert, whose taste was noticeably more catholic than that of Tonks. Tonks' antipathies included the Royal Academy – "we were left in no doubt whatsoever that the Academy was the home of the devil." Degas, Manet and Pissarro were admired, and Claude recalled a visit with Tonks to the Tate Gallery on the occasion of Monet's death in November 1926 to pay tribute to "the last of a very great brotherhood of painters".

In the 1920s Tonks WAS the Slade. Claude was awed enough by his presence to study him carefully, and with a painter's eye. "A tall figure of good build, lean but solid. He had a swift sloping walk, something between Groucho Marx and a tiger. Big hands, carefully scrubbed, long fingers with the nails cut square. The head was long and bony, the eyes, which were a little hooded, grey and appraising over the half glasses he wore. He had a Roman nose and a forelock. In totality his head and face might have been created to demonstrate the concepts and maxims of his drawing lessons. It was a lined face; the lines were careful and precise and strengthened the modelling. The forms were interesting in conjunction and as a whole. When teaching in the life room he would sometimes explain that a mouth is best thought of as a sectional line drawn across the curving pad of muscle set between nose and chin. The length of his thin, sensitive mouth demonstrated this idea to perfection."[10]

Tonks stood out even from those members of his staff, particularly Russell and Wilson Steer, who had stature and personality. As Claude remembered, "Steer was a huge amphibious bulk, like a seal or a sea-elephant at the circus squirming slowly into position. If you were lucky, he would take up a palette and look and blend a mixture of paints alternately until, at long last, and on the very edge of the area covered by your painting, four miraculous pats of paint somehow brought the dead, damned thing to life."[11] Anthony Devas, who later made his living as a portrait painter, complained to Claude that they received little technical instruction at the Slade, spending a great deal of time discussing aesthetics. On the whole no technique was taught, and Steer for example never showed anybody his methods of painting in watercolours. Only once was his system revealed, to the painter Rodney Burn, who much later told the following poignant story to Claude. "When towards the end of the first great war Burn arrived at the Slade, fresh from the army and filled with ardour to draw and paint every moment of the day, he found few students there so that he particularly noticed an older student, a solemn fellow who usually sat warming himself on a radiator in the corridor. In the end this accustomed sight became an irritant so that when one day the other spoke, asking how Burn was getting one and what he liked doing, the reply was rather sharp. Things were all right said Burn, though people as a whole didn't seem to over exert themselves at the Slade. As to what he liked doing best, he was uncommonly good at watercolours. Steer – for the other was Steer – seemed properly impressed. Encouraged by this Burn offered to show him a few useful dodges. The offer was accepted and the performance carried out in an adjacent room. 'Well now,' said Steer 'that was very interesting. In return I will show you a thing or two myself. Meet me here tomorrow and I will bring along my colour box.' 'And do you know,' Burn lamented, 'I had been so little impressed by this lazy radiator fellow – mind you I still had no idea who he was – that I cannot for the life of me remember a single thing of all the things he showed me the next day.' "[12]

Certain philosophies of painting were prevalent at the Slade at this time and one of them concerned 'subject matter'. At the Slade, subject matter was only important as an excuse for painting and had no influence on the way a picture developed. The search for formal relationships within the subject dictated the development and the method of painting. Claude recalled that "the detailed characteristics of an object were to be avoided as they destroyed formal relationships and led to illustrative effect. Details of the features of a head destroyed the formal simplicity of it. They had emotive, 'illustrative' significance. 'Illustrative' was a bad word and illustration to be avoided. 'Decoration' on the other hand – the idea of painting as the embellishment of a flat surface with formal relationships of colour – was all right. Distortion could be useful as an adjunct to decoration."

Tonks identified drawing with carving and painting with modelling, and explained that in figure drawing one could carve out the form by gradations of shading, the white of the paper representing the part of the model nearest to the eye. As the surfaces receded from this part they were 'chipped away' i.e. they grew darker. Tonks' demonstration drawings worked from inner marks and surfaces outward towards the contour and refrained from any final definition as long as possible. Claude recalled that "the eraser was frowned upon. At best it was a shameful kind of survival kit, to be used in extremity and with repugnance and reluctance. For me at that time india rubber was as taboo as bacon."[13] Tonks suffered meretriciousness badly and could not tolerate, for example, drawings in red conté crayon which could enhance an indifferent piece of work. Painting was taught in terms of tone, and by warm and cold relationships rather than by positive colour relationships. Claude often found it difficult to relate this teaching to his own experience of colour before nature. A painting started with a middle tone and extended the range towards extremes of light and dark. The white canvas was usually rubbed over with a neutral colour before starting – the sludge in the bucket was often used for this. Colour was inseparable from tone, and as a rule of thumb highlights were cold, lit surfaces warm, half tones cold and shadows warm though colder than the lights. This was still essentially Victorian painting, designed for the representation of plastic form. The notion of flat colour or of respecting the flat surface of the canvas was not encountered at the Slade. Even to students of that time these ideas began to seem stuffy and restrictive; and, despite his admiration for Tonks, Claude remembered the one visit that he made to the Professor's house in the Vale of Health leaving him with an overwhelming impression of prim stuffiness. "With the name of Ingres, Degas' name was most often on Tonks' lips when giving a lesson in the life room. Reproductions of their work, with some by Tintoretto, hung on the walls of the men's life room . . . Other staff had their pet likes and dislikes. Walter Russell's battle cry was 'the thrust of the torso against the tilt of the pelvis'. George Charlton's 'a little more hatching there I fancy'. Wilkie 'make it richer'. Mr White was silent."[14]

Because so many students were fee-paying, and many with private means (Avery Colebrook with an income of £300 a year seemed as rich as Croesus) the pace was leisurely, and exhibiting not exactly encouraged. It was considered better for the development of a painter to wait, and to be more certain what he or she was about. Tonks clearly thought a good deal of Claude as a student. At the end of his first term at the Slade, in December 1925, prompted perhaps by Claude, the Professor wrote to Mrs Rogers: "I am very interested in your son's work here. I think he shows such deep interest in it and has made such progress in it since coming here, that it would be unfair to withdraw him and it would seriously interfere with his future, for which I have every hope."[15] At the end of the first academic year, in June 1926, Claude was awarded a Slade Scholarship for the forthcoming year, worth £35. He also won a second prize, worth £10, for the Slade's Summer Composition. On the basis of Tonks' letter and these achievements, Ida and Uncle Jim were persuaded that Claude was doing the appropriate thing and his future as a painter was settled.

Claude's summer composition painting, *A Day in my Life*, clearly demonstrates his future promise. It is a low-toned painting, dimly red and green, with more than a suggestion of Slade mud, but its composition, with the swinging circular movement created by palette, chairback and open window frame, both on the surface plane and within the depth of the picture, is very assured. The group created by mother and sister is elegant in a slightly Edwardian way, but the figure of Claude himself, legs firmly apart and gazing out of the picture, has a distinctly personal note. Claude painted it at 27 Barrowgate Road, having persuaded his mother and sister to sit for him, recalling his "rage and irritation when my mother made the proviso that she would only sit if she could have her back so that nobody could see her face. The interesting thing was that, as the picture began to go along I suddenly realised that this was the making of it because if she had been looking into the room the outside would have been entirely unrelated to this figure".[16]

Another picture, painted by Claude in the antique room at the Slade, also survives. This is the *Boy with a Dolphin* which Claude began in his first year. Michael Reynolds remembered this painting, writing of it later: "At the beginning of the Easter term Claude Rogers and I were authorized by Professor Tonks to start painting. There was not, however, room for us in the Life-painting room, so we had to return to the Antique and paint from plaster casts. Claude chose one of Verrocchio's *Boy with a Dolphin* and on the first day made an extraordinarily brilliant start. It had all the atmosphere of a little masterpiece – like the first stages of a painting by Chardin. Tonks and all the other instructors were excited about it; almost everybody from the various life classes came up to see it. We all felt that a great event was pending. But there is a wide gap between promise and achievement. By the second or third day Claude had begun to run into difficulties. The drawing had to be corrected, the tone went wrong, the luscious, subtle brushwork had to be scraped out and done again, losing in the process its quality and magic. The painter's confidence faltered; he became anxious and 'depwessed'. He kept on dourly, and by the end of term had brought the painting to something like completion."[17] Claude kept this painting all his life, and exhibited it several times. Its thickly painted, dim greenish surface still holds an air of well-fought finality about it, and, as Bruce Laughton suggests, it is probable he had an affection for paintings that had been battled with.

Claude was living at home throughout his student days, and making the journey daily from Chiswick to Gower Street. This was very much the norm among the students. His home life continued much as before. Claude would take himself off painting during the days he was not at the Slade. Sometimes his younger brother Keith would be sent off with him. Claude would get onto a barge and become absorbed in a picture and Keith would grow bored and restive. Claude also painted at home in the house. The family had a parrot, a rossetti cockatoo, which only Claude could handle and which he had completely tamed. It sat on his shoulder while he painted, shredding his dressing gown and nibbling at his hair and his ears. When it became too much of a nuisance Claude would shove it upside down in his pocket, where it righted itself and remained quite happily for a while, eventually climbing back onto his shoulder. While not painting Claude haunted the junk shops of Chiswick and Bloomsbury, and collected all sorts of objects, picked for their shape, colour and texture. He also combed the second hand book shops and read voraciously. He read at meal times and eventually the family, unable to dissuade him, joined in the habit. Michael Reynolds would often bicycle over to Chiswick to compare notes with him. Reynolds spent time with the Rogers family at Hope Cove in Devon, where they had rented a cottage for the summer of 1926, and was a witness to the progress of Claude's summer composition picture. He remembered that, of the three figures, the one at the easel was the best. "It was an excellent self portrait, in a characteristic pose – legs astride, head held high, pipe in mouth, palette and a great spread of brushes in one hand, a single brush extended towards the canvas with the other. The prevailing tone was rather low, but this gave emphasis to splendid bursts of rich, glowing colour. It was an extraordinarily exuberant, joyous picture . . . The technical skill, particularly the balancing of the tone values, was remarkable: I don't really know where Claude can have picked up his technique – he had not yet had any tuition in painting at the Slade. And he had no father to help him. He had usually finished for the day by the time I arrived, but would still be pottering about his studio in the fading light, cleaning brushes and cogitating over the progress of his picture. If things had been going well, he would lead me eagerly to the easel and point out choice passages. 'There, that's not bad is it? I'm quite pleased with that.' And with a radiant smile he would exclaim 'Man! There's an absolutely delicious bit I'm going to do tomorrow. Here – the inside of this sleeve. The light shines through it. It's bright orange.' On other evenings I would find him dissatisfied with the day's work and feeling 'depwessed'. Claude's depwessions would be quite monumental, and were sometimes prolonged; though they never amounted to much during the painting of this picture. It was I more often than he who felt irritable and out of sorts of an evening; and he would put himself out to cheer me with talk of Napoleon's campaign or a reading of one of O Henry's stories. The memory of our association in those days is something I treasure. Even at the time, preoccupied though I was with my own aspirations, I was vaguely conscious of being privileged in having Claude for a friend. It was like knowing the young Courbet or the young Renoir. I am not suggesting that Claude is as good a painter as Courbet or Renoir; but he is a real painter, a born painter, in the sense that they were. I was fortunate in having so intimate a view of the flowering of his talent."[18]

Early on during his Slade days Claude and a friend decided to try for a piece of publicity and have some fun. They smuggled some goldfish into the Tate and deposited them in the pond, telephoning a couple of newspapers and drawing attention to the unaccountable appearance of the fish. The *Daily Mail* printed a small paragraph about it. Claude spent his days, and sometimes nights, in the company of his friends, and learnt to sleep on a floor with newspapers wrapping him, between his clothes – his first experience of this in Coldstream's room after a party.

Absorbed as they were in painting, Claude and his friends were fairly ignorant about current affairs. Claude was scarcely aware of the growing labour unrest and the various strikes of the 1920s. But he was forced to take account of the General Strike in May 1926. "I remember I walked to the Slade without thinking any more about it. I arrived a bit late, not very late, and there was Bill Coldstream and one or two others, and we went into the Life Room and started to draw, and Tonks came down and was horrified to see what we were doing. He said 'You must go and save the country', and so we looked at one another rather sheepishly and somebody said 'How do we do that, Professor Tonks?' and so he told us there was a recruiting office in the cloisters where we could register for work of national importance . . . I was advised to go back to Chiswick and to go anywhere locally where I'd be useful . . . I didn't want to break the strike. In fact it never occurred to me that I was doing anything of the sort. But my experience as a bus-conductor, talking to strikers, talking to the extraordinary people on the buses . . . entirely changed my conception of things. One was very frightened at times . . .

My route ran over Battersea Bridge – we came to the top of the bridge and there was the far shore black with strikers, and one's heart and bowels turned over, and the only thing I could think of doing when we got to the other side was to get off the bus and politely help off the passengers who wanted to alight, because I thought if they are going to hit me I bloody well don't want to see it."[19] Claude did not enjoy the atmosphere, which was rather like that of a bad war film, with the canteens staffed by debutantes and the men behaving like Bulldog Drummond, but for him it was a first taste of the outside world and proved an educative week. When William Townsend arrived at the Slade later that year he was astonished to hear how the students had been shooed off to help beat the strike and how they had complied. Townsend, at 17, had been a paid up member of the Labour Party for some time. Claude was later surprised and embarrassed to receive an official envelope containing a certificate covered with union jacks and touches of gold, thanking him for his services during the strike and enclosing a cheque. He considered returning the cheque, but money was short and when Michael Reynolds and Avery Colebrook suggested that he go with them on a painting holiday to Rochester in Kent, he used the money to pay his share of the tally and to buy painting materials.

This was the first time Claude had had a painting holiday with other painter friends. They took a cottage owned by a sailor's widow, paying 27/- each a week for bed and board. As Reynolds recorded, they painted all day and in the evening "would sit over the mutton-chops and tea, and with much argument, by the dim light of an oil-lamp, draw up lists, in order of importance, of great artists and great men. Michelangelo usually headed the first list, Jesus Christ the second. Looking back, it seems to me that the Slade students of my day spent a good deal of time making lists of this sort . . . Two or three times a week we would have a night out in Chatham or Rochester. Usually it was Chatham: we preferred its jolly, raucous garrison-town atmosphere to the sleepy olde-worldiness of Rochester. The evening's entertainment always started with a visit to a local music hall. There were several in Chatham in those days. The one we favoured was small and intimate – so intimate that from the stalls you could distinguish the sweat running down the nose of the comedian and the suspender-marks on the thighs of the dancing girls. Afterwards we would have a meal at a fried-fish shop, and then drop in at a sailors' pub. We went to the pub not because we wanted to drink – it was only reluctantly that we got down half a pint apiece – but because we liked watching the sailors and overhearing snatches of their talk. I don't know if they were conscious of our interest; if so, they never reacted to it. They ignored not only us, but our sketchbooks. They were quiet, well-behaved men - rather disappointingly so. We hoped - at least Claude and I did - for drunken singing, and possibly fights; all we ever saw was a darts match.

"Still, we quite enjoyed being in their company. Walking back to the village under the stars - the last bus would have gone by then - we talked enthusiastically of the Navy and its traditions. Claude and I would each in turn try to imitate a sailor's walk; and Avery - who, it turned out, was actually a member of the RNVR - would tell us we had got it all wrong . . . Before going to bed, we would stroll to the end of the little jetty and watch the swerving reflections of the red and green ships' lights. It was a pleasant time."[20]

Michael Reynolds shared Claude's passion for military history, and knew every detail of the great battles. On one occasion they joined up with a mutual friend in his flat high over Marble Arch to build the terrain of Waterloo in the big drawing room, and fight the battle step by step with the aid of hundreds of "flat little soldiers of German manufacture, perfect in every period detail".

The second year at the Slade was memorable for an exhibition marking the centenary of University College, London. King George V and Queen Mary were present at the official opening, and were escorted round the exhibition by Tonks and Steer. Claude had a watercolour painting of Hyde Park on show. That summer there was also an exhibition of paintings by Matisse at the Lefevre Gallery, much haunted by Slade students. The excellent new Brandon Davies Gallery had opened in Fitzroy Square, and it was here that Claude saw his first important painting by Henri Rousseau. In the twenties Paris was still the centre of the art world, and French painting the hard currency of art. Bloomsbury was of course wholeheartedly francophile. It was difficult to see French painting in London, and Slade students felt it essential to get to Paris if they could. In April and May 1928 Claude made his first visit there. He went with his family to stay with his uncle James and his wife, who were over from Argentina and staying in a dauntingly expensive hotel in the Rue de Berri. The visit was not altogether successful, as Claude felt, rightly or wrongly, that his uncle regarded him as an unapproved financial burden, and his efforts to speak French were largely unsuccessful. However, he did manage to see some painting - very little abstract or cubist art, but he familiarised himself with the Louvre and the Luxembourg. He was impressed by the large Renoir nudes and had to defend them to his uncle. He noted with suspicion the universal esteem in which Foujita and 'beastly Miss Marie

Laurencin' were held, and regarded with distaste the oily highlights in Derain's paintings, remembering the Slade doctrine that obtrusive highlights were sinfully destructive of form.

Perhaps the most impressive exhibition that Claude saw during his years at the Slade was Sickert's large retrospective at the Leicester Galleries in June 1929. There were 70 paintings and 40 drawings on show. Claude paid many visits to this exhibition, often with Coldstream, who was so impressed by the portrait of Victor Lecour that he induced Claude to pose for him in a similar stance and took photographs with an idea of doing a painting from them. Coldstream apparently made a start on this painting but nothing came of it.

Sickert had occasionally appeared and lectured at the Slade, and Claude had attended his talks at the East London Group, a society formed around the Slade-trained painter John Cooper in Bow, where Coldstream and Moynihan sometimes gave assistance. Sickert's clear and logical teaching had impressed them all. "We were very interested in Sickert because of the complete identity that seemed to exist between his idea of drawing and his idea of painting. We came to meet him through a group of painters who met at an evening class in East London. Sickert used to go down to this class . . . and Coldstream managed to get a bit of a job there, helping John Cooper, and I used to go along just because Sickert used sometimes to come. He'd sit on a table and talk to everybody about drawing and painting – it really was rather a wonderful experience. According to him . . . it was impossible to work from nature because nature moved about so much. So what one did was to make drawings – sometimes rapid drawings, sometimes careful drawings in detail – and one could then, later in one's studio, square these up, transfer them and build up a picture from them. One could make notes of the tone values, notes of the colour, build up a logical series of colour and tone upon this foundation. He would say 'go out and you see a scene, and it's obviously got an orange under-painting. So you start on an orange canvas.' . . . Sitting at a table, his feet in carpet slippers, he spoke amusingly for the better part of an hour . . . Coldstream told me that the students were in the main boys employed in the clothing trade and anxious to learn to draw fur, or tarts in for a rest. Sickert had no difficulty with his audience. His first talk which began 'When one considers the works of that great dramatist Arthur Pinero . . .' won them over completely."[21]

The lucidity of Sickert's ideas made clear for them much that was obscure at the Slade. Identify a point amidst the phenomena before you and mark it, Sickert would say. Then plot directions from that point as on a clockface. When it came to painting, Sickert advised "putting on the paint like a gent". Looking back, Claude realised that above all for him Sickert represented the model of a thriving modern artist. "Walter Richard Sickert ARA – or was it RA – or had he resigned again? – appeared to be the most splendid harlequinade character of all living artists in his mode of life and in his dealings with the world. Of all the painters we knew he was also the most simple and straightforward in doctrine and practice. Apart from the impact of his art as art, every painting, every drawing was clearly readable in terms of his teaching."[22]

Claude had wangled an invitation to the private view of Sickert's exhibition and was rewarded by the sight of Sickert and Munnings holding court, each surrounded by a bevy of ladies. Sickert wore his "famous ginger tartan frock coat with embellishments, and Munnings was in Newmarket garb banging at his leathers with a whip and so to say with dung on his boots. Their leathern voices competed."[23] Claude was impressed especially by the Old Bedford Music Hall paintings, and these undoubtedly influenced him both in his choice of subject matter and in his handling of paint. Pictures such as *Hannibal's* and *Chocolate-Cigarettes*, while intensely personal in their feeling, owe a great deal to Sickert, in the way they are painted and in their choice of unusual contemporary subjects.

Claude did not, however, break out of the Slade mould of painting until after he had left. A beautiful early painting, the *Spiral Staircase*, of the kitchen of 27 Barrowgate Road, painted directly onto a lightly-toned canvas in about three two-hour sittings, is still in the Tonks manner and has the gentle ambience of a leisured world. Another Slade painting, *Still Life with Reproduction of Breughel's Winter*, shows the traditional attributes of a painter's world. The aim is not to challenge, but to bring together a group of objects in harmony.

This was also the problem to be resolved in a commission that Tonks gave him during his last year, to paint a group portrait of a Yorkshire family named Coates. They had apparently applied to Tonks for a talented student to paint the picture, and Tonks had recommended Claude. The painting was to be done in situ, and Claude was apprehensive about it. Sir Clive Coates was an important figure, with a seat on the Stock Exchange, and the house had many famous visitors, including John Buchan. It was a taste of a different world. Claude made his first visit in August 1929 and was met at the door by a valet and butler. Everything was done for him during his visits to their house, Helperby Hall, near York. He made several visits and several small studies for the final painting, which was done on the spot, with the figures of Sir Clive, Lady Celia, and the four children painted at separate sittings. They appear to have been pleased with the result, and there are among Claude's papers several friendly letters from Lady Celia about the painting. He received a fee of £60, and with the help of this sum a purpose-built, asbestos-walled painting room, spotted at the Ideal Home exhibition, was erected at the bottom of his mother's garden. It was here, in October 1930, that Professor Tonks came to see the completed portrait, and bestow his blessing on his pupil. And it was here, Claude recalled, that "Victor declares he visited me . . . to discover me stark naked, smoking a pipe and working on a large abstract painting 6 foot by 4 foot with a litter of others all around. The ventilation wasn't good and it did get hot in the summer."[24]

NOTES

1 Claude Rogers, unpublished memoir version I, collection Mr Crispin Rogers.
2, 3, 4 Reynolds, Michael, *Slade Student*, unpublished MS, collection Mr Oliver Reynolds.
5 Claude Rogers, unpublished memoir version I, op. cit.
6 Claude Rogers Papers, Tate Gallery Archive.
7 Claude Rogers, unpublished memoir version II, collection Mr Crispin Rogers.
8 Claude Rogers Papers, Tate Gallery Archive.
9 Claude Rogers, unpublished memoir version II, op. cit.
10, 11 Claude Rogers, unpublished memoir version I, op. cit.
12 Claude Rogers Papers, Tate Gallery Archive.
13 Claude Rogers, unpublished memoir version I, op. cit.
14, 15, 16 Claude Rogers Papers, Tate Gallery Archive.
17, 18 Reynolds, Michael, *Slade Student*, op. cit.
19 Claude Rogers Papers, Tate Gallery Archive.
20 Reynolds, Michael, *Slade Student*, op. cit.
21 Claude Rogers Papers, Tate Gallery Archive.
22, 23, 24 Claude Rogers, unpublished memoir version II, op. cit.

Painter without portfolio

For Claude the protected Slade years were over. The world was waiting. On December 18 1930 he moved out of his mother's house and into the Norwegian Seamen's Mission at Gravesend with Avery Colebrook. They were both facing the prospect of making a living. Claude was twenty three and although he had his painting room at home in Chiswick he needed to get away from the somewhat suffocating attention of mother and aunts and to live on his own, as Colebrook was doing. Avery Colebrook, as Claude remembered "was extraordinarily varied in his activities, quite apart from his painting. As a signaller in the RNVR he went on summer cruises. He had a motor bicycle. He built a wireless set with an enormous horn at his studio in Robert Street, in order to listen to some of the first broadcasts on art given by the BBC . . . He lived in an old clap-boarded house in East Street, at that time the home of the Norwegian Seamen's Mission. This had once been the Old Amsterdam, a notorious seamen's grogshop mentioned in the sea-shanty *A-Roving*. Colebrook had the old sea bar, a vast room overlooking the moored flotillas of tugs by the Town Pier. I joined him there for six months or so.

"One day I was talking to the director of the mission, saying how much I wished I too was living there as I wanted to paint round about, when he suggested we look at the attics. There were four of them. I don't suppose anyone had been in them for some years but, although dusty, they had magnificent views of the river. Gas was laid on and surprisingly enough water. 'I don't know if they would do,' he said doubtfully 'but there they are. You can have them for – um – well – let me see. What about half a crown a week, yes? Of course that would include the gas.' This was clearly possible even for me; so I moved in with some cleaning materials, an easel and paints, a camp bed, a kitchen table and chair, and some orange boxes."[1]

The romantic associations of the place, and Colebrook's presence there were clearly irresistible to Claude, although he probably did pay more rent than his rosy reminiscences suggested. Elsewhere in his notes he mentions six shillings a week. He kept a note of his first day's expenses: Railway fare 3/-. Basin 6d. Jersey 12/11. Teapot 6d. Bucket 1/-. Soap 6d. 6 eggs 5½d. Butter 8½d. Groceries 3/-. Dishcloth 3d. Jug 6d. Matches 9d. Stamps 1/-. Exercise book 6d.[2] A further item was two meals for 1/6. Meals were to be had in a workmen's café near the waterfront – a hunk of steak pie, watery potatoes, tea, bread, suet pudding and syrup – or in a fish and chip shop. For a while this bivouac served him very well. "There was plenty to paint at Gravesend, and I learnt from Colebrook the theory and practice of washing up, a discipline I have never forgotten. Not far away along the river there was an ornamental parapet flanked by towers that must once have led down to a landing stage. The river walk widened at this point, into a paved semicircle. I liked going there; and one day poking about in an alley behind the houses, an alley bounded by garden walls on one side and palings and rusty galvanised sheeting on the other, I came upon a place where the sheeting had come away. Pushing this aside I found myself looking into an overgrown open space; and making my way through the fence, I came upon an ornamental statue of Diana, almost lost among growths of ivy and bramble. It was an enchanted place, the lost Rosherville Gardens, where Londoners used to go for an airing in the mid-nineteenth century after Cremorne had acquired a sinister reputation."[3] Claude did a fair amount of drawing and made a number of paintings at Gravesend, including one of Rosherville Gardens Pier. These paintings show flattened, simplified forms and muted, delicate colour, with a much lighter palette than he was accustomed to using at the Slade. They are intentionally rather more 'primitive' than his Slade paintings; it is possible he had seen work by Christopher Wood, who had exhibited paintings in London during the twenties.

Eventually Claude ran out of painting subjects at Gravesend or felt too isolated from his friends. He moved from the Seamen's Mission to a couple of ground floor rooms which had once been the snuggery of an old pub in Park Crescent Mews, just off the Marylebone Road. His brother, who occasionally stayed there to be nearer the hospital where he was training, remembered them as being very draughty, very cold and very small. He took these rooms over from Tommy Carr, paying a rent of 12/6 a week. He found he could dine handsomely at Bertorelli's restaurant nearby, and noted that 1/1d would cover the cost of a substantial meal: a large bowl of minestrone soup with lots of parmesan for 5d, the crusty end of a French loaf for 1d, half a spaghetti al burro for 5d, a small black coffee for 2d and a tip of 1d or 2d for a favourite waitress. It was here that a young reporter from the *Brentford and Chiswick Times* tracked him down. He was interviewing local (Chiswick-based) painters and Claude was to be no. 21. He questioned Claude about his views on Modern Art. Claude remembered trying to explain to him the bleakness which he felt had come to be associated with modern painting, and the lack of warmth and humanity in it. "Somehow these qualities should be brought back into painting but without weakening that understanding of purely formal values which had been gained."[4]

Throughout 1930 Claude had worked on a number of Chiswick paintings, noting the following in his diary: Cochrane's Revue, Coliseum Chiswick, Chiswick High Road, Nocturne (St. James' Piccadilly and tarts). These were followed up by the Gravesend paintings. In 1930 he was invited to exhibit with the London Group and showed two paintings – *Cinema Royal, Chiswick* and *Coliseum, Chiswick.* In 1931 he showed *Roofs, Gravesend.* Exhibiting with the London Group was a coveted mark of recognition shown to young painters, who joined in the exhibitions by invitation only. In the 1930s the London Group represented the tougher, more experimental face of British art and membership of it was eagerly sought by Britain's most serious artists.

The London Group had an interesting genesis. Some of its founder members had begun their artistic careers at the beginning of the century, and one of them, Walter Sickert, had been a radical member of the New English Art Club, founded in 1886 in opposition to the domination of the Royal Academy. Early in the twentieth century the New English Art Club seemed to have lost its vitality and a group of friends, meeting in Sickert's studio, proposed forming a large association of independent artists which would mount annual exhibitions similar to the French Salon des Indépendants. This was the Allied Artists Association, which survived long enough to hold eight annual exhibitions, the first in 1908, held in the Albert Hall. These exhibitions were enormous, too big for any one group to make its presence felt. Sickert and his friends formed the habit of meeting frequently at the Café Royal, where they discussed whether to try and reform the New English Art Club, now grown ominously conservative, or to secede from it and form a new society. At length they decided on the latter course and named themselves the Camden Town Group. The Camden Town Group consisted of Sickert, Gilman, Ginner, Bevan, Spencer Gore (the first president), Malcolm Drummond, Duncan Grant, J.D. Innes, Augustus John, Henry Lamb, Wyndham Lewis, Lucien Pissarro, William Ratcliffe, and J.B. Manson (secretary). It represented an extraordinary confluence of varied talent, but its very variety meant it was not destined to last long. Other societies, such as the Cumberland Market Group and 'Nineteen Fitzroy Street' were in existence, and all these groups amalgamated in November 1913 under the presidency of Harold Gilman. Thus the London Group came into existence, its name suggested by Epstein. It included Britain's new avant garde artists, Epstein, Nevinson, Wadsworth, William Roberts, and Bomberg.

Ethelbert White, in a letter dated August 10 1958, told Claude a poignant story concerning the young Bomberg and his work in the London Group. "He had climbed the stairs of the Goupil Gallery under a canvas of vast proportions and was met by Nevinson at the top who informed him, partly in joke, that no works could be hung if the member's subscription had not been paid. Bomberg with a good-tempered grin hauled his enormous canvas back down into Regent Street, and although members of the hanging committee ran down to recall him, all they saw was a great sail tacking across Piccadilly."[5]

The London Group was effectively an annual exhibiting society, dedicated to independent, non-factional art, and to welcoming experimental work. Its first exhibition was held at the Goupil Gallery in March 1914. Roger Fry was elected to its membership in 1917 and brought in the Bloomsbury painters. Fry's influence as an arbiter of taste was considerable and he had a powerful sway also in the selection of work for exhibition, trying to direct the Group towards French models. "There is something to be said for that picture," exclaimed Fry as a painting by a non-member was about to be removed after it had been rejected by the Selection Committee. "Say, it Roger, say it," was Sickert's affectionately malicious retort.[6] In the 1930s the London Group had assumed a position of vital importance in British art. Roger Fry wrote in a foreword to the 1931 exhibition catalogue: "The years covered by the existence of the London Group comprise one of the most eventful episodes in the history of British art. It has been a period of searching enquiry into the principles of design, of criticism of all the accepted standards, of daring experiment in the search for new possibilities. Throughout this period the London Group has been the home of those English artists in whom the ferment of new ideas was working." Every forward-looking artist of the time was a member, and Claude was now on the threshold. After exhibiting regularly with the Group throughout the thirties he was elected as a full member in 1938. Fourteen years later he was to become its president.

During the early thirties Claude was seeing as much as possible of his Slade friends, and a great deal of William Coldstream. Coldstream had moved out of the family home and was living at 76 Charlotte Street, Constable's old studio. Claude later lived here himself, and it had once been the work room for one of Sickert's many schools, and according to Sickert, the least successful. He told Claude that in all his time there he only managed to get two students and they were Siamese twins! It was here, in the finely proportioned room with a beautiful light from a narrow window running just below the ceiling along the whole length of the north wall, that Claude was one day asked to stay and meet the son of a doctor friend of Coldstream's father who was working as a clerk at County Hall but was very keen on painting. This turned out to be Victor Pasmore. Pasmore had become interested in painting while at school at Harrow and had even submitted and sold a picture at the Royal Academy while still there. He had great natural talent and an equal curiosity about the theory and practice of painting. Pasmore's father had died young, when his son was only sixteen, making it necessary for him to earn his living. He lived at home with his mother, brother and sister at Dewhurst Road, Brook Green, Hammersmith. His work at County Hall afforded him some measure of financial security and allowed him to develop his painting, in the evenings and at weekends, in his own remarkable way. At the end of their first meeting Claude and Victor had found a good deal in common as well as a shared interest in painting; they were each the eldest of three children, with a brother training to be a doctor, and a younger sister. Both their fathers had died young and they lived near each other in their mothers' houses. They travelled back home together by underground, agreeing to meet again as soon as possible. It was the beginning of a lifelong friendship.

Pasmore, Claude wrote many years later, "proved to be diverting and interesting. He had an amusing and aggressive cock of the head, with an unruly tail of hair sticking out behind like an Indian's feather. His eyes, large and dark, were set fairly deep in a face shaped like a cob-nut, curving from wide cheek bones to a broad, flattish mouth and a rounded, determined chin . . . [at this first meeting he] lurched around the studio, hands in pocket, head sunk in shoulders, looking at things. He didn't say much, but what he said was to the point . . . Soon after I got to know him he found an attractive painting-room, a large attic near Finsbury Park Station where I often went to see him. Finsbury Park was a choice determined by Pasmore's peculiar sense of logic after he had decided to have a work room [as far] away from home [as possible] . . . in those days Finsbury Park was the terminal station on the Central London line from Hammersmith."[7]

Pasmore made good use of his time despite having a full time job. Claude would often ring him at County Hall to find him not available – he was probably drawing or thinking out some new painting in the lavatory. "Although Pasmore was in a full time job so that he had far less time for painting than I did he was producing much more. He had no formal education in art apart from some evening classes at the Central School, drawing under Hartrick; but he was so interested in everything to do with painting, talked to so many painters and himself painted so variously that this was not very important . . . Like several Harrovians I knew, Pasmore could be aggressive, dogmatic, intolerant and provoking; but he had charm, a quick mind and talked in a lively and personal kind of shorthand, interrupted by 'static' like a faulty wireless set, so that he constantly tailed off . . . He was the best of companions. No one I had met was so discerning where pictures of whatever kind were concerned. To visit an exhibition with Pasmore is still one of the most enjoyable and rewarding things I know."[8] Claude and Victor took to meeting in the lunch hour and going to look at exhibitions together. "Victor had an eye and made surprising discoveries which more often than not were worth a look. He took in a show extremely quickly and we would see a great deal in that lunch hour of his."[9]

Many years later, at a rather rowdy party, Claude sat next to a bored Freudian psychologist, and told him that the two painters he knew best were called William Coldstream and Victor Pasmore. The psychologist perked up a bit, looked interested, and commented that when one thought about it the name of Claude Rogers fitted in nicely.

In December 1931 Claude was elected to the London Artists' Association. The LAA was a unique venture in art economics, originating from Bloomsbury. The idea owed much to Roger Fry and to the economist, John Maynard Keynes. Fry always did his utmost to help modern artists in England, and kept in touch with as many of them as possible. He was generous and interested in the young, encouraged by Helen Anrep, who had moved in with him after the failure of her marriage to the Russian mosaicist Boris Anrep. They gave parties at their house in Bernard Street which Claude and his friends attended. Fry had practical administrative experience from his years at the Metropolitan Museum in New York and from running the Omega Workshop. There were in London at that time very few dealer galleries, and even established artists could not be sure of having their work exhibited and sold. Keynes and Fry induced some of their wealthier friends, collectors of paintings, to take an interest and to put up money to guarantee certain selected artists a small annual income. In his notes, Claude kept a little verse from the *Nation and Atheneum*, written by 'Mac Flecknoe', confirming the influence of Roger Fry and Keynes:

When anybody wants to know
Who are the Nation's leading sages,
It pleases me to make reply
Well, J.M. Keynes and Roger Fry,
While Mr Leonard Woolf and I
Instruct the public in the *Nation*'s pages.

The four original guarantors of the LAA were Samuel Courtauld, F. Hindley Smith, the novelist L.H. Myers and Keynes himself. Seven artists, all members of the London Group, were represented in the opening exhibition at the Leicester Galleries in May 1926. They were mainly Bloomsbury painters – Roger Fry, Vanessa Bell, Duncan Grant, Bernard Adeney, Keith Baynes, Frederick Porter and Frank Dobson. Each artist was paid £150 per annum, plus any sum in excess of £150 made from sales, less 30% commission. At first the Association went exceptionally well, and Keynes noted that in the first four and a half years of the LAA's existence they had sold more than 700 works for an aggregate sum of £22,000, being an average of £30 each. By December 1931, however, when Claude was elected to its membership, the LAA was running into difficulties. 1929 had seen the stock market crash in America, and in Britain the economic slump was making itself felt. The public were not buying so many pictures and prices were not so good. Claude was not offered a contract or a guaranteed income. Membership of the LAA now conferred no more than entry into their exhibitions and work held in stock for public viewing at their gallery opposite St. George's, Hanover Square, or, later, at their premises at 163 Old Bond Street. For the final two years of its life the LAA was housed in a part of the Cooling Galleries at 92 New Bond Street. The prestige of being a member was important, but the rewards were minimal. Claude appears to have sold only two paintings through the LAA, one to W.A. Evill, a solicitor and well-known collector, and one to James Agate the theatre critic. Agate, in his memoir '*Ego I*', records selling his car and with the proceeds buying art at the LAA – a painting by Cox for 10 gns, an Allan Walton for 10 gns and a Claude Rogers for 5 gns. For the two paintings by Claude that were sold, he received, less commission, a total of 7 gns. Although the sales themselves were flattering, this was an alarmingly small return on about six months' work.

Two years later, in 1933, Claude was offered a one-man exhibition at the LAA. He shared the galleries with the painter John Dodgson, with whom he had been elected in 1931. He appears to have sold nothing, although the show received some critical attention. A fortnight after the opening, Keynes invited all the artist-members of the Association to his house at 46 Gordon Square for the final meeting of the LAA, or as Claude designated it, the Grand Assassination Tea. Keynes was already channelling much of his money and energy into ballet, spurred on by his wife, the dancer Lydia Lopokova, and by 1932 two of the painters in whom he was most interested, Duncan Grant and Vanessa Bell, had been taken on by Agnews as their dealer.

The Grand Assassination Tea took place on May 16 1933. At the meeting beforehand the LAA decided to go out in a blaze of glory, with a final retrospective exhibition of members' work. This show took place at the Cooling Galleries in 1934. Claude showed two paintings – *Cannon Street Bridge* and *Mr Mondale Willing*. But the tea stuck in Claude's memory chiefly for the fact that the buns were stale and rock hard, "a job lot of buns if ever there was one. Unsuitable for human teeth and Epstein's Rock Drill would have done no better. My indignation grew. The least we deserved, I felt, was a fresh, spiced, warm bun apiece. I could almost smell it. A bon bouche . . . I began to regard the cheerful Keynes as rather a scoundrel, a cheapjack".[10] This was a view Claude maintained to the end of his life, and later referred many times to Keynes' apparent meanness over the buns. At the tea Claude was determined not to go without having extracted something from the visit. He asked Keynes if he could look at his pictures. Victor Pasmore, also at the meeting, went with him into the big front room overlooking Gordon Square. They studied the paintings – mainly Camden Town and Bloomsbury, Sickert, Gore, Gilman, Grant, Bell – and then spotted a Bonnard painting, recently acquired. Claude opened his mouth to ask Victor's opinion when "from below the level of our navels came a slight stirring, and a sharp sound as though a pussycat had woken and started to stretch. We looked down. We had not noticed the chaise longue or the tiny tight curl of Lopokova asleep upon it. There was no doubt she was about to waken. Our retreat was hurried, but soundless."[11]

In 1932 both the national and Claude's personal economic situation had driven him back to living at home in Chiswick. Money from Uncle Jim in the Argentine was no longer coming through and he had virtually nothing coming in from his paintings. He based himself at home, spending his time drawing in the streets around Chiswick. There was a group of painters living in St. Peter's Square in Chiswick, among them Ceri Richards, Raymond Coxon and John Piper, and he spent a good deal of time with them, talking about art and playing chess. His diary notes that he stayed with John Piper at Chalkpit Cottage, Bletchworth, Surrey, in June of that year. He also began to visit Lucien Pissarro, then aged 70, in his studio at Stamford Brook "where the battens, which ran round all four walls, held row upon row of paintings done plein air. There was usually a group busily talking around the tea table though Pissarro himself said little. He would sit in his armchair with folded hands, the eyes withdrawn, the gold-rimmed spectacles a-twinkle, the head bowed over the benevolent white beard. Something said would occasionally catch his attention and then in an extraordinary sweet and high-pitched voice – which invariably surprised me, as though a bassoon began to tootle like a flute – he would begin to talk – about what he had heard Renoir say in the circumstances, or what Cézanne would have said since that idea was one of which he particularly disapproved. The names fluttered round the room . . ."[12]

Claude later remembered 1932 as the year he saw a Picasso painting [probably *Girl at a Mirror*] which Zwemmer had brought back to London fresh from Picasso's studio and put on display in his gallery window. Work of that quality was not easy to see in London at the time. Matisse was a considerable influence on young painters, and Claude saw what he could of Matisse's work. The Gargoyle Club in Dean Street had an interior designed by Matisse and two of his paintings hung on the walls. "A sheet of mirror-glass tessera swept over the entire interior – ceilings, walls and mouldings – giving an extraordinary light. The two great paintings hung – the one over the band – this I think was the still life, objects painted flatly and scattered over a red ground, while the other, the studio interior with the model, was over the bar. I was not, like Coldstream, influenced by them in my painting at that time but I was immensely impressed and never could quite give my attention to the food and drink and conversation . . ."[13] In order to study these paintings, Coldstream and Rodrigo Moynihan would meet and go to the club early, persuading the cleaning staff to let them in. This ploy did not occur to Claude. But John Dodgson had become a friend and several times asked him to dine at the Gargoyle, where he could look at Matisse's paintings.

One summer day Ceri Richards announced to Claude that "representation is finished". The statement puzzled him greatly at first, but he found that a group of his friends, chiefly Rodrigo Moynihan and Geoffrey Tibble, had begun to experiment with abstract painting of a unique kind, owing little to models that were to be seen on the continent. The idea was ruthlessly to eliminate all reference to the outside world, and to build up a web of colour and texture created by the 'pure brushstroke' onto the canvas. These paintings came to be known as Objective Abstractions. Claude's notes recalled: "When you looked at an Objective Abstraction you saw a soft, amorphous and somewhat crusted surface with little in the way of a focus or structure and little apparent concern for relationships between surface markings and the edges of the canvas. The colour was clean, high and simple – black strokes, greys, white areas, earth pinks, a pale ochre, perhaps were the kind of mixtures you saw. As the style developed the surfaces became exquisite by intention, with a suggestion of enamelling or of porcelain glazes. The canvases, never very big, took a long time to do."[14] In some ways Objective Abstraction foreshadowed the gestural painting of the late 1940s in America, but it never incorporated the private symbolism that painters such as Rothko and Barnett Newman developed in their work. And the paintings were very different in size (the American canvases being huge by comparison with the British) and in speed of execution. Objective Abstractions were built up slowly and deliberately, depending on the visual sensibility of the painter and the strength of his creative intuition. Claude always considered Tibble the leader of the Objective Abstraction group, as he was best able to formulate their ideas. Moynihan and Tibble produced the most work, but quite a number of other painters - Graham Bell, Tommy Carr, Edgar Hubert, Coldstream and Pasmore, as well as Claude himself - were on the periphery. Claude tried his hand at abstract painting, as did Coldstream and Pasmore, who visited Claude in his Chiswick painting room and criticised his new canvases. Claude remembered in detail the method of making an 'objectively abstract' painting. "On a virgin canvas a start was made with random strokes and rubbings of paint or if pushed to it by a system of marks suggested by any objects to hand. But representation was barred and any hint of it destroyed at once. And if in the course of work chance marks on the surface of the canvas began to suggest an image these were obliterated too. Leonardo's stains on old walls and stones had no place here. A surface was gradually built up by addition. The artist considered the marks and spreads of paint already on the canvas. Presently he felt impelled to alter what he saw. He made more marks and the balance on the surface was altered. It was a process of inspection, evaluation and change which had some resemblance to the adjustments which Mondrian made when he was at work on one of his grid pattern compositions circa 1921. But there was nothing equivalent to the philosophical 'controls' which governed Mondrian's reconstruction of reality, with metaphysical values attached to right angle and rectangle, vertical and horizontal."[15]

In 1934 an exhibition of these paintings, organised by Robert Wellington who invented the title Objective Abstractions, was held at Zwemmer's Gallery. It attracted some critical attention, mostly adverse. Brian Howard in the *New Statesman* complained that it was difficult to distinguish between the work of Tibble, Moynihan and Graham Bell, the paintings were so alike in conception; but as Claude pointed out, the art-form was so new that it was "like a negro newly arrived among white folk saying that it was difficult to see any difference in their faces". The exhibition was accompanied by a catalogue in which the artists involved made statements about their work. Claude remembered Pasmore's answer to the question "What are you trying to express?" "The painting itself is the expression." He later maintained that this reply should be memorised by every painter, being "the correct reply to so many gambits from the Philistin Incartade to the Prodnose Refused and leaves the painter beautifully poised if he can be bothered to counter-attack."[16] Despite some painstaking attempts by one or two critics to understand what was going on, most failed to do so. One critic dubbed the group 'objectionable obstructionists'; and when in the following years Tibble and Moynihan exhibited abstract paintings with the London Group the reaction was definitely hostile. "Mr Moynihan works up a mass of pigment into the consistency of raspberries and cream and calls it Painting." The painters were somewhat discouraged by the public reaction to their work, but they took to Sickert's advice on bad reviews in the press: "For God's sake don't read them, weigh them." By that criterion Objective Abstraction pound for pound did very well. However, there were very few sales, the collector showing most interest being Mr Billy Winkworth, a collector of porcelain with an eye for a fine surface texture.

Claude's experiments with Objective Abstraction left him dissatisfied. He found he could not begin the paintings without some objects to look at and to inform his first marks on the canvas. Then he became so fascinated by what he was looking at – orange boxes, a chair, a table – that he could not free himself from his subject. He was reading Herbert Read's *Art Now*, published in 1933, and he sympathised with the aims of abstract art and admired the products of his friends, seeing it as the only kind of English abstract painting to develop spontaneously while owing nothing to continental models. But he decided that it was not for him; he needed the motif, the outside object, to look at and think about when he painted. If he began to think more about the painting than the subject he was looking at, he tended to dislike the results. Much later he wrote "Today, although I like looking at non-figurative pictures I cannot imagine painting them, but between 1932 and 1935 I was seriously painting abstractions. I remember a series of formalised still life, abstracted from nature rather than abstract in conception; and another series, purer in intention, and based on flat geometric shapes . . . I cannot now imagine doing them; my own idea of painting is coarser and more earthy. I like looking at all kinds of pictures and drawings. Not that I go to every exhibition. I look at them where I find them, maybe in a dealer's gallery or a public building or a famous collection; maybe in a private house, or a junk shop, or one of those pubs where pictures are hung on the wall."[17] Claude deliberately tried to keep his subject matter firmly in mind, while avoiding the dangers of illustration. The purely formal side of his painting – the selection and combination of shapes and colours – was arrived at semi-subconsciously while his visual curiosity was focused on the subject itself.

Instead of pursuing his abstract studies, Claude reverted to his preferred subjects – the sights around the river and the streets of Chiswick. He haunted the cinemas and the fun fairs which had sprung up within shop premises forced into bankruptcy by the economic depression. He got to know many curious people and places and his painting became more dependent on them. "I had found a pencil with a torch attachment, used by students for notetaking at lectures, and began to try and draw in one of the small cinemas, The Cinema Royal, during the show. The management who discovered me at my work because of the torch were interested enough to give me a free pass. As a result I spent a great deal of time there, drawing and savouring the atmosphere. Like the fun fairs, which were beginning to grow in number, it was a loitering place for the unemployed (was I not unemployed myself?), warm, too, in winter. The number of people present, their mood, their awareness of one another, their absorption in or apathy to the film being shown varied unaccountably and was to me quite extraordinary. Normally the front row or so was rowdy with kids. Behind, a scattering of people. On some days they seemed to sit as far apart as possible, on another a little group might fall into a whispered discussion, during an entire performance with God knows what drama and catastrophe of nature whipping by on the screen. Very occasionally there would be a hint of violence. Management appeared. A few words. A shabby figure left . . . Of the oddities, the two cigarette girls had soon drawn my attention. Each had her 'station'. They guided people to a seat with their torch and occasionally made a slow round up and down the aisles, their torches illuminating the trays which held their wares, with a low monotonous chant 'chocolate-cigarettes'. Otherwise they went to their stations. They froze. They were in love with the cinema, mesmerized. Hour after hour they leant against the wall, content to see the same film again yet one more time till, come Thursday, come Saturday, the programme changed. Their tray was slung from their shoulders and they wore black dresses, rather loose, a bit short, and aprons and caps like waitresses.

"The one I drew was called Arleen. She was very obliging, once she discovered what I wanted she made a careful note of where I wanted her to stand and whenever her duties permitted, there she was for me frozen in place. The lighting was subtle, the pose slightly off balance – Arleen about to stir. There she stood, crucified against a long vertical and some horizontals of the architecture. Well, that was what the painting was meant to be about. I would take my drawing home and work from it and see what I needed to try for in the next drawing. The painting was 16 inches by 8 inches and went on and on forever. I put it into the Exhibition with the title *Chocolate-Cigarettes.* I took Arleen a private view card. She was flattered, excited, but doubted she could go. She had never been further from Chiswick than Hammersmith Broadway in one direction and Kew Green in the other. I never found out if she went. She had begun to frighten me."[18]

Another favourite place of Claude's was Hannibal's Fun Palace near St. Peter's Square. It had once been a drapers but now "the whole interior had been roughly plastered, sometimes in great bosses of form and then covered all over with shimmering metallic papers which were illuminated by batteries of lamp bulbs, the poor man's Gargoyle no less! Against this interior full of queer corners, were the rows of pin tables. A large clear space was given over to the Bumper Cars. These chariots had attendants connecting them to an electrified mesh ceiling. They were an extravagance and were not often in use in great numbers, but would glide about when in action with a crackle of overhead sparks. Their shape especially in conjunction was beautiful. I did several paintings in which they appeared with silent figures grouped behind them on the cinder verge. On what had been the long blank wall behind them someone had painted a long abstract design in distemper, freely done and truly remarkable. The boss knew nothing of its author, one of the workmen in his spare time, he thought. Part of it came into some of my paintings."[19]

Claude's wanderings around Chiswick resulted in a series of potent small paintings – *Hannibal's*, *Cinema Royal*, a painting of the cinema with its blue dome, large display of placards and magnificent commissionaire, and an aeroplane in the sky, a daring introduction, Claude thought, in order to emphasise the space. This was the first of Claude's paintings to show an aeroplane – a theme he was to develop later on. There were also the *Grand Organ of the Commodore Cinema*, *Fun Fair*, a painting of the bumper cars, and others. Five of them were in Claude's show at the LAA, nothing bigger than 25 inches by 30 inches. As Claude admitted, they owed their idea and method largely to Sickert, but updated to the current time. Cinemas replaced music halls; Sickert's subject matter of music hall and dingy interior had by that time acquired a romantic patina, and Claude looked for subjects that were new, awkward and raw. Without losing any of the immediacy and authenticity of the subject Claude succeeded in creating strong and satisfyingly constructed images in unusual and very beautiful colour. He remarked later that he had no socialist realist thoughts while making these paintings - "there was something about the atmosphere, it was very moving in some queer way, while the actual shapes and things to be seen were extraordinary."

Claude was rather stranded in Chiswick with effectively no income. He saw a lot of Pasmore and the St. Peter's Square friends, but he missed the Fitzroy Square crowd, and especially Coldstream who was now married and living in Regent's Square. "By now I really was getting rather isolated in Chiswick, living in an aunt-haunted house and . . . cut off from my north London comrades. It sounds absurd, but with no source of income and hesitations about cadging from my mother it had become difficult to make the journey very often. Of course I did go to the occasional Hampstead party, and so home to Chiswick in the early morning by my own patient route which passed, about half way, the best coffee stall in London . . . I still saw Pasmore. That meant a lot. But somehow I missed the chitchat with the Fitzroy Square crowd and with Coldstream. The St. Peter's Square people were intelligent and charming and good artists but I had far less in common with them. When it came to choosing work for my show, I decided to show figurative work only. The experimental work seemed too uncertain and disconnected. I had no confidence in it as a whole . . . Maybe I had learned something doing them but I could not think what and they depressed me . . ."[20]

In his LAA exhibition, with the cinema and fun fair pictures Claude also showed some landscapes of Cumberland. These were the result of a long walk Claude undertook with Michael Reynolds and Avery Colebrook. Avery, who liked seeing things for himself, decided it would be of interest to have a look at England in the year 1932 in an unprejudiced and exploratory spirit. "After studying his maps he decided that if one took a long slant, from just outside London with somewhere like Keswick in the Lake District for a destination, a varied prospect would day by day unfold, since the walk would be across the geological stratification of the country . . . Avery then persuaded me and Michael Reynolds to go with him. I know I was told that we would make time on the way for the occasional watercolour and that the constant change in the type of landscape would delight me, and indeed I brought back quite a batch of drawings. I seem to remember that I was able to finance this working holiday on a picture which Kenneth Clark bought from the Palser Gallery for Southampton Art Gallery [*The Spiral*

Staircase, 1927] . . . We started off on July 7th, each carrying light sleeping kit in a rucksack and a share of the food and cooking gear. As Colebrook had promised the kind of landscape we walked through continually changed – some of the little towns where industry was still almost a craft seemed fairly prosperous. There was a lack of paint everywhere but that was more noticeable in parts of the countryside where thatch and fences were in some disrepair too. Townees though we were, we realised that some crops were choked with weed. In a bigger town I noticed a small listless group of unemployed on a street corner, just as in the Chiswick High Road.

"I was made treasurer and had a notebook in which I recorded all items of personal expenditure. The first entry I had to make reads: 'July 7th – Colebrook Vol. 2 Karl Marx – 2/4.' I am impressed. Three really serious young men . . . Michael kept his 6′4½″ going with many extra lunches and it was anything up to 2/9½d at a go. From July 7th to July 29th Colebrook smoked 230 cigarettes at sixpence for 10. I smoked 6 oz of pipe tobacco and bought some viridian water colour (a whole pan) and a drawing pencil from the Howe Farm, Keswick. I sent for paints, canvas and an easel, already packed and awaiting dispatch by Mr Shea . . . the colour man in Fitzroy Street. On August 1st, Avery and Michael set off again making for the Roman Wall. I next saw them in London."[21] The half dozen or so paintings made as a result of this trip are low toned and very green. Slade colour but with a firm grasp on the simplified shapes of the landscape.

Pasmore at this time was spending his leave in Dieppe, where he liked the associations, so near to and yet so very different from England. However, when not in France, he and Claude saw a good deal of each other. Claude sat to Pasmore for a portrait not long before his exhibition opened. "I had sat down in a bentwood rocking chair he had and he began to squint at me and then asked if I'd mind sitting. He hadn't a suitable canvas but rummaged about until he turned up a piece of ply some twenty inches by twenty four and then found he'd run out of turps. There was an oilman in the terrace of shops nearby but Victor wanted to make a start and decided to use paraffin. The chair in which I was sitting with its tight curves and scrolls was to provide him with a motif which he explored for some years . . . The piece of ply he used already had on it a Matisse-like still life of two white fish, like opened-up haddocks, upon a dark ground. He set to work on this in a relaxed unhurried way giving the impression of a class batsman with his eye in and plenty of time for his strokes. He painted with great economy, making full use of the dark grey-green ground . . . For long periods he would sit head cocked to one side, left leg crossed almost at right angles upon his right thigh, thoughtfully regarding his canvas. Occasionally there would be a long slow look at me. He would choose a brush with care, make a slow mixture and then draw a carefully calculated line or define a small area. It was a pity about the paraffin. In the course of time . . . the surface has deteriorated."[22]

Sometimes Victor and Claude would go off for the day, walking and drawing along the Sussex coast, by the Seven Sisters or to Newhaven. In July 1935 they had a holiday together in a punt on the Basingstoke Canal. One end of the punt was laden with canvases and paint and food and the other end with tins of paraffin for cooking and a stove. Despite having to bale out the punt after a great thunderstorm, they managed quite a bit of painting. They had both been looking at Bonnard's paintings, and his influence can be seen in both painters' work of this time. Pasmore's picture *The Quiet River* was a product of this trip.

By 1933 the world depression and the first stirrings of rearmament had begun to make their impression even on the art world. Free speech was being stifled in Germany, and writers, artists and scientists as well as the working classes were being persecuted. Liberal thinkers in England were moved to indignation by the menace of the fascist philosophy of racial hatred and the idealisation of war. Claude was among them. He noted Mussolini's remark that "war is to man what maternity is to woman" with repugnance; and he rallied to the cause of the Artists International Association. The AIA was founded in September 1933 by about twenty committed left-wing artists and writers, among them Percy Horton, Edward Ardizzone, Hans Feibusch, Misha Black and the three Jims - Jim Boswell, Jim Fitton and Jim Holland. It was a politically conscious body of artists, socialist in spirit and motivation. Their brief was "to oppose The Imperialist War on the Soviet Union, Fascism and Colonial Oppression" with their art, and to hold fortnightly discussions on communism. In that climate communism offered a very attractive alternative to the prevailing ideology, and many flirted with it or became committed communists. Members also tried to help artists get out of Germany and find homes in Britain.

The AIA held its first exhibition, *The Social Scene*, in premises in Charlotte Street, and subsequent exhibitions were held either there, or in Frith Street or Grosvenor Street. In 1935 there was an important exhibition in Soho Square - *Artists against Fascism and War* - which included work by Robert Medley, Paul Nash and Henry Moore. By the end of the war the Association had over a thousand members. The powerful communist lobby had been checked by more moderate members who, while not afraid to support political causes, were fully aware of the defects of communism, and were reluctant to be drawn into an extreme political stance. The AIA became less political and more of an exhibiting society. In 1947 Claude found the premises at 15 Lisle Street where the Association established its gallery and where it flourished until 1971. Claude was involved from its inception with the AIA's activities but kept out of the politics, believing that the artist's job was to make art. He made the following note: "The political point of view of the AIA was during the early part of 1935 very fully discussed and the opinion of many representative artists was sought. It was generally thought that the manifesto issued in 1933 was both narrow and out-of-date. It omitted many matters about which artists as a whole cared deeply, and about which they might be prepared to cooperate with such a large and uneven group as the AIA. For although aiming in the right direction, the AIA had been taking a too specialised point of view. It had not considered the artist *qua* artist. It had thought of him only in connection with the needs of the working class. This point of view carried with it the assumption that all artists must recognise that their future is bound up with the success of the working class movement. . . It was discovered that very few artists were prepared to accept this outlook."[23] Later, in about 1937, Claude noted that the immense improvement in the May Day processions and meetings for Spain in Trafalgar Square had been largely due to the AIA who designed and executed banners, posters and tableaux, and that "considerable numbers of members have attended all outdoor demonstrations of this kind which were in accordance with the aims of the Association, which has its own banner for such occasions." At the exhibition held in Soho Square in 1937 about 500 artists contributed; money was raised for the Spanish Medical Aid Committee, and a lorry was sent to Spain. Later Claude amongst others backed a scheme to produce lithographs at a price everyone could afford, and in 1940 AIA Everyman Prints were published at 1/- and 1/6 each.

One Saturday in 1934 Claude met some of the Hunger Marchers in Hyde Park. "An idea for a painting had been germinating, the result of previous visits, and now I wanted to make drawings for it - simple enough really, people asleep, lovers - lying in the long grass. That afternoon there were an unusual lot of people sitting about in clumps. I sat down against a tree to watch and gradually realised that they must be a body of marchers recently arrived, grubby but in good shape and spirits, some still accoutred with knapsack and blanket roll and too tired for the moment to get rid of them. I began to draw. It was a fine, natural group. A banner rolled up leant against a fence, another was half draped over it. My interest quickened. These people were more interesting than the sleepers in the grass . . . It seemed urgent that I should have a go, the other could wait."

Claude engaged them in friendly conversation, and it struck him that he might be able to offer one or two of them a wash or some hot food. "I had enough money for the bus fares home and a nest egg there. I could manage hot water - not in the house - Good God! the enormity of the enterprise suddenly dawned on me, but it seemed that I had already made an impulsive proposition of some kind because they were looking at me differently and a small group were smiling and carrying on a confabulation. 'If it's OK with you we'd like Nel Oldershaw to go. She's found it worse than the rest, and a real wash up and a proper kip down for a night or so is what she needs . . . Set her to rights, OK?' If the redhead had sloshed me with a hammer I could not have been more stunned . . . I made an attempt to get Nel a companion but my suggestion was brushed aside . . . presently Nel and I set off for 27 Barrowgate Road . . . Somehow I should have to convoy my precious Nel across the garden lawn and into the hut. This was the hut where Victor had discovered me, a pipe-smoking, naked, abstract painter. If only, I thought, I dare come clean with my mother, if only there was the half chance she would understand. But the miseries over each day's *Daily Telegraph*, of unemployment, of the marchers and bolshevism, and ultimately the wicked Argentine, daunted me. Then there were the Neighbours and the two Aunts. On my side, I suddenly realised, was the fact that they were accustomed to the occasional professional model coming to work for me. At a pinch Nel would pass for another Nellie Tanner or Elsie Cecilia Dennis - somehow that was wrong; and then the whole thing became something I very much wanted to do, a bit of help to someone I might never see again but had warmed to. I was going to carry it through no one the wiser, as adroitly as I could - come hell or high water.

"We had been chatting on our bus top as with part of my mind I reviewed the problem and of course I looked at her too. She was charming and unaffected and had begun to perk up. I suddenly saw her in all her pallor of dust, and her tangle of grime and sweat and with this aliveness, in the middle of a painting, of her and her mates in a casual group under the tree, the banners too, the blanket rolls and pile of haversacks. I really wanted to paint that. This must have lent me confidence. I had no trouble getting her and her paper parcel into the studio-hut, left her with a warning to keep inside and out of the way of the house dwellers, marched indoors and filled two huge galvanised pails, one with warm, the other with scalding water . . ."

Claude provided her with washing things and food, and returned from further provisioning to find a completely different figure. "Gone entirely was my heroine of the long march. Clean, kempt, hair washed and combed, no make-up but bright-eyed, a contented and composed young lady tried to thank me . . . Why the hell hadn't I done one drawing before filling those buckets? I did do some drawings of her while she was around. I suppose they were alright . . . I was astonished what a couple of nights' rest and perhaps the food did for her. When I took her back to the Park some of her friends had drifted off. The others welcomed her in an incuriously matter-of-fact way and smiled at me. We shook hands and she ventured a light kiss. We waved. That was that."[24] Presumably the painting of the Hunger Marchers never materialised as there is no record of it in Claude's papers. The drawings he did of Nel may still some day come to light.

Claude was never really politically committed although, in sympathy with his peer group, he was socialist in inclination. Although he was possessed of a natural sympathy towards all sorts of people, he cannot have identified strongly with the working class – his background was too sheltered and his natural leanings too academic. Although at times he was comparatively hard up, he was never actually as poor as he imagined he was, and he never suffered real hardship. As he became increasingly a figure of the establishment, his natural socialism was probably tempered by practical realities of getting on and making a living and a reputation. He never took part in any political societies except when painting was involved. He simply did not operate in that way. He was, however, acutely aware of the political situation in the 1930s and followed world events with increasing alarm.

When in 1933 Hitler was Chancellor in Germany, and Britain was in the grip of a severe depression, Claude noticed that "the texture of life seemed to alter". Many of the paintings he did in 1933 were signed R 33. This signature held a special meaning for him, referring to the great airship disaster of that year and to the ominous times. As a Jew, he belonged to a minority group within Britain; this may have inhibited any political inclinations on his part. Whether by nature or by upbringing, his tendency was to conform, to follow tradition, rather than to deviate from the norm. In the early thirties he began to meet with anti-semitic prejudice, which he had hardly encountered amongst his liberal set of friends. Amongst Claude's papers was a letter to the *Times* from a Mrs Rosa Henderson which Claude cut out many years later (October 29 1968) and kept as a reminder – "Surely there must be enough people, like myself, who can still remember the slogan PJ (Perish Jews) painted alongside the fascist encircled lightning flash, throughout Britain before the war . . ." Claude did remember. In 1933 he was for the first time deliberately insulted because he was a Jew; and in a letter dated March 3 1936 he wrote to his future wife about another incident at Bertorelli's restaurant, where he was going regularly to a particular table to make drawings for a painting. "[I] found my place occupied by a lousy couple, so I sat with my back to them. Presently a familiar figure came in. I thought I knew him but although we casually eyed one another we were ships that passed in the night. And then Robert Medley came in and I realised the first chap was Rupert Doone. Rupert's face slowly smiled.

–Hallo.

–Hallo.

–It's a long time since I've seen you.

–Yes, I don't come up very much.

–Is this place taken? We may as well sit here.

"It was indeed a long time since we had met. Except for one occasion, the last time had been after a London Artists meeting. It was summer 1933 I think. Anyway Hitler had just become Chancellor that spring and there was a good deal of discussion about him. And of course the Jews. Jew-baiting was becoming an Aryan national sport over there. It's awkward on these occasions. With my name you know. Although I imagined that everyone knew I was a Jew and I certainly have never been ashamed – why should I? – or attempted to hide it. But Doone said 'what I loathe about them is that they are one and all so hideous'. Medley agreed. John made some mild criticism. I was scarlet with rage. I looked at Coldstream and he at me. Well, they might not know. If they didn't then better to tell them as it would only make them more uncomfortable if they continued the conversation and found out afterwards.

–You know, I said, I'm a Jew.

–Yes, answered Doone with a smile, We thought so."[25]

When Munich came it acted on Claude like a slap in the face. He recalled the indescribable feeling of let-down and horror for the Czechs, as well as a sort of guilty relief that war was inevitable. He felt he had to make some sort of gesture and on impulse went into a barber's shop and told the barber to take off his beard. The barber queried "All of it?" and Claude replied "Yes, all of it." So "he lathered me up and after taking parts of it off with scissors, he lathered it and began stropping his razor.

He lifted my nose and said between his teeth 'A funny thing sir . . . only once before can I remember somebody coming in like that – that other chap who had it off – he was a murderer. I saw he was taken by the police two days later.' "[26]

NOTES

1 Claude Rogers Papers, Tate Gallery Archive.
2 Claude Rogers, unpublished memoir version II, collection Mr Crispin Rogers.
3 Claude Rogers Papers, Tate Gallery Archive.
4 Claude Rogers, unpublished memoir version II, op. cit.
5 Claude Rogers letters, collection Mr Crispin Rogers.
6 Read, Harold J., 'The Respectable Rebels – A Survey of the Origin and Development of the London Group' *Art* June 15 1956.
7, 8, 9 Claude Rogers Papers, Tate Gallery Archive.
10, 11 Claude Rogers, unpublished memoir version II, op. cit.
12 Claude Rogers Papers, Tate Gallery Archive.
13 Claude Rogers, unpublished memoir version II, op. cit.
14 Claude Rogers, unpublished memoir version I, collection Mr Crispin Rogers.
15, 16 Claude Rogers, unpublished memoir version II, op. cit.
17 Claude Rogers Papers, Tate Gallery Archive.
18, 19, 20, 21, 22 Claude Rogers, unpublished memoir version II, op. cit.
23 Claude Rogers Papers, Tate Gallery Archive.
24 Claude Rogers, unpublished memoir version II, op. cit.
25 Claude Rogers letters, collection Mr Crispin Rogers.
26 Claude Rogers Papers, Tate Gallery Archive.

School meals and Little Else

In June 1933 the young painter Elsie Evelyn Few entered Claude's life. They met at Nommie Durrell's flat at 10 Smith Terrace in Chelsea. Nommie Lazenby, who married Harry Durrell, had been a student at the Slade with Elsie. Elsie had studied at the Slade for the session 1928–9, and then at the Bartlett School of Architecture, next door to the Slade, from 1929–1931. She was at the Slade during Claude's last year there, though it is unclear whether he ever met her at that time. What is clear is that their meeting in Chelsea had a dramatic effect; they were immediately attracted to each other, and a passionate love affair developed. Claude was certain that Elsie was the right person for him, and they certainly discussed marriage during that year. However, it was over four years before they finally committed themselves.

Elsie's family were of East Anglian farming stock. Her father, Jethro Few, had been brought up in the little village of Villingham in Cambridgeshire, but had sought his fortune in Jamaica, where he set up a drapery business. His three children, Elsie, Margerie and James, were born in Kingston, Jamaica. Elsie was born on February 4 1909. Her mother died when she was ten, and her father remarried. At about fourteen she was sent to boarding school in England. By the time she went to the Slade she was thoroughly anglicised, although she never quite lost the expectation of servants to do the work, and she never really took to cooking. She was, however, marvellous with her hands and an expert seamstress, often making her own and her sister's clothes. After leaving the Bartlett School of Architecture she travelled extensively in Czechoslovakia, Austria, Yugoslavia, Greece and Italy, studying folk art there. She also studied pottery, lithography and weaving at the Central School of Arts and Crafts. Although she did a certain amount of painting all her life, she was as much a potter and craftswoman as a painter. She had fine features, a calm manner and an intelligent, slightly *grande dame* air. Like Claude she was inclined to fat.

Elsie met Claude at a critical moment in her career. After two years of travelling she had completed her studies and had no immediate plans, being undecided as to whether to stay in England or return to Jamaica. Claude was bowled over by her and pursued her with zeal. Elsie's father was informed of Claude's attentions, and in July Jethro Few came over to London and stayed at the Regents Palace Hotel, where Claude was taken to meet him. What he made of Claude is not known, but there seem to have been no obvious objections on his part. In September Dennis Browne, a contemporary of Claude's at the Slade, who had unexpectedly inherited the title of Marquess of Sligo, invited Claude to stay at his house, Annagloy in Boyle, in Ireland. Claude went, but not before wangling an invitation for Elsie to join them. At the time of their meeting, Elsie had a top floor flat in Hammersmith Terrace overlooking the river (for which she paid £1 a week), but in September she took a flat at 103 Barrowgate Road to be near Claude. Claude spent as much time as possible with her. According to his sister Beryl, Claude could be heard, with his springy yet heavy-stepping walk, coming all the way down Barrowgate Road at three in the morning.

Marriage was certainly in the air. Both Coldstream and Moynihan were already married, both to contemporaries at the Slade (Nancy Sharp and Eleanor Bellingham Smith), and both were already fathers. Michael Reynolds, writing to Claude on July 27 1933, says "I have hardly enough energy left to congratulate you on your marriage – that's a charming way of putting it, but I hesitate to say 'engagement', not knowing if it has gone as far as that. . . In fact, just what is the situation? I'm getting married on September 2 so you will have to buck up if you're going to beat me to it. I'm glad you're getting married . . . the least pleasant part of my own marriage is that it threatens our intimacy. Is your girl Jewish? Elsie Few sounds Aryan to me . . ." and he adds "This morning my engagement is acknowledged by a firm of french-letter makers who sent me a catalogue . . . Could KBR [Claude's brother Keith] help with advice before MR makes his purchases?"![1]

Claude could hardly bear to be away from Elsie and when separated he tried to bridge the gap with letters. In August 1933 he wrote: "Victor Pasmore was here this evening. We dined at Bertorelli's and came back home afterwards. He is a charming fellow and I do hope we shall see him often when we are married . . . What really impressed him was the nude I did of you. I pulled it out by chance having quite forgotten it and was very surprised at it myself."[2] Whether this is the nude of Elsie which has been tactfully dated 1938 or another painting is uncertain. The 1938 painting is a tender but accurately observed rendering of Elsie's soft, full forms, and shows great relish in the physical character of the flesh.

Claude's warm and physically passionate nature was allowed full force with Elsie. He had always been strongly attracted to women, but being rather fat and clumsy, had not always had a great deal of success. He also had an earthy streak which, combined with an excellent sense of humour, could be very amusing. In glum moments he worked out his frustrations by writing doggerel, at which he became rather adept. One poem that survives in several drafts and clearly had some sort of a tune, goes as follows:

> I am not ambi-dextrous
> Homo I mean to say
> And when I get good and sextrous
> No-body comes my way
>   tra lalalala
> Everyone has their pleasure
> But no one alas! with me
> Still I won't be cas-tra-ted
> Beastly you know, I mean
> Some day I may be may-ted
> Sometimes I want to scream
> Nobody loves my penis
> Nobody loves my balls
> Dear oh dear I very much fear
> The old urge calls.[3]

Claude had always been prone to sudden and intense passions for girls, but on the whole he was the pursuer rather than the pursued. No one, it seems, had unequivocally loved him back. Elsie's reciprocating passion must have been wonderful, releasing all his capacity for love and appreciation. When separated they both experienced the pain common to all lovers, and in July Elsie wrote miserably to Claude from Villingham, where she was staying with her family, adding: "I have 350 relatives in this village, one of the oldest families in Cambridgeshire, they have lived here for over 400 years and are supposed to be descended from a certain fiery Baroness 'de Few' she was called who took refuge in the Isle of Ely." Claude wrote to comfort her: "Little Else (I love calling you this for I think of little else) I want to kiss you until you are no longer at all miserable but feel warm and lazy with happiness. I want to kiss all your dear, passionate, beautiful woman's body . . . Try to cheer up, we won't be separated for very long in reality; although each day does contain so many hours of emptiness and clocks ticking . . ." Claude begged her to come to London for a few days. "I told Mother you might be coming and asked her if we could not put you up in the studio; she said it would be alright . . . Sorry things seem so communal. It is always the way in family life. Luckily Keith, Beryl and I all like privacy of sorts but the aunts don't . . . If only I could get a small job we could marry tomorrow . . ."[4]

It is difficult to gauge what Claude's mother thought of Elsie.

Presumably she was disappointed that Claude had not found himself a Jewish girl, but she maintained that she had had religion rammed down her throat as a child and was not going to inflict the same treatment on her children. She appears to have accepted Elsie quite readily as her elder son's choice of a wife. It is quite possible she reconciled herself to the idea better than Elsie's father. Elsie did not get on well with her stepmother. Either Elsie's own doubts about Claude, or parental pressure, made her consider going back to Jamaica. Claude had no job, and although Elsie received a quite handsome allowance from her father, her parents may have felt that this alone would not support the pair of them, and that marriage was impossible. When Elsie talked of going back to Jamaica Claude was desperate enough to consider going out with her. He wrote almost daily, keeping her in touch with his doings and his thoughts: "There isn't much to tell you. Saw Pasmore, and the Moynihans just back from Dieppe. Queer how the whole lot, even Tibble and Co, make me feel slightly inferior at times. We went to the Marquis of Granby and I drank cider. Crowds of intellectuals . . . and Nina Hamnett getting her evening souse of gin. I like Nina, she's an artist and a gentlewoman . . . I wish celebrities did not strike me dumb . . . What could we live on in Jamaica and what could I earn at the bottom of the rope ladder? Would I have spare time to paint in (is there early closing for instance?) Would you hate it if, in our spare time, we went painting and I painted you or anyway PAINTED instead of visiting people much? I have to consider my people as well. As I told you, if money from Argentina got a lot less (they might try and prevent it coming out of the country) I should have to send what I could back to help. Putting things at their bloody damndest, if we were both broke, would you be willing to live at home and to let me send all I could home to England and live in some tiny place near you . . . I personally feel I have found something we must not lose but I don't really think you are absolutely sure. You seem to have doubts which I hate. I have jettisoned all my sentimental associations I think – I know they die hard in women . . . Don't be rash. If you aren't sure you probably will be sure sometime – in Jamaica or England or Austria or somewhere. There's all the world you restless creature and I am only Claude Rogers, 26, white, semitic, painter (not even sure if good yet) but he tries and probably has some tiny spark in him. So be analytic blast you. My only doubt is an odd fear of uprooting myself . . . I believe, if you really want to, you could make me completely happy. Do you believe I could make you so too?"[5]

Elsie firmly dismissed Claude's ideas of living in Jamaica, and decided to stay in England for a while, telling him "Anyway, my sweet I shall try to get a job in London. I think it would be preposterous for you to go out to Jamaica, it would not do your work any good - your work comes first."[6] Claude worried about this separation and courted Elsie with another poem "Sweetheart, I really don't see any reason in our separation, and as for rhyme

I want to be with Elsie - shure;
Upon the Bill of Selsea - or
Wherever she may be
And does it really matter much -
My bed is in the rabbit hutch
And only pork for tea?
Lor luv you - No! I'll paint the view
And buss my Elsie, Elsie Few -
'Tis just the life for me.
I want to be with Elsie - shure
Upon the shores of Elsinore,
Wherever that may be."[7]

As well as writing verse, Claude also started writing children's stories, often with a girl named Elsie as the heroine. For Claude, Elsie seemed to have sparked off a period of extreme creativity, and the writing was a way of using up excess energy, and possibly of making a mark on the world in a different field. In one of the stories entitled 'Steamroller or Peace with Honour' the friendship between the little girl heroine and the steamroller is too clear an analogy of his relationship with Elsie to be ignored. He was full of doubts about himself as a worthy recipient of love. Some of these doubts emerge in his writing. ". . . although Elsie could walk anywhere Steamroller could not. Gentle as he was he couldn't help rolling everything flat - and that meant trouble."[8] In another of the stories, 'The Man in the Moon', there is a long argument between Elsie and the painter hero, Billy Rill, which transparently reflects Claude's doubts and fears. These stories were interesting and unaffected, with a lot of pace. He showed them to Elsie for her comments; what their eventual fate was is not clear, and although Claude was to commit himself to various pieces of writing at all stages of his career, often draft after draft being written, much of it remained in semi-embryonic state. Elsie also acted as his muse for doggerel which sometimes reverted to baby talk and sometimes to a sort of extended clerihew. One such ponders on music - Claude was not at all musical, but his mother was a musician and as both his sister Beryl and Elsie's younger sister Margerie were training as pianists, he was presumably subjected to hearing quite a lot about it.

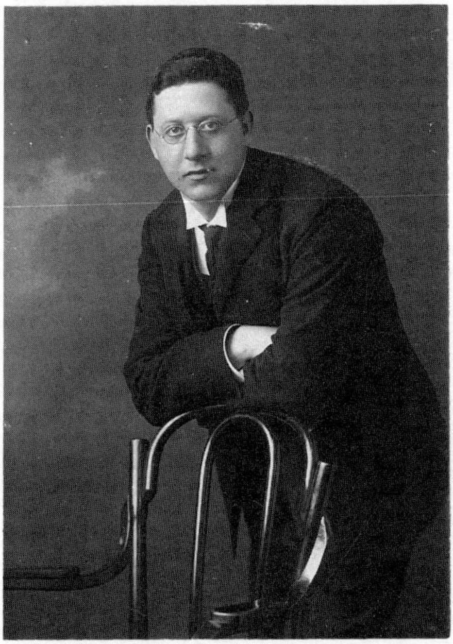

1. Claude's father, David 'Dick' Rogers.

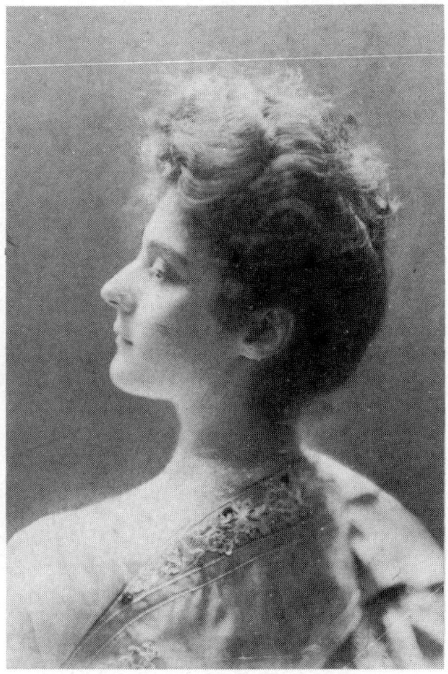

2. Mother, Rebecca Rubinstein.

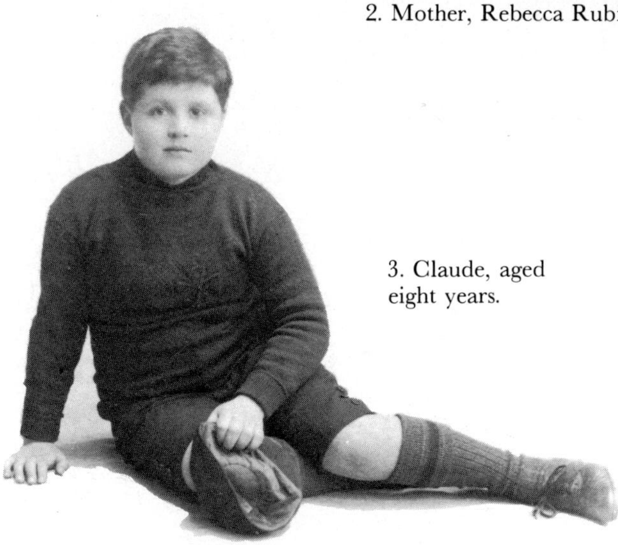

3. Claude, aged eight years.

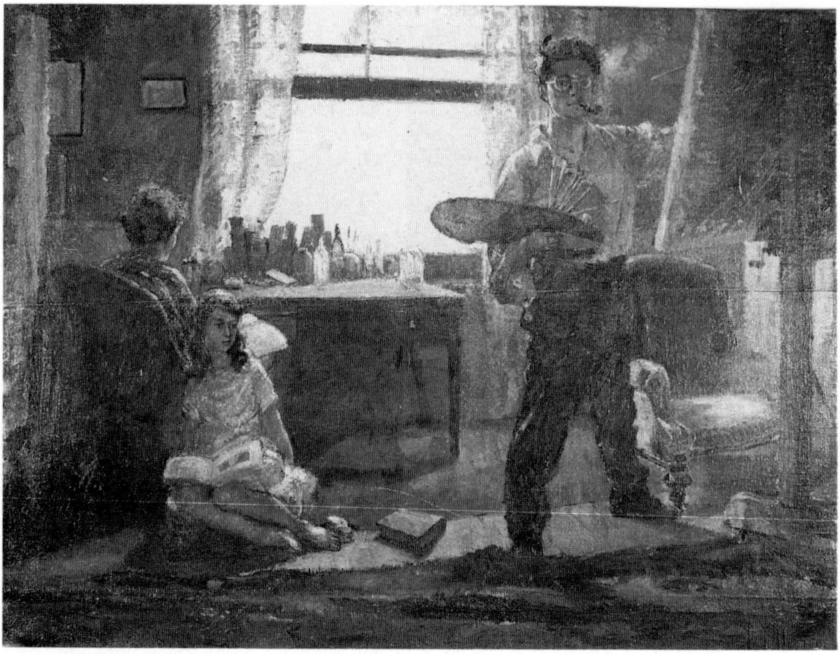

4. *Family Group*, 1926.

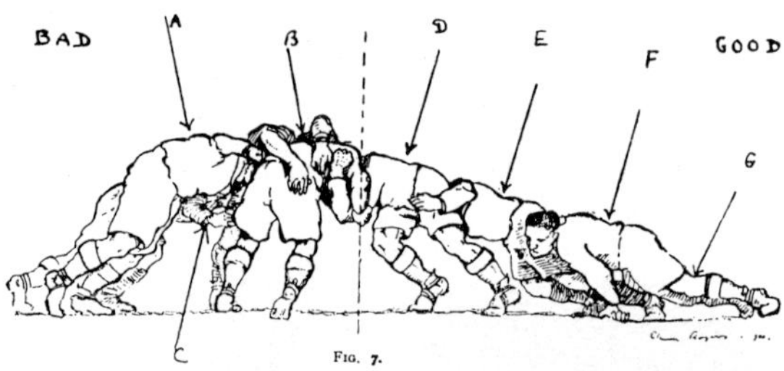

Fig. 7.

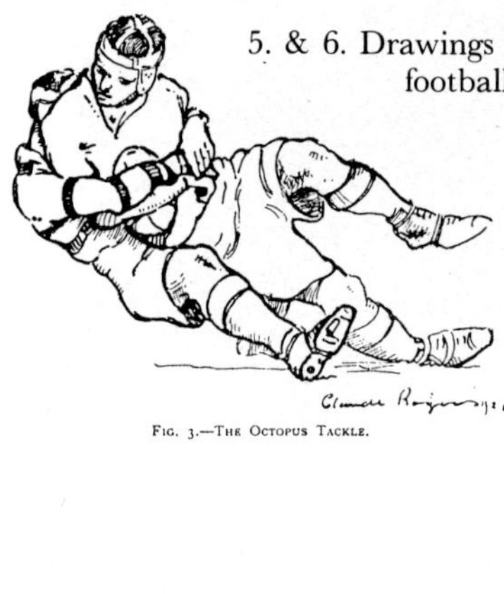

5. & 6. Drawings for rugby football manual, 1926.

Fig. 3.—The Octopus Tackle.

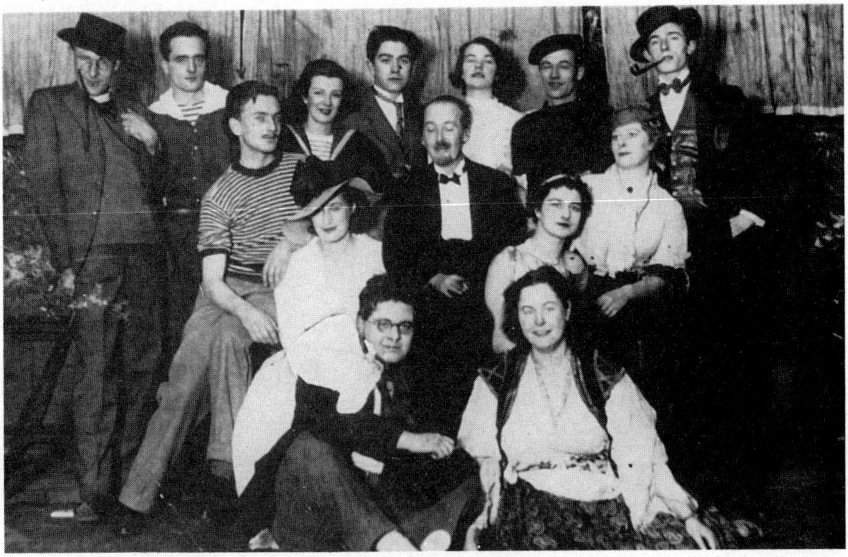

7. Slade Dance c 1933. Claude and Elsie seated in front.

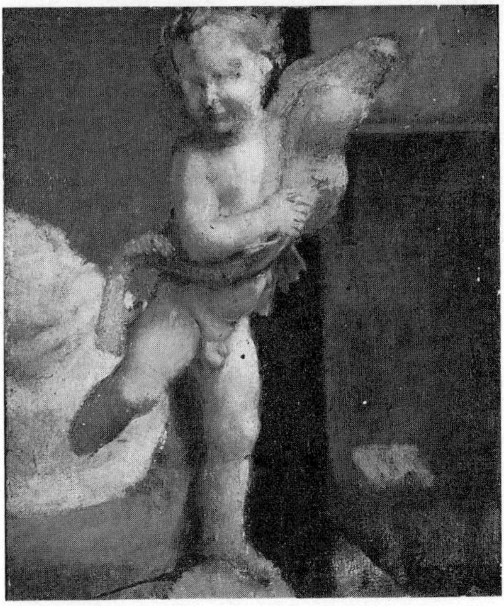

8. *Boy with a Dolphin*, 1926–27.

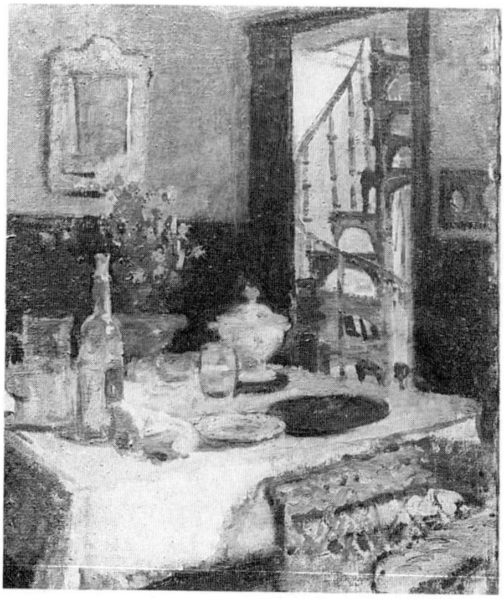

9. *Interior with Spiral Staircase*, 1928.

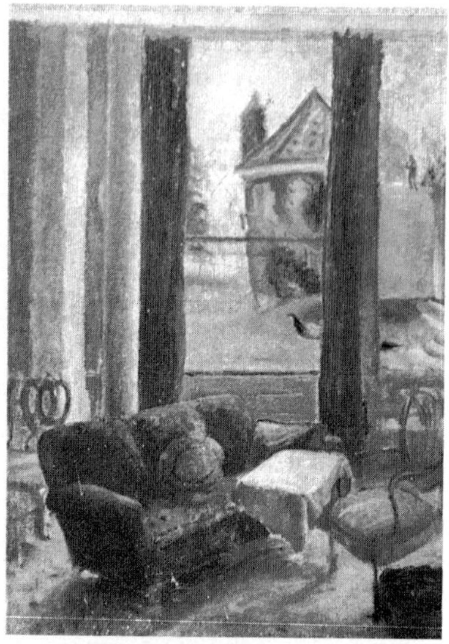

10. Study for portrait of Sir Clive and Lady Coates and family, 1929.

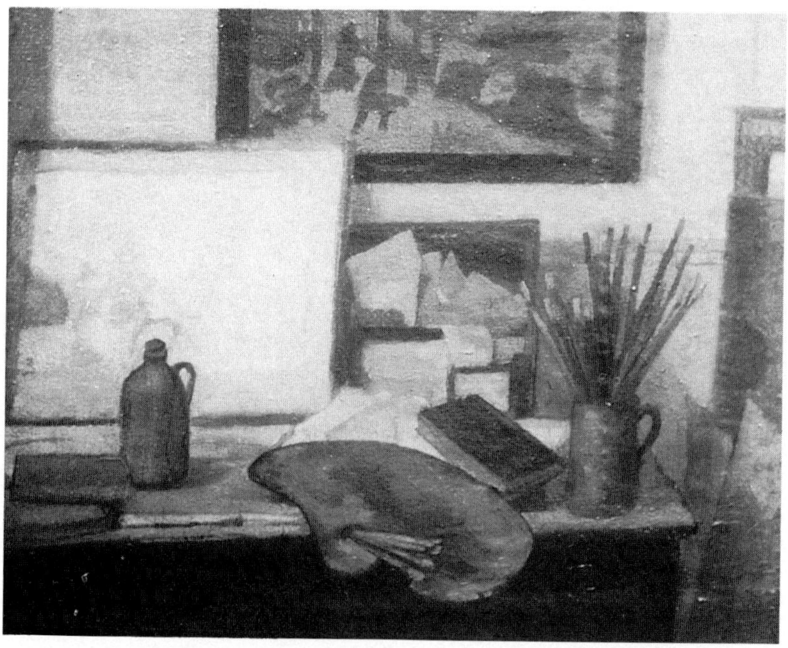

11. *Still Life with Reproduction of Breughel's 'Winter'*, 1929.

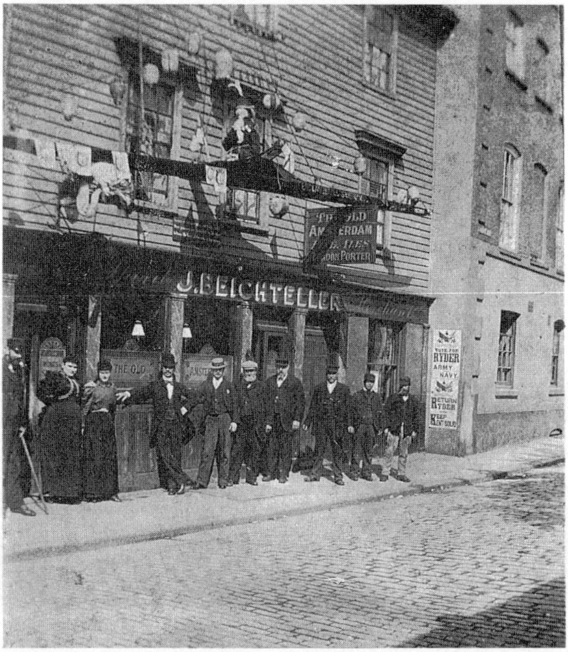

12. The Old Amsterdam in Gravesend before it became the Norwegian Seamen's Mission. Claude took a room in the Mission after leaving the Slade in 1930.

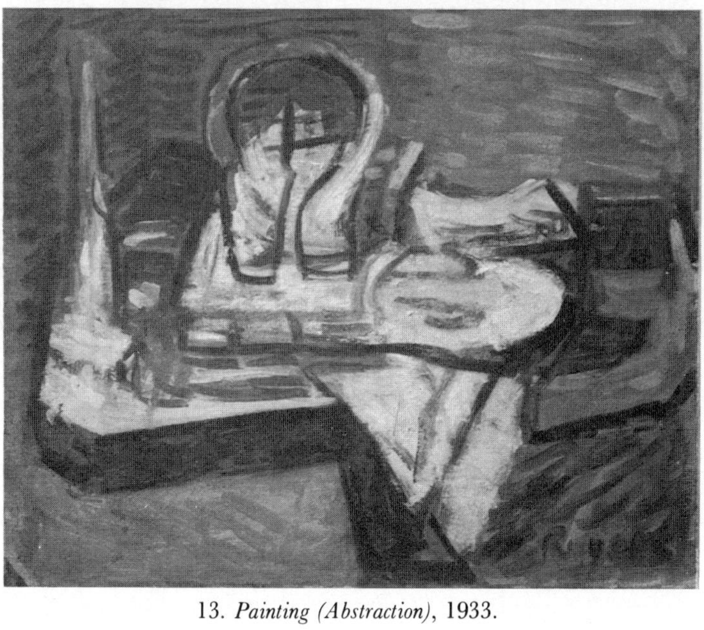

13. *Painting (Abstraction)*, 1933.

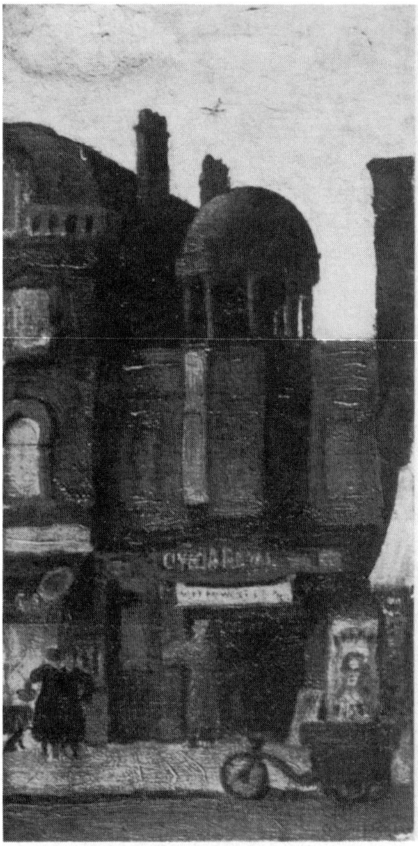

14. *Cinema Royal*, 1930.

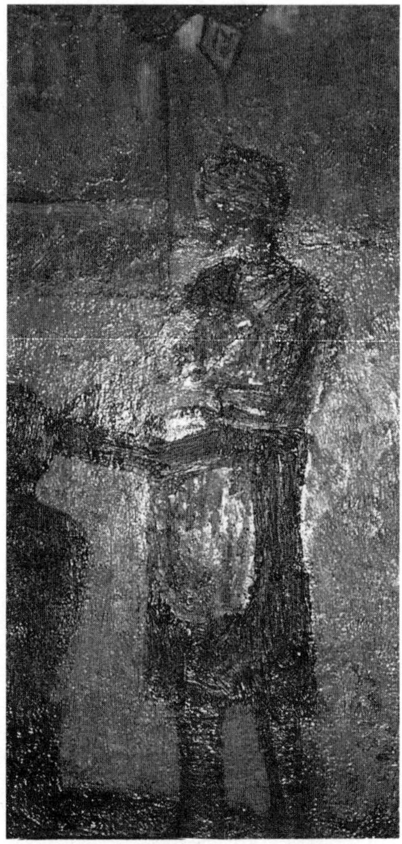

15. *Chocolate-Cigarettes*, 1933.

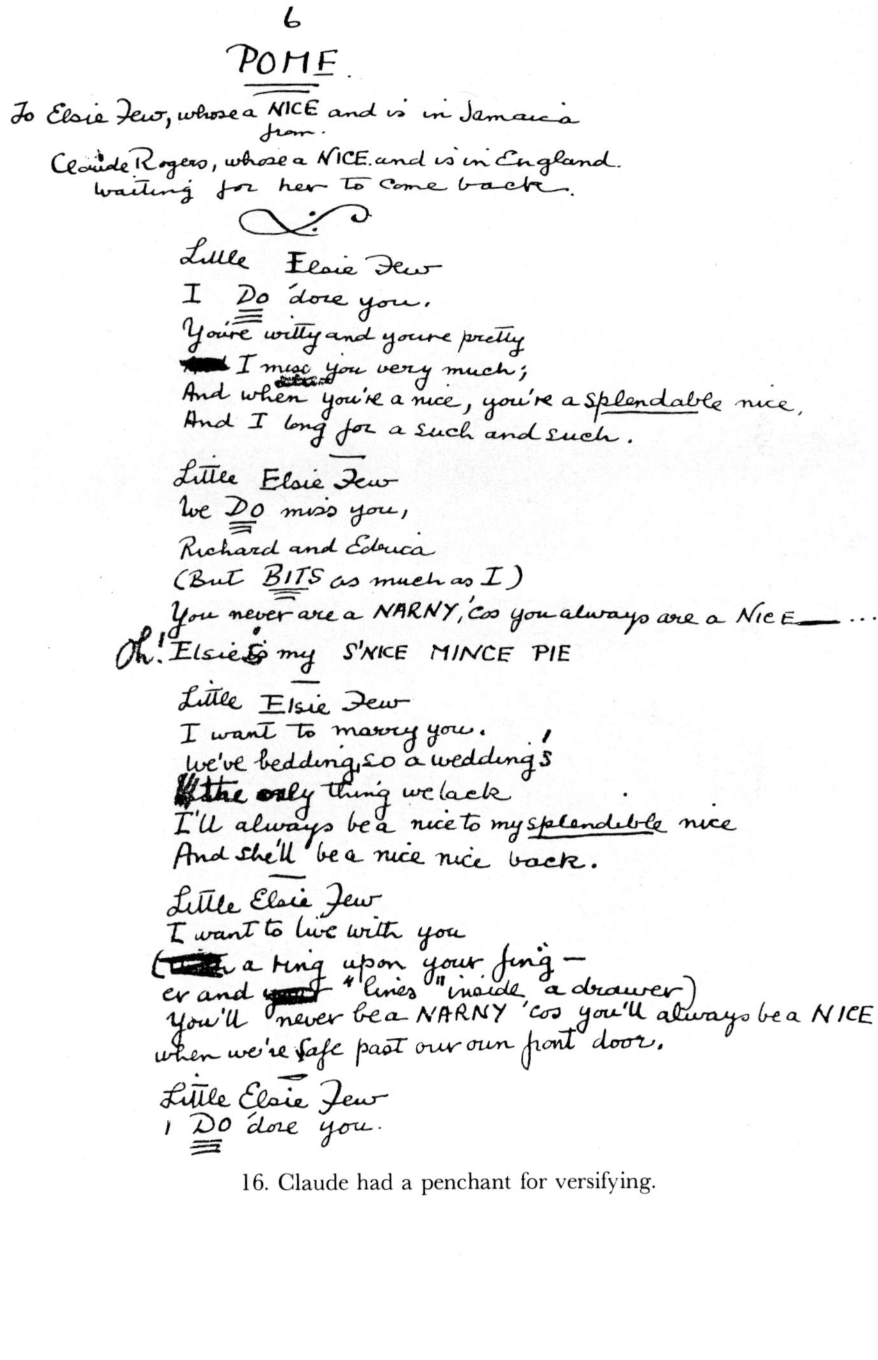

6

POME.

To Elsie Jew, whose a NICE and is in Jamaica
from
Claude Rogers, whose a NICE and is in England
waiting for her to come back.

Little Elsie Jew
I DO 'dore you.
You're witty and youre pretty
I miss you very much;
And when you're a nice, you're a splendable nice,
And I long for a such and such.

Little Elsie Jew
We DO miss you,
Richard and Edwina
(But BITS as much as I)
You never are a NARNY, 'cos you always are a NICE— ...
Oh! Elsie's my S'NICE MINCE PIE

Little Elsie Jew
I want to marry you.
We've bedding, so a wedding's
the only thing we lack.
I'll always be a nice to my splendible nice
And she'll be a nice nice back.

Little Elsie Jew
I want to live with you
(a ring upon your fing-
er and "lines" inside a drawer)
You'll never be a NARNY 'cos you'll always be a NICE
when we're safe past our own front door.

Little Elsie Jew
I DO 'dore you.

16. Claude had a penchant for versifying.

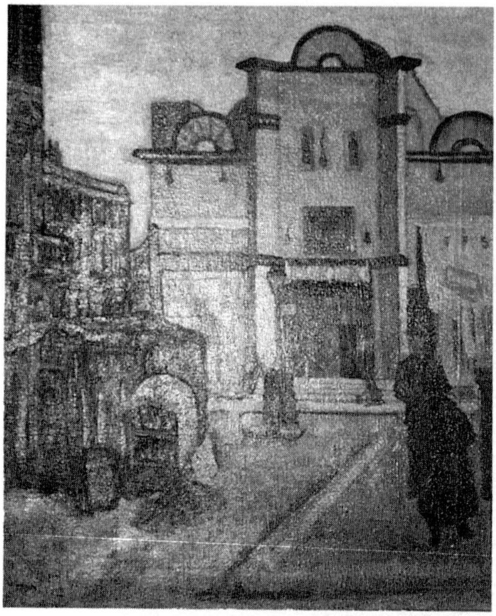

17. *The Tolmer Cinema*, 1931.

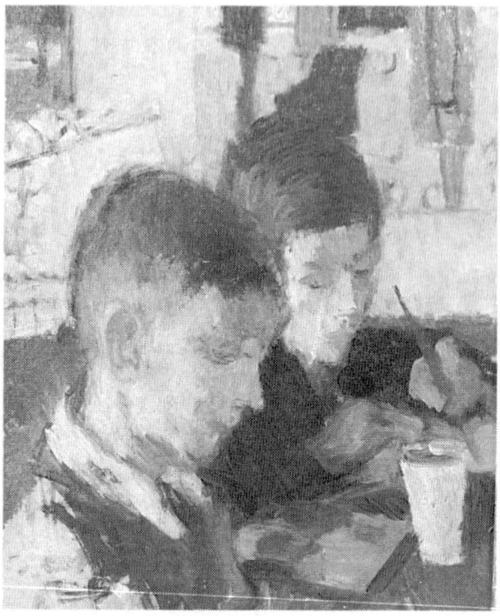

18. *Two Boys Working*, 1936.

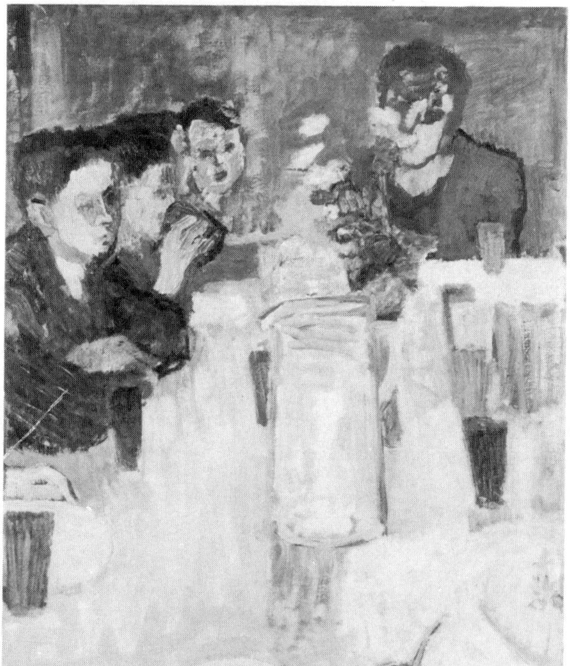

19. *Dinner at Raynes Park School (Glasses)*, 1937 version.

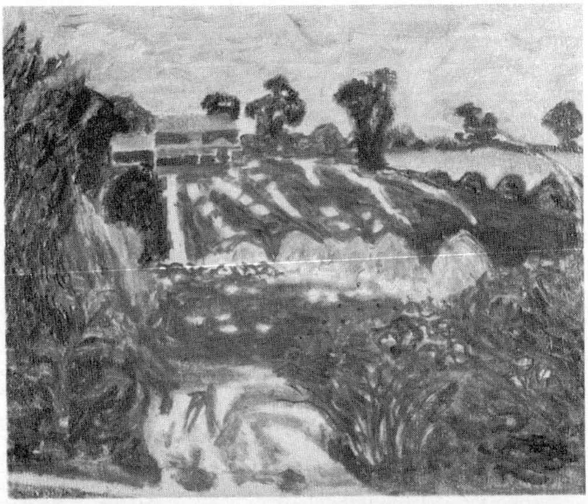

20. *Landscape*, 1936.

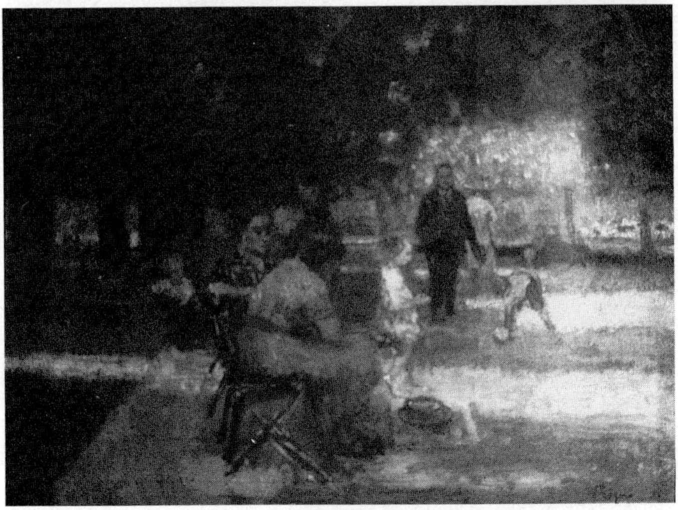

21. *The Chestnut Avenue, Regents Park*, 1938.

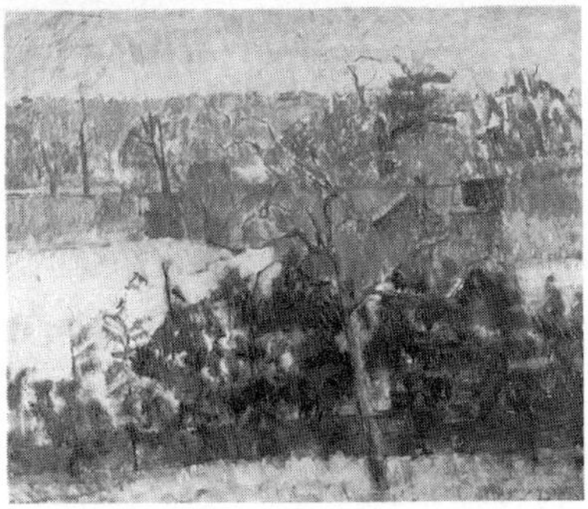

22. *Snow at Rodwell*, 1939.

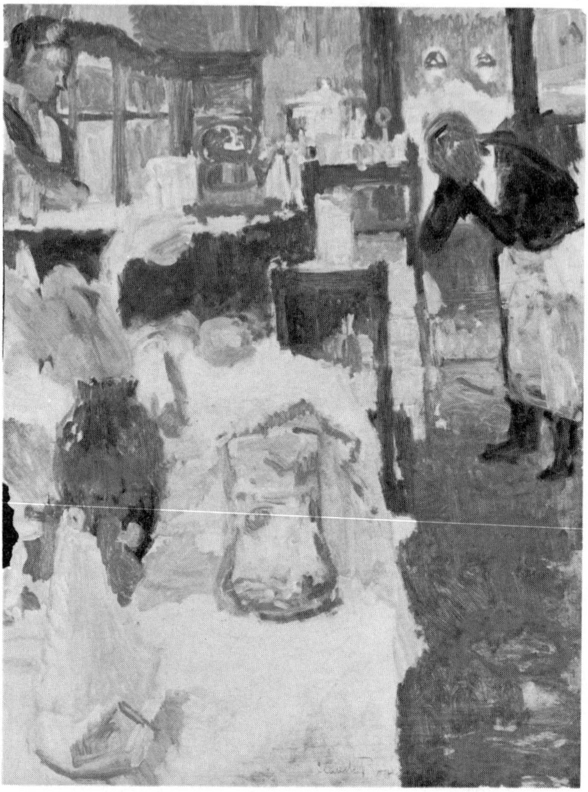

23. *A Mirror in Bertorelli's*, 1936.

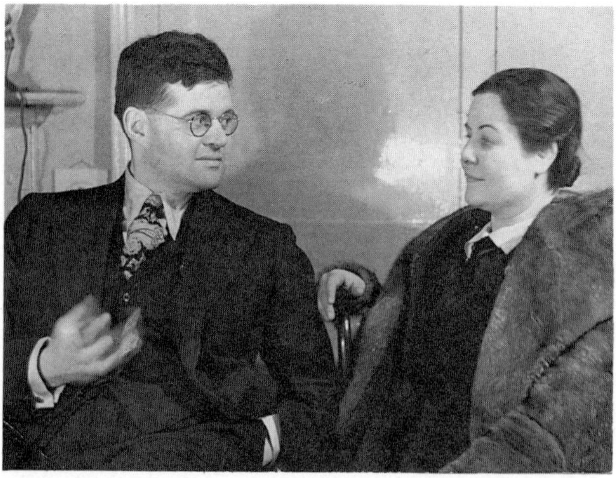

24. Claude and Elsie on their wedding day, 1937.

A NEW SCHOOL

for a limited number of pupils of

Drawing and Painting

under the direction of

CLAUDE ROGERS

VICTOR PASMORE

WILLIAM COLDSTREAM

associated with

Vanessa Bell · Augustus John, R.A.

Duncan Grant · John Nash

25. Prospectus for the Euston Road School, 1937.

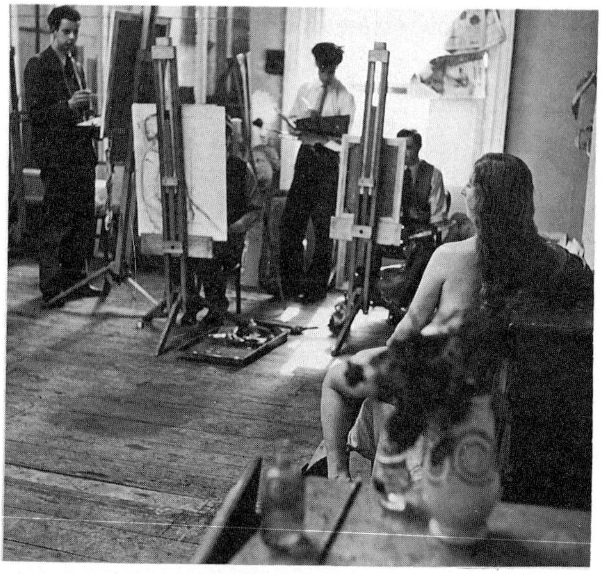
26. In the Euston Road studios.

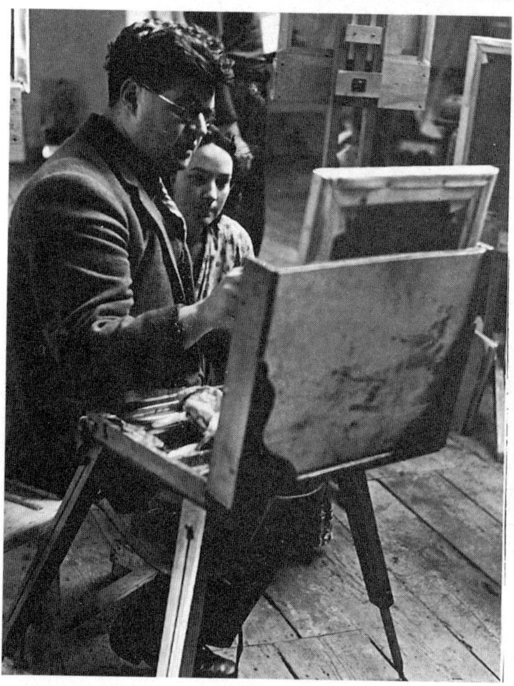
27. Claude teaching.

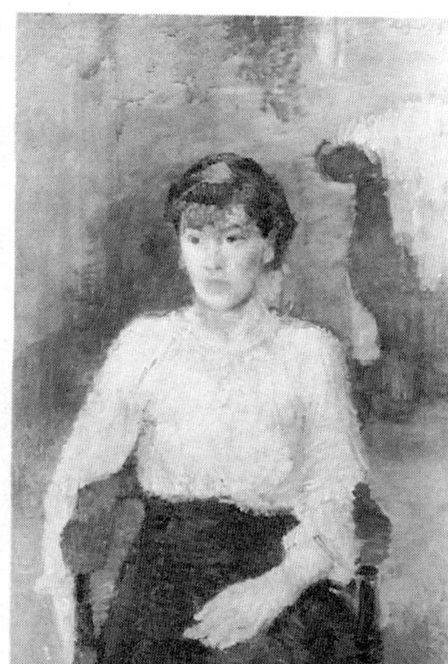
28. *Mrs Richard Chilver*, 1937–38.

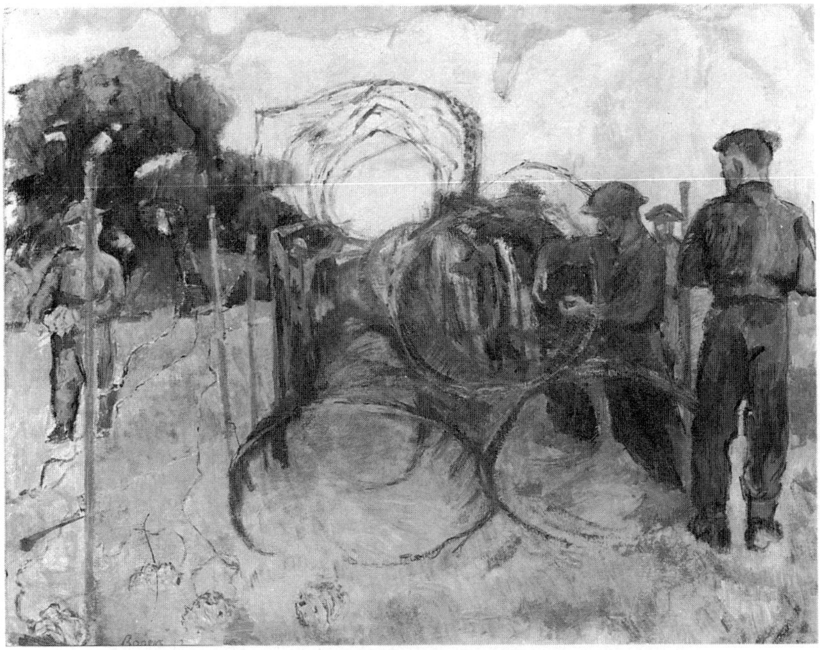

29. *Sappers Wiring*, 1942.

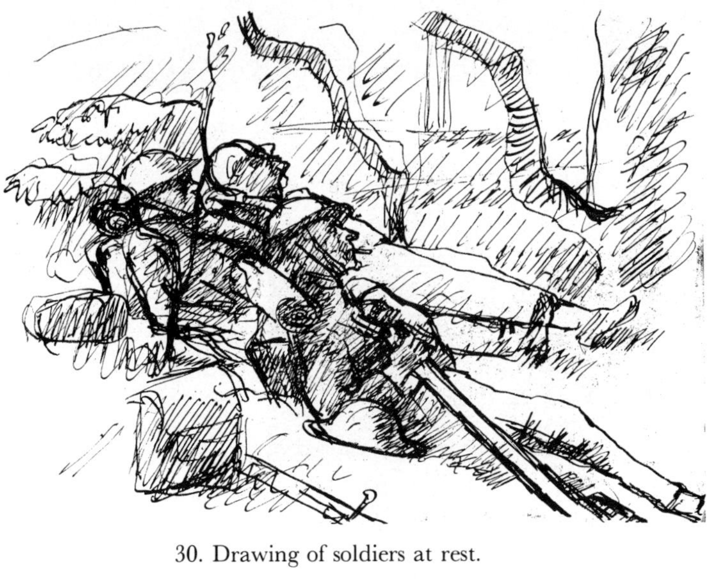

30. Drawing of soldiers at rest.

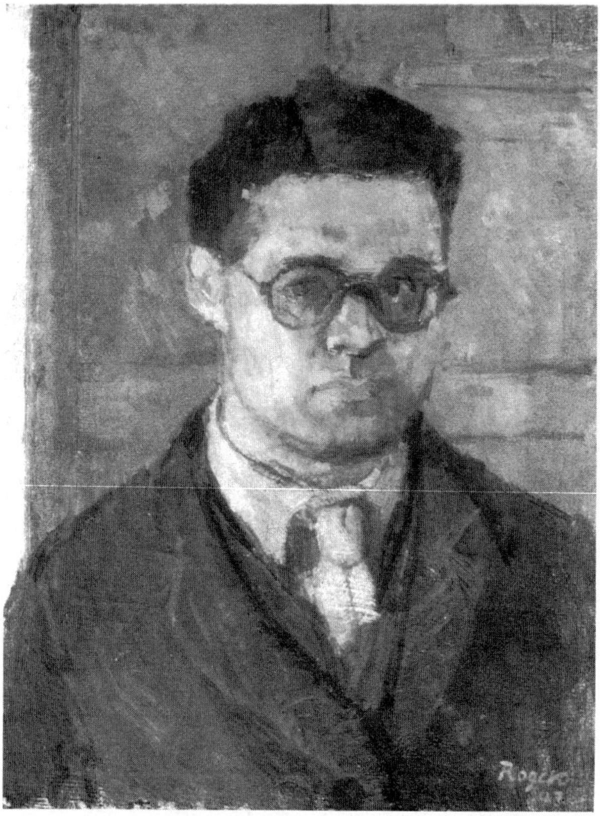

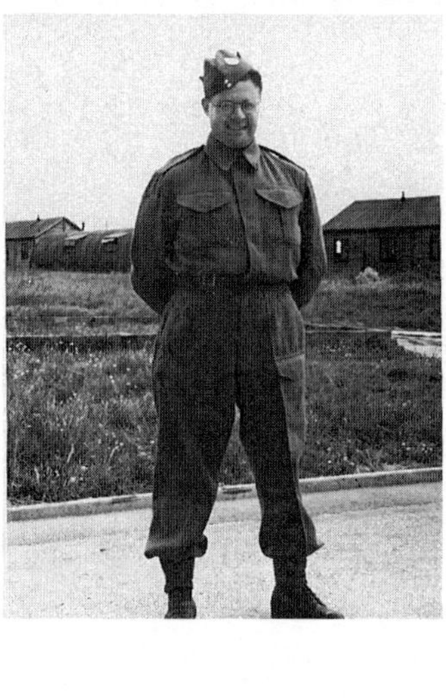

31. *Self Portrait in Hospital Blue*, 1943.

32. Sapper Rogers.

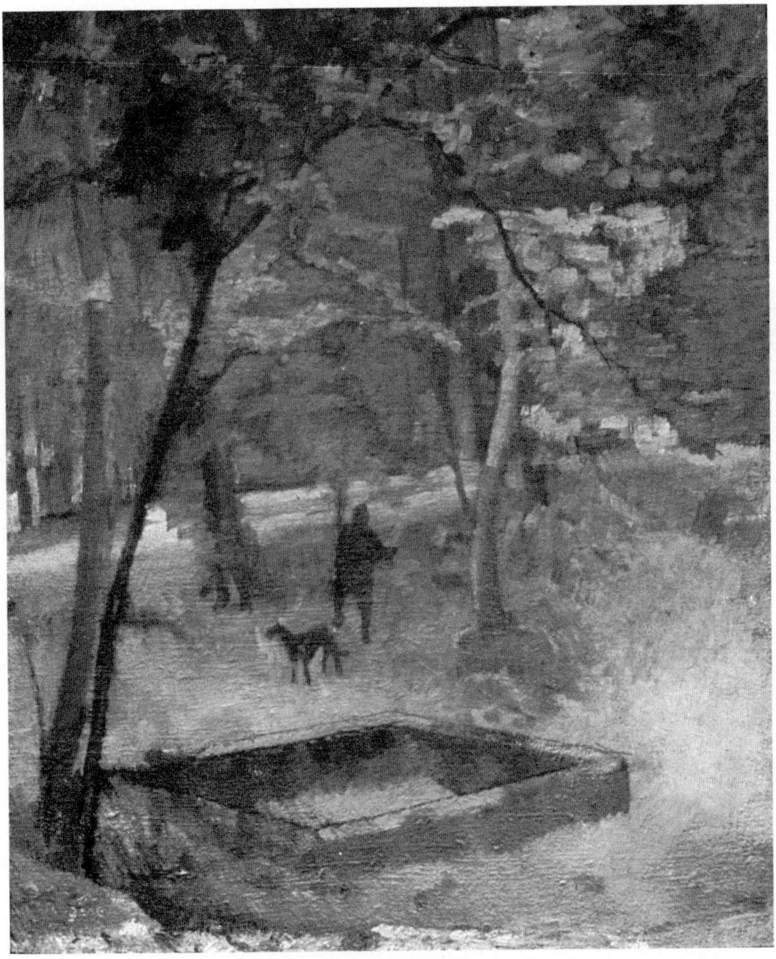

33. *The Poacher*, 1945.

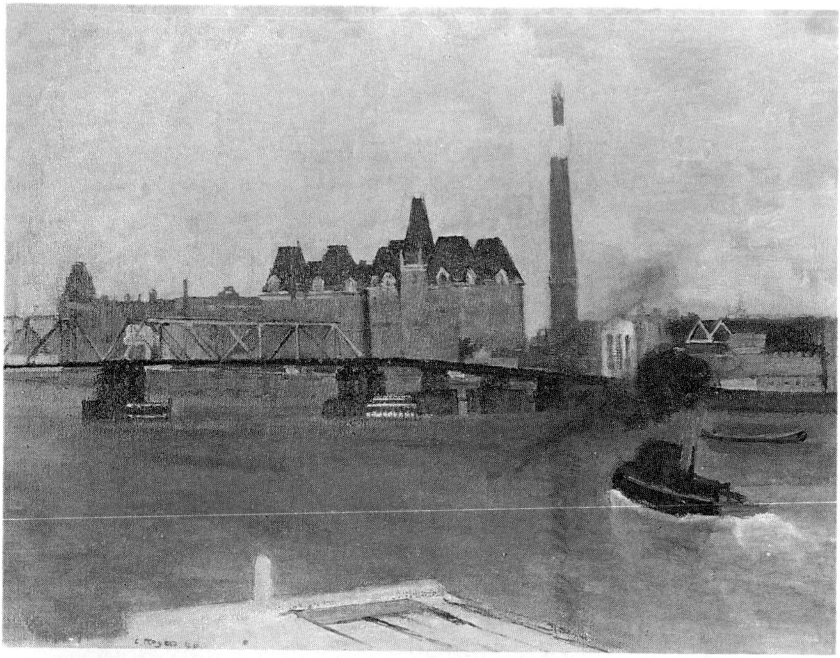

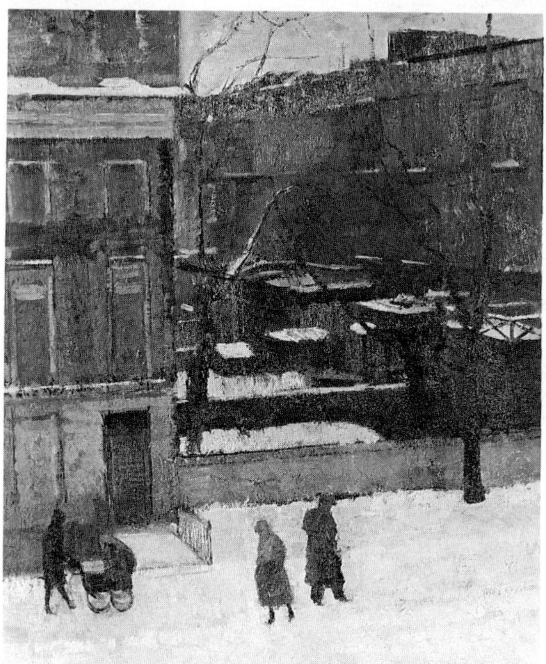

34. *Vauxhall*, 1946.

35. *Bloomsbury under Snow*, 1945.

Music hath charms they say
When that chap Brahms they play
But if I must listen at all
Play Duke Ellington or Henry Hall

Then there's someone called Cesar Frank
Who is put in the foremost rank.
Well! these days more might be written
About a young man called Benjamin Britten

There's some chaps are real rude
About Rachmaninoff's Prelude
But I'm an admirer
When it's played by Miss Scharer

I can't abide Wagner
Even in the edition of Augener
But oft, on the slopes of Jura
It's played to the Fuhrer

Few men
Have written stuff like Schumann
But I always muddle Schubert
With Schumann and Eggshirt

John Sebastian Bach
Certainly made his mark
It is open to doubt
If it will ever be rubbed out

The songs of Ravel
Are all very well
But I'd sooner my pussy
Sang Debussy

The symphonies of Brahms
Are frequently shalms.
His sonatas in parts
Are less ersatz.

They complained that Franz Liszt
Was frequently pissed
Perhaps said he
But oh, what a Rhapsody!

Cesar Frank
Is a lot of swank
What has he written
Like Benjamin Britten.[9]

Did Claude suffer from all the musical talk? It nevertheless had its uses, and he noted in his diary of 1935 "one evening, before Elsie left for Jamaica . . . we went to supper with the Coldstreams in Upper Park Road. After supper . . . Bill asked Elsie if her sister Margerie (the pianist Margerie Few at that time I think still studying at the Royal College of Music) happened to know anyone who might be able to compose music which could fit film. Elsie at once said 'Yes as a matter of fact there is a man at the College who Margerie often talks about who might easily be able to do that. Margerie says he composes effortlessly and is awfully good. I'll ask her to find out if you like whether he'd be interested.' 'I wish you would' said Bill, 'What's his name?' 'Benjamin Britten'."[10]

In August 1934 Elsie, still in London, moved to a flat in St Peter's Square in Chiswick. Both she and Claude were looking for jobs, but not having much success. Coldstream was working in the General Post Office Film Unit making documentary films with Grierson, and Pasmore was still at County Hall. Claude noted that refugees such as Naum Gabo, Walter Gropius, Moholy Nagy and Mendelsohn had begun to arrive and settle in England hoping to find a welcome and a home. These visitors had all left by 1938, mainly to go to America. Claude spent a month with Avery Colebrook in the Norwegian Seamen's Mission at Gravesend, sharing his studio and typing his 'Elsie' stories while Colebrook typed his articles at the other end of the room. In a letter to Michael Reynolds, asking his advice about a publisher, Claude described the scene; "We, Avery and I, used to sit at opposite ends of the room typing – I working at these stories and he at his articles about the Unemployed. Every now and then one of us would turn round for advice on some minor point, and it was curious to be dragged away from some fantastic situation in order to unravel a complicated sentence about 'the scope of the town committee' . . . I have been working hard, have not been up to town, so of course I have seen nobody. One of my ambitions, I think, is to become so famous that crowds flock to Chiswick every evening; train loads of intellectual young men and women in the guerrilla uniforms of their cult alighting at Chiswick Park and Turnham Green Stations and streaming up Sutton Court Road."[11]

When Claude met Elsie he was beginning to make his way as a painter. His exhibition at the London Artists Association's galleries at 92 New Bond Street had just taken place and had received some critical attention. This exhibition was shared with John Dodgson, elected to the LAA at the same time. Claude showed a small self-portrait and some of his Chiswick paintings, and attracted some critical attention. The exhibition was reviewed in the *Times* at some length. "At first glance and in the mass the paintings of Mr Claude Rogers . . . seem very serious but rather bleak. He has a preference for cold, dark colours, and in particular for those disquieting greens and purples which were popular with the upholsterers of the last century. And his designs, though thorough, are often strict and academic. But all this is what one would expect of a serious painter at the beginning of his career, and it is best to ignore the obvious asperity of many of these works and to look for signs of a freer sensibility which will no doubt have more play when he allows himself to use it. Though the prevailing impression of his *Still Life* may be sombre, it contains many delicate passages. His *Self-Portrait* seems to be an essay in the manner of Cézanne and the range of colour is extraordinarily like Cézanne's. But it is a sound and original imitation, very solid in its modelling and it is clear that Mr Rogers has really understood the colours which he has borrowed. His essays in the manner of Mr Sickert, of which perhaps the best is *Chocolate-Cigarettes* are by no means superficial."[12]

The small self-portrait was certainly painted in a deliberate attempt to learn what he could from Cézanne's 1880 self-portrait, which Claude had first seen only a few years earlier. The direction of the head is reversed but Claude used the idea of the long vertical of the wall against the back of the head and the mass of the shoulder in the foreground, pushing the figure firmly back into its surrounding space. Above all he tried to establish the planes of the head by colour, and, keeping the painting generally low-toned and cool, has used similar patches of red on the cheeks. He later talked to his students about this painting, pointing out the colour relationships - the patch of red on Cézanne's nearer cheek glowing warm among its neighbouring light-toned colours and establishing the raised edge of the cheekbone, and its counterpart on the shaded side, a cooler patch of purple which still reads as red within its cooler context. Claude's painting was clearly done direct from observation, in the way Cézanne worked. Very sensibly Claude did what many young painters did at the start of their careers - that is, pick the painters they most admired and try to paint in their way in order to learn as much about their methods of construction and use of colour as possible. Claude's 'Sickertian' paintings are constructed from drawings, as Sickert recommended and practised in his teaching, done in his wanderings around Chiswick. In *Hannibal's* Claude used the three groups of people, carefully observed in drawings, to establish the sharply receding space within the painting, at the same time preserving the freshness of characterisation. The colour combinations are very beautiful, red hat against lilac wall, with the yellows of the door frame setting off the lilacs. A 1933 still life adopted a Sickertian method of simplifying flat areas of tone.

During the thirties salaries were subject to the nationwide economy cut of five percent. As the numbers of unemployed soared, incomes fell and so did the cost of living. Claude noted that it was possible to buy large quantities of food at the late night markets on Fridays and Saturdays. He bought his socks at Woolworths, two pairs for 6d. He could also buy piles of *Amazing Stories* with titles like 'Black Mask' for 3d. each. These were necessary reading to lift him out of one of his depressions. He remembered that after he got to know Alan Clutton-Brock, the art critic, in 1935, he went with him to Woolworths to choose a new pair of reading glasses – "there were lenses and test cards and one fitted up a pair for oneself." He managed to afford a painting room in an old loft built out of the back of one of the shops in Goodge Street, approached by a rickety ladder. Life seemed liveable with work and painting. But at the end of the year Elsie decided to return to Jamaica to visit her family over Christmas and stay for an indefinite period. She and Claude were still engaged and she seems to have hated leaving him as much as he hated her going, though he tried to keep cheerful, writing to Elsie the week after her departure on December 2 on ss *Carare* "All things considered I think this is one of the best things that could have happened to us. We were getting a little take-me-for-granted. Anyway I don't half miss you . . . so don't stay too long . . ."

Both Claude and Elsie wrote to each other regularly, keeping each other in touch with their doings. Claude, writing from his mother's house, visited Victor Pasmore's house which he describes as "same sort of atmosphere as here – almost – the drawing room is furnished a little worse than ours, but the bedrooms (pure Edwardian) are a little better . . ." And "Saw Victor yesterday – he's all het up as he's planning proposing to a girl. Wonderful man! I was treated to a very full account of the campaign so far – it is entirely on classic lines by both of them. Everything done with extreme dignity; sort of 18th century war rules."[13]

It was dangerous to leave Claude on his own in London. He had an enormous appetite for pretty girls and an endearing way with him. He was inclined to dive after anyone, but he was good-natured about it if they objected. He must have confessed some of his temptations to Elsie in letters, eliciting the reply "darling dear, you can kiss and squeeze etc as many girls as you like I don't mind at all as long as you go on loving me. I will tell you if anyone kisses me but I don't want anyone to anyway. Every bit of me is used up in loving what I see and wanting to put it down."[14]

Elsie painted a great deal while she was in Jamaica, and once out there she had nothing to think about except her painting. She found it hard to make the move to go back to England, writing in February to Claude: "I have been considering staying on a few weeks longer, if you would not mind? You see money is in rather a mess and I shall probably have to look for a job of some sort when I get back . . . As you can imagine it is a prospect that does not please. Especially as I feel that I am just beginning to paint. I love you and long to be with you, but I just passionately long to paint . . ."[15] Eventually she made the decision to return and took the first step away from her easy life in Jamaica, booking her return passage for May. "Oh little dear it is a wrench, if I didn't love you as much as I do, I think I might stay ten years for I am not at all sure that if I did I wouldn't amount to something as a painter. I feel that I want to paint here and there is nothing to distract me as I have absolutely nothing else to do."[16]

If Elsie wanted to claim Claude for herself, she had to return to England. He had fallen for another girl, Peggy Rose, and true to form had told Elsie all about it. She was upset: "Dearest Claude, I don't know what to say when you tell me that you are three quarters in love with Peggy Rose – I feel so miserable I wish I could cry but I can't, you don't seem to realise that I would have come back to England long before this but I haven't been well . . . and there hasn't been any money until this month. I could have fallen in love with someone here if I had wanted, only being loyal to you seemed to me to be more important . . . When I met you I had been crushed by something of this sort . . . I was very bitter and unhappy. You were very kind to me Claudie dear I loved you very much. You gave me back myself and a feeling of assurance and that I have a place in the world."[17] Elsie's money worries were serious as her father had suffered a set back in business as a result of the bankruptcy of one of his tenants; Jethro Few's children depended on their father's allowance to them, and Elsie was not sure how her own income would be affected. However, the problem seems to have been resolved satisfactorily.

While in Jamaica, in 1936, Elsie organised an exhibition in Kingston entitled *Exhibition of Modern Paintings* containing work by herself, Victor Pasmore and Claude Rogers. Claude sent eight watercolours, Pasmore five, and the exhibition had a considerable local success.

Claude tried to revivify his single life in London, and kept Elsie informed: "I began to run about like anything and visit people. All the Charlotte Street crowd, and Mrs Anrep and William and Rodrigo; and Victor and I saw one another about twice a week at least. People seemed to like me which was nice . . . It's Passover and I'm full of motsah. For the first time in my life the service meant something to me. What – it is difficult to say . . . I had supper with the Anreps – Mrs Anrep is such a dear. Nancy says she has a very warm soft spot in her heart for me; I should like to think so because I've always liked her. She's going to get me a commission to paint a Russian count or something . . ."[18] This turned out to be Count Benckendorff, whose portrait Claude painted while staying at the Anrep's house, Rodwell, in Suffolk. And "Tibble is a preposterous bird. I went to see him one day . . . in his immaculate studio. There is a tale that he is in the habit of jumping up and catching bits of smut or fluff that come drifting though the skylight on a plate. I can quite believe it."[19]

Claude, now in his late twenties, was not making much money from his painting and was still looking for some sort of a job to give him a bit of financial freedom and to enable him to get married. He managed to get one term's full-time teaching as the assistant art master at the Polytechnic Secondary School in Regent Street at the beginning of 1935, and taught occasional evening classes at the Borough Polytechnic, the City Literary Institute and Hackney Down Evening Institute. After this rather hand-to-mouth existence, he was delighted to be offered the job of part-time art master at Raynes Park School, to start in the autumn term of 1935. He was the first art master appointed at the newly-built school, and his appointment seems to have been suggested by friends of the headmaster, John Garrett – notably Wystan Auden. A former pupil at Raynes Park, Paul Vaughan, has given a lively description of Claude's days there.

"For the first art master, Claude Rogers, working at Raynes Park proved a turning point. Uncertain how it was supposed to be done, he had worked out for his first lessons a series of questions to ask the boys which would tell him about their experience of art. First they had to write down the names of any three pictures hanging on the wall at home. None of them seemed to have any . . . 'I realised you had to start from scratch. Almost anything you could show them would be a revelation.'

"Claude Rogers, a short, round man usually dressed in a ginger suit, was not the stuff of which great schoolmasters are made. Art lessons . . . took place in a prolonged uproar . . . Complaints came from Geography and Chemistry along the corridor, and so Claude thought up a system of his own for keeping the boys in order but without making the lessons absurdly repressive. He announced that for each period there would be one forbidden activity; one week there'd be no talking in class, the next no sweet-eating, then no walking across the room without permission, and so on.

"It didn't work. Garrett's patience snapped and he told Claude he would have to go . . . At this point, through Claude's friend William Coldstream, news of Garrett's plan came to Auden's ear . . . and when he heard of the plan to dump Claude Rogers, he at once took Claude's part . . . Auden told Claude not to worry – HE would have a word with Garrett. He added melodramatically 'I know enough to see him in Hades.'

"Whatever Auden said to Garrett after this encounter, it did the trick: a few days later, Garrett stopped Claude in the school corridor. 'Ah, Claude, I've been thinking things over. I really think we can't do without you. We shall have to find a way round this problem.' He would keep him on, but there was a condition. Garrett insisted Claude should make a point of being at school for Morning Prayers. Since Claude lived in Chiswick and he was no early riser, he heard this instruction with foreboding: nevertheless, he duly managed to turn up for nine o'clock assembly but the result was quite unexpected. 'As soon as I took my place,' he said, 'I was absolutely fascinated by the scene in front of me. All these little boys in their blue blazers and their pink faces, stretching back to the other end of the very large hall.' The result was a picture called *Boys at Prayers*; it mystified the pupils when he presented it to the school and for many years it hung in the hall; then it was vandalised, restored, and at length given a safer home in the headmaster's study.

"Claude Rogers had a similar experience when Garrett told him he should stay to School Dinner, a mid-day ritual to which Garrett attached a lot of importance. Masters as well as boys were expected to attend School Dinner, and to get to know the boys socially they had to put up with the overcooked meat and vegetables routinely provided by the kitchen staff of three unsmiling women in white overalls . . . It was probably no worse than any other school food of the time but it so happened that the meals would be helped down with draughts of water, and brightly coloured bakelite beakers were set round the tables. It was these that transformed Claude Rogers' lunchtimes. He would sit there doing his best to engage the boys around him in conversation, but with his visual sense vibrating at those splashes of vivid red, green, blue and yellow. More than one painting emerged from this. One was exhibited at Agnew's in their Coronation Exhibition of 1937 – a picture with the coloured beakers in the foreground, boys at table, and a master's face, probably Garrett's, almost completely obscured by a large vase of flowers."[20]

John Garrett bought *Boys in Assembly* for Raynes Park School in 1940, writing to Claude on January 4: "I think the historic significance of the occasion of your seeing the boys at Prayers in terms of paint is quite enough to weigh the scales in favour of that picture . . . I will send you a cheque for £5."[21] Seven other Raynes Park paintings were made: of boys at dinner, boys in class working or talking and boys painting. The subjects are seen from a high viewpoint, implying the master/pupil relationship and the enclosed world of the boys observed from an outsider point of view. The compositions are unusual and off centre, owing something to Degas and the chance capturing of a moment by the camera eye. The action within the picture is cut by the edges of the canvas, suggesting a continuum outside the picture frame. Claude was obviously taken by the unusual shapes he could find in the schoolboy scenes – the painting done with a mixture of firm and tentative touches, with passages of extreme delicacy in the handling of the boys' heads.

As Paul Vaughan wrote, "Teaching at Raynes Park drove Rogers back to what he considered his true métier as a painter. He had flirted with abstract art, but now began to paint what he saw in front of him . . . His enthusiasm growing, he organised an exhibition at the school, to show boys and parents and anyone else who turned up what contemporary English painting was like: he borrowed works from Duncan Grant, Vanessa Bell, Rodrigo Moynihan, Victor Pasmore, William Coldstream and others, and for security's sake hung them in the Masters' Common Room. Boys were allowed to enter at fixed times, and view the paintings in the fug of stale tobacco."[22] This exhibition was so good that other schools lusted after it, and Claude received a begging letter, sent on to him by Garrett, from Sevenoaks Grammar School: "I hear you have an exhibition of modern pictures at your school which fairly makes my mouth water. With the greatest difficulty I have scraped together a dozen Medici prints for our school and should like to know if this exhibition is a permanent collection which could be borrowed by us also . . ." The exhibition was reviewed in a local paper, and the review included in *The Spur*, the school magazine. "The exhibition was representative in the sense that it gave an opportunity for seeing work of every school. Representational, however, is not an adjective that can be used to describe some of the pictures. The . . . Art Master was often to be heard saying to some earnest enquirer, 'But it isn't supposed to represent anything exactly'. And the writer must confess to have been entirely out of his depth when examining Ceri Richards' *Construction* and Rodrigo Moynihan's *Painting*, though they were very well worth seeing, when one remembers that one of the functions of education is the enlargement of experience. Elsewhere we were delighted by Roger Fry's *Mantelpiece* . . . by Walter Coldstream's [sic] dismal scene at Dieppe, by Augustus

John's head, and particularly, by the fascinating colouring of Ivon Hitchin's [sic] *Garden in a Window* . . . Included were pictures by Mr Rogers . . ."[23]

Claude had collected the latest work from all his friends and it must certainly have been a sight to make any connoisseur's mouth water. Claude, with Elsie's help, had clearly put a great deal of work into organising the exhibition, and John Garrett wrote at the end of the summer term, on July 29 1936, to thank him for it. "Since you will miss tomorrow the general expression of praise and gratitude which I am handing out to my staff, let me write a line to tell you how full a share you have yourself commanded. In particular thank you most sincerely for the exhibition and all the work which it entailed. In this I must include your fiancée's splendid efforts. But also I thank you - and more important still it is - for the general enrichment of their lives which your patient work in art throughout the year has brought to the boys. Finally, for the way you have identified yourself with all aspects of school life and have made yourself so much more than a 'visiting master'."[24]

To Claude's surprise, he enjoyed teaching schoolboys. He would turn up at the school invariably late, often in a taxi which must have somewhat depleted his wages, and launch into the business of teaching. His classes were noisy and unruly, but he was oblivious to the hubbub. Boys on the whole did what they wanted. A former pupil, Robert Chapman, remembered one of Claude's set subjects: "In the foreground was a large cut glass bowl of sugar standing on a café table, and in the background a serving area with people queueing up and being served."[25] This subject, obviously revolving around Claude's head, was probably of Bertorelli's restaurant which both he and Graham Bell were to paint. Claude became famous in the school for the unusual subjects he set for painting - 'A dog taking a man for a walk' or 'A fly swatting a man'. He was rarely at a loss. Paul Vaughan recalled an incident when Claude was patrolling the aisles of the art room and came across a boy painting his penis bright blue. "Put that away," Claude said, completely unruffled. Claude discovered that Paul Vaughan's father was secretary to the Linoleum Association, and, never one to ignore the potential usefulness of acquaintances or to miss a free sample, he persuaded Mr Vaughan to supply sample squares of lino for the boys' linocuts.

Claude was amused by the boys and collected small items from their work, finding in one boy's diary the following plaintive entry: "Dec 27. Forgot to go to church. Ate Christmas cakes instead of Christmas Day. Dec 29. Vic's birthday. Forgot to give present. Played billiards. Dec 30. Got up late. Had a row with somebody. Went to bed." He was a popular teacher and appears to have extracted some excellent work from the boys. He also joined in the life of the school, as well as attending prayers and organising exhibitions, running the chess club, painting sets for the school play, playing rugger or cricket. There was mention of his sporting activities in *The Spur*. "On Monday, July 27th [1936], as part of the end-of-term festivities, the Headmaster led the Staff into the field against the School XI . . . Robbins and Clayden batted steadily and well until Robbins was bowled and Clayden edged . . . from then onwards the batting was unworthy of the school side . . . and the end soon came when Mason charged down the pitch to a slow full toss . . . to be well stumped by Mr Rogers, whose wicket-keeping had been a feature of the day's play . . ."[26] When Claude retired from the job two years later, in 1938, John Garrett expressed sincere regrets; ". . . you have been so valuable in many ways beyond even your own department, on the rugger field, playing wicket, with the play, with chess . . . on open night . . . the whole common room has asked me to say how sorry we are . . . is there any chance this may be temporary?"[27] Claude admitted it would have been "utterly impossible to do anything without the extraordinary free hand I have been allowed". In his review of the book *Art and Regeneration* by Maria Petrie, John Garrett made mention of his protégé: ". . . there have been great teachers who knew how to bring to birth the child's own idea by advice and encouragement - Willi Soukop at Blundells and Claude Rogers at Raynes Park were such . . ."[28] Claude must have known of Sickert's remark that "his own talent, if you can help him to find it, is the most interesting gift you can make to a student"; this was to become the principle on which his teaching was based, and the foundations of his philosophy of teaching were laid down at Raynes Park.

The boys benefitted from his encouragement and enthusiasm for painting, but he in turn learned a great deal from teaching them. He pondered on his experiences in an unfinished manuscript that he was working on during the 1930s. Having learned relatively little history of art at the Slade, he had latterly become extremely interested in it, and had come to believe that it was a duty for artists to be conversant with the traditions of their own and previous ages. "It is because I believe that understanding of tradition in European painting really does offer a standard, primarily to painters, but also to the critic and the connoisseur, that I am writing this essay." The essay, given the temporary title of 'The European Tradition in Painting', rather ramblingly discusses the growth and development of painting traditions. Claude drew his personal conclusions. "Just as man goes through stages of development – through childhood, youth, adolescence, manhood, maturity and old age, so may the pattern of all things be. In the Tradition, Byzantine would correspond with childhood, Giotto with youth, Titian with adolescence, Cézanne with manhood. I suggest this because I have been thinking over my experiences when I was Art Master at Raynes Park School. The boys I taught were from the age of ten upwards; and the youngest had distinct Byzantine tendencies in the work they produced. One of the subjects I found most useful in rousing interest – especially in children who had just arrived from a school where art was taught on naturalistic principles – was 'A London Character'. The procedure was to get each child to choose some different character, typical of the people he saw every day, and to make a drawing in colour of this. As each child decided what he wished to do, his choice was written up on the blackboard. This satisfied the sense of possession, and at the same time eliminated most of the competitive feeling by working it off at the start. The results these children produced were conventionalised figures in silhouette, good colour with a firm contour, with well marked features and with any accessory it was possible to use as enrichment turned into pattern.

"I was at the school about three years and invariably got the same result. In fact the monotony was itself discouraging. I began to see that it was always possible to get a large proportion of the form to produce work which, though interesting and quite good in itself, was fundamentally the same. My wife, who has been concerned for several years with the training of art teachers, had a theory that it was the personality of the teacher which was reflected in the work. I myself came to believe this at the time, especially as I was in the habit during my rounds of the class of suggesting, in order to make the interest grow and to stimulate the creative effort, that appropriate backgrounds should be put in – such as a street scene for a postman etc – I am inclined to think differently now. The children were in the first stages of The Tradition, and any suggestions I offered – they were never more than the one I record above and no work was done by me on their drawings – were nothing more than the suggestions of a more mature person helping them to grasp the next stage in the Tradition. Inevitably the introduction of appropriate objects behind their figures began to suggest, firstly a sense of scale and secondly a sense of space. And so quite soon far more realistic drawings which included these qualities to some small extent, began to appear. In these however there was little sense of 'light' – they were really Giottoesque, but spoilt in many cases through recollection of light effects in pictures they had seen."

He further added: "Children rely on facts that are known or felt rather than on visual appearances. For instance buttons, which offer a problem and therefore are peculiarly important, are represented as early as three or four years of age, and long before a convention is evolved for fingers . . . It seems probable that the Byzantines worked to a mental concept rather than to any external standard of vision."[29]

Claude's theories about art were tested by his teaching; he thought hard about it and probably discussed it exhaustively with Elsie, and he generalised from his experiences. His idea of Tradition in painting as a set of preordained rails along which the train has to run is interesting. He related the development of painting closely to other human activities, natural growth, religion, science, and feared for it going off the rails. He clung to the idea of a tradition in painting from which progress can be made as from a springboard but which must not be overturned. His own work was very much within the European tradition and he was content that it should be; he was less rebellious than many of his contemporaries. Perhaps as a Jew he felt more pressure to belong to the English tradition of painting in which he found himself. Perhaps he was naturally conservative in his tastes. It is likely that he subscribed to the old idea of the 'unities' - that the greater the constraints on art, the more condensed, richer and tougher the art that emerges. In all his painting the bones of the European tradition underlie his observation. The Tradition acted as the framework for the development of his individual expression; it was part of the essential permanence of art, and he sensed a sort of immorality in acting at odds with it. "I believe instinctively in slow change. Iconoclastic reformers, driven by their various devils, psychologically warped, cannot achieve anything permanent because they are driven by hate. The quality of life which corresponds to the painter's 'love interests' is what we must build on."[30]

By February 1936, Claude's letters to Elsie were filled not only with his general escapades but also with a wholly new idea. "Victor, Rodrigo and I want to start an art school . . . If only we can find someone to back it for a year we shall start this autumn. We reckon to spend (with model) about 70 pounds a term - heat, light, rent, everything. That is about £200 a year. Victor has some idea of approaching a rich bloke he knows and offering him one picture from each as part security - value per picture £30. We buy 'em back. He has to risk the other hundred. Fees - 10 gns (full time a term) 2/6 a session part-time: 3 sessions daily, morning, afternoon, evening. This seems wrong somehow - perhaps I have magnified expenses. I saw William and Nancy [Coldstream] on Friday, and Carr (they have a most extraordinarily malevolent looking infant, but I understand they improve invariably) and Tibble who has moved to a sumptuous studio downstairs . . . I met a delightful and natural young woman called Geraldine Fitzgerald the other day . . . she's only about twenty. I wouldn't mind a kiss . . . I'm getting almost out of practice making love, you know, so when you return I may be frightfully rusty. I send you heaps of kisses. You will have to teach me how you like them when you return. I'm not quite rusty in this art yet, having put in a little target practice at parties; but we have special sorts of kisses I only like doing with you . . ." Back to the idea of the school again, he continued ". . . it had been agreed that we should all three try approaching people to see if they would be willing to back us for part of a year. None of us has a bean, but we have plenty of pictures . . . Rodrigo was to approach Mr Billy Winkworth. Victor tried Mr White of Lefevre and Mr Coxon for information about someone who would help . . . All I could think of was Mrs Anrep who might know someone . . . It was decided to look for a studio. The area – from south of Regents Park, Charlotte Street one way, Selfridges the other . . ."[31] This idea was eventually to give birth to the Euston Road School of Drawing and Painting, and Mrs Anrep was to play a vital role as midwife.

NOTES

1 Claude Rogers Papers, Tate Gallery Archive.
2 Claude Rogers letters, collection Mr Crispin Rogers.
3 Claude Rogers Papers, Tate Gallery Archive.
4, 5 Claude Rogers letters, op. cit.
6 Elsie Rogers letters, collection Mr Crispin Rogers.
7 Claude Rogers letters, op. cit.
8, 9, 10 Claude Rogers Papers, Tate Gallery Archive.
11 Claude Rogers letters, op. cit.
12 *The Times*, May 16 1933.
13 Claude Rogers letters, op. cit.
14, 15, 16, 17 Elsie Rogers letters, op. cit.
18, 19 Claude Rogers letters, op. cit.
20 Vaughan, Paul, 'John Garrett and Raynes Park', *The London Magazine* December 1992 – January 1993.
21 Claude Rogers Papers, Tate Gallery Archive.
22 Vaughan, Paul, 'John Garrett and Raynes Park', op. cit.
23 *The Spur*, October 1936.
24 Claude Rogers Papers, Tate Gallery Archive.
25 Letter from Robert Chapman to J Pery, December 6 1992.

26, 27 Claude Rogers Papers, Tate Gallery Archive.
28 *New Statesman*, August 1946.
29, 30 Claude Rogers Papers, Tate Gallery Archive.
31 Claude Rogers letters, op. cit.

Measuring points

In the summer of 1936 Claude again stayed with Helen Anrep at Rodwell. Generous with her hospitality, Mrs Anrep was an 'enabler', supporting and encouraging the young writers and painters who stayed with her. It was she who obtained the commission for Claude to paint a Suffolk neighbour of hers, the émigré Russian Count Benckendorff. Claude went to his house for sittings, and he painted two portraits of the Count, one for his sitter and one for himself, the first while the Count discussed his business affairs and looked serious and the second in a lighter mood, with the Count talking about his love life. A small oil sketch also exists. Coldstream was staying at Rodwell at the same time, working on a painting of Helen Anrep's daughter Barbara. In the evenings Claude and Coldstream discussed painting. Claude's experiences at Raynes Park had drawn him back from abstract into figurative painting. Coldstream and Pasmore had meanwhile been experimenting with portraiture, taking turns to pose for each other, and Coldstream, after a terrible first attempt, had started working by measuring. As Victor Pasmore remembered, Coldstream had become fed up with the film world and longed to return to painting. The question was, where to start? Pasmore found a photograph, a very nice one, that Coldstream had taken and suggested painting with a similar documentary approach. They started on each other's portraits. "We tossed up who should sit and who should start painting. I sat, and Bill produced a third-rate picture, rather like something by Sargent. We thought, there's no future here, we'll have another try and start again next Sunday. By that time Bill had a plumb line and ruler and started measuring. We had a look at that one. It was a bit rum but a little better - the first Euston Road picture."[1] It was this method that Coldstream was developing in his painting of Baba Anrep. He and Claude agreed that nothing equalled the satisfaction of actually painting directly from a motif, even a motif that had not necessarily aroused interest in the first place. The satisfaction was to sit down in front of it, look at it with as few preconceptions as possible and "put down what one could about it". The 'Baba Anrep' portrait, Coldstream's first major work of this kind, is a wonderfully considered and controlled painting. Although he confronted his subjects in the same way as Coldstream, Claude's approach was rather different. With Cézanne's paintings in mind, Claude was trying to see the subject in terms of flat shapes which were tautly interrelated to produce a unified surface and a coherent design. While the creation of form in Coldstream's painting was through the accumulation of a web of measured touches, in Claude's it grew from solidly painted interlocking shapes. But in both cases the desire was to be objective in looking at the subject. The idea of unprejudiced observation was to become the keynote of the work done in their school.

Elsie, back from Jamaica at last, visited Rodwell for the first time during this summer. One weekend Coldstream's wife Nancy came, and Claude remembered that the Coldstreams tried hard to talk him out of marriage. "Nancy, William and I went for a walk, one of them on each side of me. They set about persuading me not to get married (to Elsie or anyone else) on purely economic grounds, really, and in terms of avoidable responsibilities. You are far less likely to be asked away for a weekend or, as now, much longer if you have a wife as well or a wife and family, argued Bill. And it's very pleasant and convenient to be asked away, isn't it? It's that kind of thing I mean, Claude."[2] It was advice that Claude did not follow.

"August was hot and dry," Claude remembered. "Apart from working on the portraits I painted a number of landscapes, somewhat Bonnardy in their outlook . . . One day I came back tired from painting and found the Clarks had arrived (he was appointed to the National Gallery in 1934). He seemed friendly and was very enthusiastic and encouraging about my work which Helen (dear Helen) made sure I took him to see – bought one on the spot and asked me to come and see him in Portland Place on my return to London with any I liked to show him etc . . . The incident was heartening and even exciting and I suppose I read more into it than was intended, being somewhat disconcerted by the coolness of my reception when, in a tentative sort of way, I attempted to take Clark up on his invitation . . . Later there were various guests such as Eddie Playfair and Alan Clutton-Brock who had not so long ago lost his wife: with the result that Baba, whose behaviour was normally eccentric and neurotic to a degree at this time, took it into her head that Helen and Alan were in league to conscript her into matrimony as the second Mrs CB. She rarely left her room, even eating and visiting the lavatory were agonising expeditions to her. Sometimes I, when alone, would become aware of an elemental, lonely figure in thin garments, fluttering on tiptoe at the door, her great luminous eyes entreating, her moist lips – and nose – rabbit working 'are they gone out?' – the ghost of speech. And one day before I left . . . I told Helen about my idea of starting a school for drawing and painting only, with Victor and perhaps Bill . . . Helen was tremendously excited and promised to help . . . But you must do it, she said, it's just what's needed. She was off to Charleston and would canvas Duncan and Vanessa and Maynard . . . It was as though a great rocket had gone off, that sort of enthusiasm (and yet she was so quiet)! And she did as she said. Bloomsbury were captivated . . . Helen got Marion Richardson [the educationalist] among others interested and Miss Richardson sent some eager people who wanted to come to the school as soon as it should open . . . In the spring of 1937 Clark, prodded by Helen perhaps or Charleston – offered to pay and actually paid for a beautifully produced Prospectus . . ."[3]

Helen Anrep's help was invaluable. Her friends were persuaded to back the idea. She insisted that Claude should go to Charleston to see Duncan Grant and Vanessa Bell, who both, she maintained, had great confidence in Claude. Both Grant and Bell, with Augustus John and John Nash, agreed to have their names used on the prospectus and to teach occasionally if required. Claude was advised to go and look for possible premises as quickly as possible. Helen Anrep had a conscious gift for bringing out the potential of others; in a letter to Claude, Elsie quoted "a wicked story about her someone once told me. One night at a dinner party when the conversation turned on Raphael she is supposed to have remarked to Kenneth Clark 'Ah Raphael, I could have made something of that young man.' "[4]

Claude, who at that time was back in London and teaching at Raynes Park, decided that marriage was possible at last. Despite all friendly advice to the contrary, he and Elsie decided to take the plunge. They were married on January 11 1937 at Marylebone Registry Office, with a couple of friends as witnesses. Elsie had found herself a job teaching part time at Southlands Training College in Wimbledon, and she started work at the beginning of the January term. The two of them rented a second floor flat at 28 Charlotte Street over a Chinese art shop at a rent of 25/- per week. The shop was run by Billy Winkworth's father who collected Chinese art objects, including, apparently, a Chinese mistress. Claude was delighted to discover that the flat used to be a rather disreputable whorehouse. The top floor of the house was inhabited by the painter Frederick Gore, son of Spencer Gore, and the first floor, below the Rogers, by the painters Cedric Morris and Arthur Lett Haines, who later founded their art school in East Anglia. For the first time in his life Claude was living in his own home. And with both he and Elsie bringing in part-time salaries, plus Elsie's allowance from Jamaica, they were not too badly off.

Claude kept on his painting room at 9 Goodge Street, and was doing a fair amount of painting, learning what he could from looking at the work of other painters. The landscapes done at Rodwell during the summer of 1936, with their loose touches of broken colour, clearly show the influence of Bonnard. The schoolboy paintings suggest Degas, Bonnard and Vuillard, as well as Sickert, in their handling of paint and their composition. Another painting, now lost, entitled *A Mirror in Bertorelli's*, was handled in a similar way. It was shown in an exhibition of contemporary British artists at Agnews in the summer of 1937, and also at the London Group exhibition, and was noticed by Raymond Mortimer in his review of the show in the *New Statesman*: "The Cinema Attendant is one of the most satisfactory paintings in the show and the Italian Restaurant one of the most charming . . ."[5]

Claude painted Elsie many times, but never as successfully as in the early years of their marriage. *Breakfast in Bed*, *Elsie in a Black Cape*, and *Elsie at Rodwell* are all powerful small paintings, and stand amongst the best of his work. He started work on a nude of his wife at Charlotte Street, trying to paint a nude which did not smack of the studio. Painting directly from observation, he recalled having difficulties in establishing the pose, with its twist in the back. The result is a lusciously soft and fleshy rendering of the body, delicately painted with a small brush. This picture was later given to Kenneth Clark in exchange for the landscape he had acquired at Rodwell (of which he claimed to have grown rather tired), and then given by him to Sheffield City Art Gallery. *Breakfast in Bed* has a similar high viewpoint and shows a close-up scene of Elsie reading in bed with cup and jug on the table in the foreground. It is a beautifully organised painting, with the light touch characteristic of his work at this time.

By the spring of 1937 Coldstream was desperate to get away from his film job and return to painting. Equally eager to paint full-time was his friend Graham Bell, a handsome South African of Scottish descent who had come over to England in 1931 with the determination to become a painter. Bell made his living by writing for the *New Statesman*, *The Listener* and *The Left Review*, while continuing to paint. He had been one of the group of painters who had experimented with abstract painting in the early thirties. Coldstream and Bell, anxious to find some kind of support for their project to return to full-time painting, composed and sent off a document entitled 'A Plan for Artists' to Kenneth Clark. In it they explained their standpoint as artists and their needs, and proposed a guaranteed bank overdraft in favour of artists, suggesting ten guarantors contributing £40 each. Although their plan never gained wider interest, as a result of this document and in return for a first choice of work Clark agreed to provide some support for them both, at the same time inviting Bell to take up quarters in his house in Portland Place. Coldstream and Bell were thus financially freed to devote themselves to painting.

In the summer of 1937 Claude and Elsie again spent some time at Rodwell. Igor Anrep, Helen Anrep's son, remembered that they brought with them a huge tiger skin bought from Simmonds junk shop. They draped it over the bed at Rodwell and lay on it half the day eating chocolates and cream buns. Both were fat and they seem to have encouraged each other to grow fatter. Later in this visit Claude's weight was drastically reduced by catching pneumonia; a self-portrait done at this time shows him unusually long and lean and pale. Unable to take part in the plans for the school, he remained at Rodwell until he had recovered, but wrote to Coldstream that "lying in bed here it gives me much quiet satisfaction to think how, in busy Hampstead, the business of measuring points is going steadily forward."

Plans for the School of Drawing and Painting (later nicknamed the Euston Road School by Clive Bell) were now taking concrete shape. Premises had been hired at 12 Fitzroy Street and the Prospectus widely circulated. Claude noted: "that summer at 13 Charlotte Street I had interviewed and accepted at least five full-time pupils - Jack Shadbolt, Jenny Watson, the American who went back to run a museum in California [Kenneth Ross], Basil Rocke, Sylvia Melland and one or two part-timers, not to mention our scholarship lad L. Gowing . . . Their fees were banked and we started on that and some very nebulous premises. John Dodgson, incidentally, met one very important lack. He suddenly came up with an extra and belated wedding present for EE and me - a dozen radial easels. The other furniture, chairs etc. was second hand and cheap . . . The fees from students always just about covered expenses - as the numbers grew we had to find a bigger place and this just about ate up all we took. As a result the initial idea (Victor's and mine) that such a school as ours would support three teachers at a salary of, say, £120 a year each proved nonsensical. But we benefited in kind - principally with sales and materials from the shop, some free, most at the discount price."[6]

The magic figure in their original plans of £150 a year for each of the three teachers as just about enough to live on had been completely unrealistic, but with Coldstream financially self-supporting, Claude still teaching part-time at Raynes Park, and Pasmore still at County Hall and teaching in the school in the evenings, they were able to get going.

As Claude noted, the original idea for the school had been his and

Pasmore's. With Coldstream freed from his job in films he was able to come in too. The three painters were at that moment thinking very much alike about painting and were all painting using measurement. Coldstream suggested bringing in Graham Bell as a fourth teacher, and this created a bit of difficulty which Claude recounted in his notes: "[Coldstream's] reason for the suggestion was, in part at least, because he that autumn when we were committed to start - studio bespoke and all - would be engaged on several portraits - the Auden I think and the Mrs Auden and perhaps the Spender. He therefore was doubtful if he could manage a really regular attendance as one of the teachers. Graham as VP and I knew was intelligent and lively. But the same thing occurred to us both I think. Bring in emotional Graham and there was bound to be a clean schism in the management - Bill and GB on the one hand, VP and I on the other. GB was intensely partisan. He needed a Christ and a Devil in his cosmology. From the reviews he wrote it was clear that WMC was his at any rate en passant Christ: and VP and I were only too aware how close to the Devil-line we trembled. Mentally we shied like horses at Bill's idea and he may well have read our faces. In the event, Graham was never acknowledged as one of the founders of the school . . . And yet Graham did an immense amount for the school, using it and making it go somewhat in his own way. It was he who arranged the astonishing series of mixed exhibitions at a variety of important Bond Street galleries during the two years of the school's life. He it was who inspired Victor and me to get hold of lecturers. His influence in my opinion turned what otherwise is likely to have been just another not-without-interest private school into a real centre of the liberal cultural life of that time."[7]

A letter from Pasmore to Graham Bell, written in 1941, illustrates Bell's position in the group, and his importance as theoretician to the school: "I realise now how much the Euston Road owes to you. I know very little of your association with Bill and how much his great genius has been influenced by you. But I do not forget that, while he was imitating Matisse in Fitzroy Street and Regent Square, you and Nuttall-Smith and to a certain extent myself were slaving away at cabbages and coffeepots in Devonshire Street and Claude was painting similar subjects in a shed at Chiswick. That we should all succumb to the fashionable conventions of modern painting was, I suppose, inevitable, but my quarrel with you started when as a supporter of Tibble's objective abstractions, you announced that painting from Nature was finished. This I held to be going too far. Although I had no idea as to what extent, I knew that Nature had something to do with painting. It was therefore with some suspicion that I regarded your next announcement that painting consisted of meticulously copying Nature! Your persistence, however, in this latter statement in the face of half-hearted support from Claude and myself has resulted in the best work of the Euston Road School . . ."[8]

As both Pasmore and Claude recognised, Graham Bell put the Euston Road School firmly on the map. "The teaching . . . processes that prevailed were certainly unusual for those times and interesting in themselves; but they were given true point by Graham. Through his efforts the work done in the studios and the students working in them became related, and naturally, to the world of art outside and to professional artists other than the teachers . . . It was his civilising influence which was largely responsible for the stream of visitors - native and foreign painters, poets, critics and others - who found their way at one time or another into the studio".[9]

Copying Nature was to be the main item on the agenda for the next two years. The School of Drawing and Painting opened on October 4 1937 with twelve students. On the opening day Claude was still writing to potential new students, and the copy of a letter amongst his papers to a Miss Hutchings gives details of the school's facilities: "The school opened today at 12 Fitzroy Street, Fitzroy Square, W.1. The first evening life class is tomorrow, October 4th [5th], 6 to 8 . . . The model poses each morning and in the afternoons students can work at still life, or at pictures from drawings, or they can bring along work they are doing for criticism and work at that. A limited number of tickets are issued to practising artists to work from the model without instruction. Part time pupils have the option of buying these tickets if they wish and also tickets for the evening life classes. We are thinking of arranging a special evening for pupils who desire instruction at the evening life classes."[10]

The teachers worked with the students in the studios as a matter of course, and the atmosphere was that of a group of artists studying together. The prospectus emphasised that the chief discipline taught would be observation, and that the looking was more important than creating a likeness, for there was no certainty what a likeness was really like. The idea was to pursue an objective study of nature with no thought of the kind of picture this would produce. The method of exploration was by measurement, and the approach empirical. William Townsend, in the introduction to a later exhibition of Euston Road painting, noted that all the Euston Road painters had in common "an attitude of mind that distinguishes them from a great many of their contemporaries . . .

they are intensely interested in what they see around them: people, buildings, landscapes; and they try to paint this outside world without imposing on it any kind of pattern or feeling or atmosphere that they do not find in the things they are looking at . . . While they had no fully worked out doctrine to preach, nor rules of practice that they wanted their students to follow, they did feel that an unprejudiced approach to the objective world still had a great deal to offer the artist."[11]

In a radio broadcast made many years later, on March 4 1970, Denis Duerdon interviewed Victor Pasmore, who recalled the doubts that he and his friends had about the validity of modern art and their ability to make it. Duerdon commented: "When most of the important painters in the world were preoccupied with a radical break from the traditions of the European Renaissance it seemed as if the Euston Road School had suddenly decided to turn in on itself and quietly pursue an insular variety of an unfashionable and derided classicism." Pasmore replied that their painting grew out of a feeling of "revolt against what we felt was an excessive subjectivity on the part of modern art. Our experience of what we had of Fauvism and Cubism, also abstract painting, had led us to believe that modern art had kicked away all its objective footholds. We felt rather like drowning men clutching at straws".[12] The Euston Road painters decided to try and revive a form of classical naturalism, thus hoping to recreate a link between the artist and the public, which had been alienated by the phenomena of modern art. They were subject to socialist realist influences from Spain and Russia; communism was a fashionable ideology and many of their friends were communists. The involvement in the school of the poets Auden, Spender and MacNiece kept the ideology of left-wing politics in the forefront of their minds. For Stephen Spender the experience of painting brought home two lessons. One was "that it is possible entirely to lack talent in an art where one believes oneself to have creative feeling . . . The other and much more significant lesson was that the art in which one may hope to excel is that in which one can take immense pains over detail."[13]

The Euston Road painters believed that the contemporary artist should work for his public and serve public needs. The most obvious public need in a secular society appeared to be portrait painting, so portraits became the focus and the symbol of the school. Coldstream's method of measurement became the school's method; his was undoubtedly the dominant influence of the group, and his style became a sort of 'house style'. Paintings were built up by the slow accretion of marks which were quarried from the painter's observation of the model. Coldstream always had difficulty in reaching a final, definitive statement, and this difficulty was common to all the painters at the school. They could in fact no longer be classical artists, but were faced with the problems of modern relativity. As Pasmore saw it, "Classical art put it in simple terms, of course; it was like a camera, in a sense, the object was out there and the artist was, or considered himself, as reflecting the object. The two were separate entities. In modern art the two things have become amalgamated so that there is no clear division between the artist, the sensibility and the mind of the artist and the object he is painting."[14] Pasmore was eventually to see realism in painting as too limiting and he later professed an interest in "creating ambiguity, so that you don't know quite where you are. This ambiguity stimulates the imagination . . ." But during the years the School was functioning all the painters were involved in similar experimentation.

Claude felt that it was the painter's 'exploration' that mattered – the discovery of what a shape is really like and how it related to its environment. A degree of 'likeness' was bound to occur as a result of the process of painting – the eyes scanning to and fro across the objects and their environments, the determination of distance between one point and another, the calculation of colour relationships thought about as locations in space. These, expressed as notations of colour, lines and marks on the canvas, built up an equivalent to likeness near enough yet distant enough from common likeness to be disconcerting. Claude was convinced that Coldstream's ideas about objectivity had stemmed from his work with Grierson, the director of the Post Office Film Unit, who had above all wanted his films to be authentic and had apparently coined the word 'documentary'.

Grierson's view that it was important to get absorbed in the work and forget about the art was interesting, and the Euston Road painters began to wonder if it could be applied to painting. Grierson had written a book, *First Principles of Documentary*, which Coldstream denied having read; but everyone at the Slade had been interested in film, and Grierson's ideas must have had some influence, for they closely paralleled the ideas at the school, especially that 'beauty' was impossible to achieve as an abstract target, occurring only as a by-product of the effort to realise. In many ways the school's attitude to painting, though reactionary, seemed revolutionary; and as Claude indicated, "it broke sharply with current ideas, which favoured picture-making, and permissive distortions and fragmentations of the image in the interest of invention, design and effect."[15]

Picasso and Matisse had had a *succes de scandale* early in the century with their flat, distorted images, and they had had an overpowering influence. Their powers of invention were formidable, but they were not easy to imitate. Painters in England, however, studied their work avidly, and Clive Bell's theory of significant form was hard currency. By the late 1930s painting from nature without distortion began to seem old-fashioned. But modern painting often seemed generalised or full of tricks designed to shock or charm, and to have no real connection with outside life. "It was to break with what they had come to think of as the dogmas of the School of Paris – which at that time seemed to offer no more than a choice of mannerisms – that the Euston Road painters sought an alternative. If they took French painters as their models, it was from an older generation. Someone was said to have written on the walls of the school 'The Drawing of Degas, the Colour of Cézanne'. They found their interest quickened by the act of observation, and so had resort to that ancient remedy, the return to nature. Despite all the art they had seen they made an attempt to look at things afresh, without prejudice as to where it would lead. It was the looking that was important . . ."

The Euston Road School was not only unusual in its strict emphasis on looking, but also in teaching only drawing and painting, skills that could be taught entirely in relation to looking. Students were equipped with a twelve inch rule which, held at arm's length, verified distances; a plumb line was set up in front of the model to verify the verticals and the points on the model that fell below each other vertically. Close observation was important, and verification by measurement rather than guesswork was essential to impel students to look harder, to find the subtler relationships and to avoid the obvious. It was a toughening but rewarding discipline, and stood many painters, even those who later changed their methods of work, in very good stead. Lawrence Gowing, the scholarship lad, was a case in point. As the youngest student at the school he had probably the most to learn, and he relished the opportunity. As he was to point out later, the School "opposed to an aesthetic of discrimination an aesthetic of verification". In January 1939 in the first issue of the magazine of the newly formed Art Students Association, devoted chiefly to criticism of existing art school teaching, he wrote: "I am a student . . . I have always supposed that William Coldstream, Claude Rogers and Victor Pasmore began the school as a definite constructive criticism of existing schools rather than an aesthetic manifesto or a commercial proposition . . . The normal process of most art schools is, for the student faced with the profound mystery of art and the endless frizzle of talk about it, to settle down to imitate the tricks of his favourite master . . . The teaching at the School of Drawing and Painting is based on a slower and to begin with less impressive method, the training of the only artistic faculty which is open to training, the power of observation . . . It is only necessary to add that the School . . . is not only the smallest and wisest school but the pleasantest too. The directors paint there themselves at regular intervals. The stove in the big studio explodes at times. The heating is sufficiently erratic to make the climate the natural as well as the conventional topic of conversation. The parties are already famous. The models are invariably good. The secretary is delightful not to say accomodating. You should come."[16]

After a successful first term, the School of Drawing and Painting began to find the premises in Fitzroy Street too small for its needs, and the staff began to look for new premises. They were still short of funds, however, and in December 1937 Helen Anrep gave a party to help raise money for the school. Two pictures were contributed by each of the teachers to a raffle, and tickets were sold at 15 guineas each. Paintings were won by Virginia Woolf, Hugh Walpole, Violet Bonham Carter, Countess Benckendorff and Marjorie Fry. Bloomsbury had come to the rescue again. Virginia Woolf is reputed to have given the school £50 per annum for two years, and to have paid the overdraft Helen Anrep had run up for the school. In some ways the Bloomsbury connection with the school was ironic. The Euston Road painters were in quiet revolt against contemporary French painting, which was fundamental to Bloomsbury thinking about art. Euston Road ideas on art could be seen to undermine those of Duncan Grant and Vanessa Bell, and it is a credit to their generosity that Grant and Bell supported the school so staunchly.

In February 1938 larger premises were found at 314/316 Euston Road, in a building which had been a garage and car saleroom and now housed a fun fair with pin tables on the ground floor. There had been a car lift which ran up through the middle of the building and opened on to the top floor, to a vast studio at the back overlooking some derelict gardens. Claude had the car lift glazed in and it was possible to stand at the top and look down on the funfair, with its flashing lights and circling bumper cars below. Next door was an excellent ironmongers with tools of all descriptions available. Students entered the school from the Euston Road through a doorway capped by a Moorish arch. A long, narrow, dusty staircase made two turns on the way up to the top floor where the school's premises were. Most students painted in the rear studio, which had a skylight. The stair head opened into it and there was a shop there for the sale of materials; faint mechanical music could be heard from the ground floor and sometimes when the model took a rest, staff and students would hurry into the rear studio for a brisk game of soft ball cricket.

The staff worked hard; they were up early and, canvas under arm, would go into the Café Conté for a cup of coffee and be in the studios by nine. The Café Conté in Charlotte Street was conveniently placed for breakfast meetings and for joint reading of the *Daily Mirror*, especially Cassandra and the cartoons. The normal gathering for breakfast was Graham Bell, Igor Anrep, Elsie, Claude, Olivia Popham, Pasmore, Coldstream, Baba Anrep and later Sonia Brownell. Later in the day the café became a resort of chess players and a cab drivers' pull-up. Claude often played chess there, and found some of the players up to the standard of the lesser professionals at the Café Regence. Graham Bell's painting of the Café Conté, done from drawings made over a long period of time, reflects the life of the group, including in the painting, apart from the girl behind the counter, figures of William Coldstream, Igor Anrep, Claude Rogers, Victor Pasmore and Tommy Carr. The girl was the proprietor's daughter, charming, alert and deaf. Her father, a French/Belgian provincial, used to sit carefully slicing vegetables for the soup every day. Claude also painted the café, filled with cab drivers. This picture was reproduced in the *Studio* in colour, but has since disappeared.

By the time of the move Pasmore, with the help of Kenneth Clark, was able to resign from his job at County Hall and work at the School full time. Claude also resigned from Raynes Park in 1938. He and Pasmore worked all day in the studios, teaching and getting on with their own paintings. Duncan Grant and Vanessa Bell made a habit of coming in to paint, sometimes doing some unpaid teaching. Augustus John appeared once or twice, but John Nash, named on the Prospectus, seems never to have put in an appearance. Claude enjoyed working alongside the students; he had worked with his pupils at Raynes Park School and found it fun, and he saw no reason why he should not continue to do so. Pasmore had no objections either, but Coldstream hated people seeing his work, and although he taught in the School, he did not usually paint there.

The school was run very informally. An American, Kenneth Ross, had a free place in return for looking after the studio, lighting the stove, booking the models and so forth. Thelma Hulbert was appointed the Secretary and although she was an excellent liaison officer between staff and students and adept at arranging parties and functions, she was self-confessedly hopeless at gathering in the money. The teachers would admonish her 'Thelma, you must TRY', and before taking friends out to lunch they would request money from the kitty, imploring her to find some somewhere. Valentine Ellis, an accountant friend from the St.

Peter's Square days and a fellow chess-player, became the School's accountant and tried to keep the finances in some sort of order. Claude noted that between October 4 1937 and July 13 1938 at least 116 people worked in the studios. About 25 of these came regularly and about six full time. Augustus John came on special occasions, and was there when Sickert came to lecture to the students. Sickert, by then aged 75, was given a good lunch in the company of Augustus John, Duncan Grant and Vanessa Bell. When he gave his lecture he was convinced that Roger Fry, who had died in 1934, was sitting in the front row and he addressed his remarks to him. As a reciprocal gesture Sickert invited the Boys to have lunch with him at his home in Broadstairs. They were delighted, as they had always held Sickert in great admiration and affection, and they sent Thelma Hulbert out to buy a box of good cigars to take with them on the great visit. The visit, in October 1938, was a success and they returned roaring with laughter. Enquiry revealed the reason. Sickert had shown them all his work and talked at length. At lunch, according to Pasmore, Claude drank two or three glasses, Victor three or four, and Sickert the remainder of five bottles of hock. Halfway through the meal Sickert started singing French songs and went on for a long time. Finally he had said to them "Well, young men, you seem to have been enjoying yourselves very much but I have to confess that I haven't the slightest idea who you are."[17]

This story was later written up by the painter Basil Jonzen and published in *Horizon*, causing a certain amount of trouble. Jonzen generally made trouble; he was a great storyteller, but not noted for his accuracy. Claude remembered Jonzen as "the great bohemian of our generation. Swirling black cape, black hat and silver headed cane he would . . . swagger into the Café Royal, putting groups of friends and acquaintances into an uproar, always trailed by the dogged O'Keefe who was employed full time by the Redfern Gallery (at this time Basil had at least two shows at the Redfern a year, and they were sell-outs) to see that he arrived at his home eventually, a studio underneath an arch of Waterloo bridge, no matter how drunk or with what female entanglements. Basil's status of ex-Harrovian rather than old-Harrovian had something to do with a letter from Lord Byron which he purloined for some perfectly good and genuine reason of his own and with every intention of returning, until [panicked] somehow by a hue and cry he lost his head for the only time in his life and flushed it down a lavatory."[18] Basil Jonzen was often present at the great parties held at Bertorelli's restaurant, occasioned by private views of exhibitions. Claude recalled that "the restaurant would be closed to outsiders and the casual diner. The tables, rearranged into a single line, stretched down the centre of the room, with a T at the tail and a bigger one at the head. These dinners took place spontaneously – after, say a lecture or an occasion at 314/316 Euston Road, or after the opening of one of the exhibitions Graham Bell arranged, biggish mixed exhibitions which included some of the school staff, and maybe three students and a diversity of friends." People would make speeches, and on one occasion Claude, never a confident public speaker, was forced to his feet by the assembled company. He later recounted "presently I was on my feet, paralysed, with a haze of laughing faces round about and not a thought in my mind, until suddenly, some words that had been teasing me in an incomplete way for some days clicked into a form so that I said, while I couldn't make a speech I'd recite a poem. I could, I said, only give them a chorus, the rest was incomplete but, when done, it would be about a lonely, penniless, friendless young randy son-of-a-bitch musing as he sits in a hot little room. Apart from everything else, he woefully thinks,

> It's much too early for the tarts
> It's much too early for the tarts
> At present they're at home
> Sitting all alone
> A-washing of their tits and private parts.

Somehow this developed a tune and was a great success."[19]

During these years Victor Pasmore lived in the attic of the White Tower, looking straight down the perspective of Charlotte and Fitzroy Street, a scene he often painted. In Claude's view it was he who made best use of the School, relishing the combined roles of teacher and student. Unlike the others, he had never had a period of sustained work in an art school and he used it thoroughly, setting up the poses for his own convenience, usually to everyone's delight because they were invariably beautiful. He was a brilliant intuitive teacher, conveying his ideas by a sort of osmosis. "He had a system of Don't-you-knows and nods, and somehow those great big black lambent eyes of his at that period seemed to force you to comprehend some series of signs and slight verbal indications . . ."[20]

At this time anti-Jewish feeling in Britain was increasing and Claude and Elsie became very concerned. Elsie's sister, Margerie Few, was studying music in Vienna and when Hitler walked into Vienna in 1939 they helped to get her back. She went to the British Consul who advised her to get out immediately. She had no money except three English shillings, on which she managed to get trains across Europe, arriving at

Victoria Station with threepence in her pocket. Claude and Elsie took her in, and she stayed with them at 76 Charlotte Street, where they had moved in September 1938. Margerie did the cooking - neither of the sisters had ever learned to cook, but Margerie had been taught to cook three dishes in Vienna; these she produced to great sisterly praise, as Elsie avoided cooking whenever possible. Margerie and Claude got on well, and Claude was extremely supportive to her in her work, advising her to do an hour and a half's practising at the piano every day before anything else. He went to her concerts and later arranged for her to give a concert at Reading.

The Euston Road School and the painters involved in it formed a close network of friends among whom the primary business was painting. The Euston Road was then a byword for grime, squalor, traffic jams and confusion, and the nickname seemed to suit the low toned paintings with vertical lines of 'drizzle' which emerged from its portals. The teaching, anti-idealistic, anti-sentimental, and impersonal, was intended to discourage 'manner'. It was not always easy to live up to these ideals. A former student, Colin MacInnes, wrote that "the most practical teacher there was Claude Rogers, whose brisk, brusque method was to paint the canvas on top of your own version. This was humiliating, but of all these tutorial devices the one that helped most in practical terms."[21] The exhibitions that centred around the group's work were important in disseminating the ideas and achievements of the painters. Apart from exhibitions round the walls of the studios, several outside exhibitions were arranged by Graham Bell. The first of these, held at the Storran Gallery in Piccadilly in October-November 1938, was entitled *Fifteen Paintings of London.* Claude showed a painting entitled *Young Women and Children in the Broad Walk, Regents Park.* This painting was built up from drawings and oil sketches done on site, and the squaring up lines are still visible on the canvas. His main interest in making the picture was the fall of the dappled sunlight on the figures, and the space beneath the trees. The picture, although painted in soft loose touches of paint, is carefully composed and Claude notes the compositional importance of the man in the middle distance. The figures, which form a knot of activity in a tranquil setting, were made from drawings, except the two women on a bench in the foreground painted direct in the studio using Sonia Brownell (known as the 'Euston Road Venus') and Elsie as models. Claude saw them both sitting talking in the studio one day with the light falling across them exactly how he wanted it, and painted them straight into the picture.

The pictures in this exhibition were large for the time, none of them smaller than 3′ by 4′, and there was a socialist realist ethic behind the show. This was noted in a review by Clive Bell, who felt that ideology behind painting should not be visible or "flop out like a bit of untucked shirt". But, unlike Raymond Mortimer who dubbed the show 'The Coldfeet School' of painting, Clive Bell summed up the fifteen paintings as "a hopeful portent in a world that badly needs something to look forward to". Claude's picture attracted a favourable mention; "he is sensitive and intelligent; and this is important because, whereas uncontrolled sensibility can lead anywhere an intelligent artist - and an artist Rogers certainly is - may be expected to go from strength to strength. It is a joy to study this picture and to realise how well the artist knows what he is about. Sensibility has supplied the delicate movements and charming harmonies; but it is intellect which has manoeuvred the figures into the centre of the canvas and then prevented them from becoming a crowd . . ."[22] Most of the paintings, by Coldstream, Pasmore, Tibble, Carr, Gowing, Medley, Moynihan and others, were straightforward London scenes, although Bell's painting *Sunday Afternoon in Whitehall* was an attempt at propaganda, depicting a group of demonstrators being broken up by mounted police. Graham Bell felt strongly that the exhibition should appeal to the ordinary man, and in order to entice this mysterious creature into the gallery he sent private view cards to all the Smiths in the London telephone directory. Seven Smiths actually came.

Pasmore showed his painting *The Flower Barrow* on which he worked for many years, changing it radically in reworking. Pasmore had ideals of 'beauty' which the other painters did not share; Claude noted that "unlike me, unlike Coldstream, Pasmore then (as now) firmly believed in Beauty as a goal anxiously to be aimed at in painting . . . in my case beauty is a by-product that possibly may be found in the end."[23]

Only two exhibitions of the Group's paintings ever carried the name 'Euston Road Group' on the cover of the catalogue. Both were retrospective exhibitions. The first took place after the outbreak of war, in the spring of 1941, at the Ashmolean Museum in Oxford under the auspices of the Contemporary Art Society. The second was an Arts Council touring exhibition for the north of England, originally arranged by William Townsend for Letchworth Garden City, in 1948. The first of these elicited a long article by John Piper in the *Listener* in which he discussed the aims and merits of Euston Road painting. "The first impression that the show gives is one of dullness, drabness. But first impressions are not always reliable . . . these painters are not pictorial isolationists. Coldstream and Pasmore and Graham Bell have been as excited by Picasso as anyone and, in their own way, as much influenced by him. But they have said to themselves something like this: All this excitement in the cultivation of a painter's personality is not the only begetter of good painting. There are qualities in good painting that are being neglected, and are in danger of being lost. Painting has been splitting up into sections, each of which has been posing as the only real thing. It has been splitting up into the ideal purity of abstraction, into the luxury of decoration, into the news-prophecy of surrealism. All these are parts of painting, but there are other parts too. So they are striving, and sometimes fumbling, to make small statements about reality, influenced as little as possible by the distractions of over-developed personality or over-cultivated imagination . . . William Coldstream is the member of the group who has the most obvious 'direction' . . . A Coldstream portrait is above all tentative. There is no easy brilliance or dash, nothing hit-or-miss about it . . . But it is Pasmore and Rogers in this group who keep the picture alive at all costs. They are likely to preserve it against inroads of theory, research, intellect, over-refinement . . . The initial drabness of the whole show is certainly misleading; but before this painting has developed much further it will have become more natural to the onlooker. It will have to sound its voice more clearly among the loud individual shouts of European painting. Today, its shock seems too much like the shock of a damp sponge. It will have to shed its remnants of reaction and its legacies of theory. It will have to pay off some of its remaining debts to the French masters, continue to avoid politics and train itself not to shrink from the personal, positive statement, and not to exaggerate it. Meanwhile, although its voice may be low, its influence is considerable."[24]

During the Euston Road School years Claude painted consistently, producing some very beautiful paintings. In July 1937 he and Elsie had spent ten days in Aldeburgh staying with the painter Alison Leplat, an occasional student at the School. Among the results of this visit were at least four paintings of Aldeburgh beach in delicate colour. Claude painted the wave forms as solidly as he was beginning to paint other objects, looking for the structure. He also painted a portrait of Sally Graves, a niece of Robert Graves who married Richard Chilver in 1937. He remembered this painting as "a semi-demi-commission which did not come off at the time. Many sittings during which Sally made much intellectual conversation and I . . . tried to get her eyes in the right place . . ."[25] It was a classic Euston Road portrait, and when Claude showed it in a wartime exhibition at the Royal Academy (one of only two occasions in his life that he showed at the RA) it was mentioned in a review in the *Times*: "The actual paint is very subtly handled, an intricate web of seemingly monotonous colour which gets its life and pungency from many carefully contrived adjustments. It is certainly a picture to be studied as carefully as it was painted, so entirely is it without any flourish, and with all its effects so discreetly calculated."[26] Another portrait was of Avery Colebrook, which John Dodgson reserved for himself, saying "I should really like to have it as I think it a very good picture." Unfortunately this was destroyed by enemy action in September 1940, although it had previously been exhibited at Rosenburg and Helft's gallery in September 1938. At the same time Claude painted a portrait, never finished, of Marjorie Rogers, his brother Keith's wife, and the portrait of Elsie in a black cape, which remained one of his favourite paintings.

The Euston Road School was a great success. Although it made no money at all for its founders it was popular and its influence was spreading. More pupils were attracted to it and the teachers were painting at the top of their form. But its life, after a mere two years, was dramatically cut short by the outbreak of war.

NOTES

1 Interview with Victor Pasmore, April 23 1992.
2, 3, 4 Claude Rogers Papers, Tate Gallery Archive.
5 Mortimer, Raymond, *New Statesman and Nation*, July 3 1937.
6, 7 Claude Rogers Papers, Tate Gallery Archive.
8 Pasmore, Victor, letter to Graham Bell 1941, collection Mrs Quentin Bell.
9 Claude Rogers Papers, Tate Gallery Archive.
10 Claude Rogers Papers, Tate Gallery Archive.
11 Townsend, William, Introduction to exhibition catalogue *Euston Road School*, Arts Council 1948.
12 Radio interview with Victor Pasmore and Denis Duerdon, March 4 1970.
13 Spender, Stephen, *World within World*, Readers Union 1953.
14 Radio interview with Victor Pasmore and Denis Duerdon, op. cit.
15 Claude Rogers, unpublished memoir version II, collection Mr Crispin Rogers.
16 Gowing, Lawrence, Arts Students Association Bulletin, January 1939.
17 Interview with Thelma Hulbert, May 23 1991.
18, 19, 20 Claude Rogers Papers, Tate Gallery Archive.
21 MacInnes, Colin, Introduction to exhibition catalogue, *Thelma Hulbert*, Whitechapel Gallery 1962.
22 Bell, Clive, *New Statesman and Nation*, November 5 1938.

23 Claude Rogers, unpublished memoir version II, op. cit.
24 Piper, John, *The Listener*, May 29 1941.
25 Claude Rogers, *Modern British Catalogue Vol II*, Tate Gallery 1964.
26 *The Times*, May 1941.

Drill and knots and lashings

The prospect of war with Germany had been getting closer. Even in the relatively cloistered world of art everyone was only too aware of the political situation and most were anti-appeasement. British artists had entered the political arena during the Spanish Civil War, and two of the Euston Road circle, Julian Bell, Vanessa Bell's son, and Felicia Brown, had been killed in Spain. Hitler made his Nuremburg speech in September and this was followed by the Munich agreement. Claude's diary entry for May 1938 states that the painter Julian Trevelyan and three other surrealists wore Chamberlain masks (made by F E McWilliam) and paraded in top hats and umbrellas carrying 'Chamberlain must go' placards.

World affairs were naturally much discussed among Claude's friends, but normal life teaching in the School and chess evenings at 76 Charlotte Street continued. Claude's pianist sister Beryl gave a concert at the Wigmore Hall, and her brother and sister-in-law were in the audience. Claude's brother Keith was now a young doctor and it seemed the three Rogers' careers were happily launched. Friends were getting married. Adrian Stokes, the writer and part-time student at the Euston Road School (*Colour and Form* was published in 1938), married one of the other students, Margaret Mellis, in July. The Stokes decided not to remain in London, and in October Claude saw them leave for Cornwall perched on a lorry heaped with paintings and household goods bound for Carbis Bay, St. Ives, Cornwall. The new term at the School began on October 10, and life was busy. The exhibition of *Fifteen Paintings of London* was showing in October, and in November Claude was elected to the London Group. At the beginning of 1939 the Euston Road School was in full swing, and despite the ominous international situation, in north London the business of measuring points was going well. At Easter Claude and Elsie went to France with a friend, Janice Loeb, driving to Aix-en-Provence via Nonacourt. On this visit Claude painted six or seven small canvases, including some views of Mont St. Victoire, attempting to paint it as if innocent of Cézanne's work. Cézanne's painting still had a powerful effect on him. Claude, freed from teaching schoolboys and able to paint while teaching at the Euston Road School, was very productive. It seemed that the impending threat of war concentrated the mind wonderfully. Claude felt the increase of tension and noted that the face of London was changing. Gangs of men dug slit trenches in the parks, a crisscross of white tape appeared on windows, and sandbags around the bottom of buildings. Claude calculated that he painted about forty canvases between the spring of 1939 and the summer of 1940, noting that other painters were also working unusually well. On March 6 1940 William Townsend wrote to Claude, saying "I hear of one friend after another and they are painting with more gusto, or better, with more assurance and serenity than ever before and more of them merely with that obstinate determination to get something done before premature death . . . The shock and the general dislocation seems to have led many of us to getting our thoughts on painting straightened out, and the release from the kind of tension which was not an artist's tension empties a stream of energy into painting . . ."[1] In February, Claude showed his portrait of *Elsie in a Black Cape*, painted at Rodwell, at Wildenstein's gallery and received letters of congratulation from his friends. William Townsend wrote: "your picture at Wildenstein has given me as much pleasure as anything I have seen in London . . . I thought it so good that it would be mean not to let you know . . . I expect you know it is much admired among our friends." He went on: "I find the uncertainties of the painter's profession since the war started do not seem in the least to have affected the absorbing importance of the painter's job. The less important things . . . now seem so utterly trivial that one can abandon them without twinges of conscience . . ."[2] Pasmore also congratulated Claude on this painting, and on the paintings he showed in March at Agnews, in an exhibition of small pictures designed by their size to suit war time austerity. The full fruits of Claude's labours were displayed in his first one-man show at the Leicester Galleries in April 1940, sharing the galleries with the landscape painter John Aldridge. Claude showed 33 paintings, most of which were painted with the soft, loose touches of his Euston Road style. But Claude combined Coldstream's rather tentative approach to creating form with a sheer love of colour and paint. This point was picked up by a reviewer writing for *Apollo* magazine. "Claude Rogers, whose first exhibition this is, seems strikingly French, of Bonnard's circle. Not that he is in any sense imitative; but he seems to possess a similar love of colour and indeed of PAINT. That has been apparent in the stray paintings one has seen of his in the London Group and elsewhere. Most of his pictures seem to exhale the pleasure he has felt in the handling of his paints. 'Exhale' seems the right word to describe a quality which is airy, like breath, and a sense of colour which is more like a pleasant odour than associated with the paste squeezed from a tube. It is a picture called *The Floral Hall, Covent Garden* which suggested this comparison to me, because it has no tangible subject; it does not present an architectural view of the hall, nor does it expand on the flowers therein; nor is it a social comment of Covent Garden flower-sellers; yet there is the suggestion of architecture, of flowers and even of a flower-seller. The real meaning is the reflection of colour upon colours, the colour of the light that falls through the glass from the sky and touches all the colours within, making for example, the touch of red on the cheek of the flower-seller as important a constituent in the design as the gold on the flowers or the silvery hue in the skylight. In two paintings *Interior with Spiral Staircase* and *The Boy with the Dolphin*, colours are severely restrained, but the impression nevertheless atmospheric. The plump little *Nude* is soft and fleshy. In the subject *At the piano* the sketch is more coherent than the finished picture, but in both cases the green palm in the foreground almost forces the delightful 'piano' part of the picture out of existence; and something of the kind happens in the *Still Life, Dish of Fruit*, where the white cup and the red apple seem engaged in a fierce struggle for precedence. All this only means that the painter has so sensitive a perception of colour values that the slightest increase or decrease of emphasis would suffice him in cases where others can 'pile it on' without risk."[3] This perceptive review points up Claude's chief preoccupations in painting at that time, those things which he had learnt from Bonnard and Cézanne – the creation of colour as an equivalent for light, and the making of form by patches of colour. Other reviewers, not perhaps so enthusiastic about his work, nevertheless noted his burgeoning sense of colour, and the unusual mixture of solidity, even lumpiness, and delicacy in his painting, a characteristic peculiar to Claude. The *Times* reviewer remarked that "the defect of Mr Rogers, in whose work is felt a belated influence of Whistler, is to be just a little 'dim', though the warmly atmospheric *Nude* lent by Sir Kenneth Clark shows that there is no lack of solidity under his diffused manner of painting."[4] Raymond Mortimer, writing in the New Statesman and Nation, seemed to aquiesce in these views, but made mention of his love of experiment, while acutely pointing out the influence that Claude's friends had on him. "He seems in danger of mistaking frugality for refinement, so that one feels a lack of urgency or intensity in many of his pictures. He stands torn, like Garrick in Reynold's picture, between the imposing frigidity of Mr Coldstream and the fascinating coquetry of Mr Pasmore. But if he has caught from his colleagues a caution that is not native to his temperament, he does allow himself a wider range of colour and he shows greater readiness to experiment. His texture is usually delicate, though he suffers from the drizzle that seems chronic in the Euston Road, his construction is sometimes brilliant, his colour sense is sure – all that he lacks is a certain impetus or ardour . . . his best pictures express a sensuous delight in the visible world".[5] This exhibition was a success, and Claude sold over £500 worth of paintings in the first few days. There is good evidence for believing that critical opinion affected Claude, that he took it to heart and thought about it; he certainly took note when the opinions were those of someone he knew. One of the most touching letters of congratulation came from John Holden, his former art master at St. Paul's School. He wrote "in my opinion, if it's worth anything, I rank you with Sickert, Duncan Grant etc. Without a doubt you have certainly arrived. I'm so pleased."[6] Another letter came on April 10 from Tommy Carr: "Graham took me to see your show, of which he is an enthusiastic admirer, as soon as I arrived in London. I shared his admiration and cursed your success. I liked your recent Suffolk landscapes . . . but seem to be unique in preferring them to the portraits, perhaps this is because I am a landscape painter . . . I'm benefitting in an indirect way from your success. Other galleries are searching feverishly for young artists and I'm Wildenstein's hope . . ."[7]

One letter which arrived as a result of this show had a lasting effect. It was from Fryern Court, Fordingbridge, Hants, April 25 1940: "Dear Mr Rogers, I went to see your exhibition and liked it a lot. I think you have a very good feeling for colour and character. If I may venture to make one criticism, I feel what appeared to be your deliberate avoidance of the CONTOUR to be mistaken, but I would like to know what you think about this point. With all good wishes, Yours sincerely, Augustus John." Claude's reply to this letter can only be speculated on, but John put his finger firmly on the chief weakness of Euston Road painting – the dislike, even distrust, of committing oneself to the final statement of the contour. It was a point which Claude thought deeply about and would return to after the war was over.

On the whole the reception of Claude's first one-man show was encouraging, and it spurred him on. He was feeling his power; small wonder therefore, when the war curtailed and even stopped, his artistic practice, that he should feel such acute distress.

During the pre-war years Claude, always susceptible to female charms, had developed a passionate attachment for Alison Leplat, née Debenham. Four years older than Claude, married to the painter Réné Leplat, she was one of the Debenham and Freebody clan. She was already a fully-fledged painter, but used the Euston Road studios to work from the model. Although Alison was not a beauty – loose-limbed with red hair always falling down – she had great character and gave excellent parties at her flat in Russell Square, where the walls were papered with different patterns of wallpaper, tartans and checks, rather like a doll's house. Claude's attachment – the first of many throughout his married life – caused friction between him and Elsie. While staying at Rodwell, Claude would go off on his bicyclc to visit Alison, and there were tremendous rows about it. Claude was guilty but defiant; he himself was puzzled about his attachment to two people at the same time, having not yet come to terms either with the nature of love or with the excessive warmth of his own passionate temperament. His confusion drove him to seek psychiatric help from Dr. Ronald Macdonald, who later helped him through his wartime depression. Claude's attachments were sudden and passionate, developing into long-lasting loyalty, characteristic of his warm and generous temperament. He much later wrote a glowing account of Alison Debenham for an exhibition catalogue. Claude's affectionate nature made him generally fond of his fellow men. He adored women, regarding them, unusually for that time, as equal to men. He was always encouraging to women painters and made the effort to take their work seriously. In his notes he admitted "I suppose we had inherited some of Tonks' ambivalence about women and art; that they were not to be considered quite on a par with men when it came to making up a list for an exhibition. Certainly Coldstream was very peculiar at times on this subject. At any rate Graham [Bell] mentioned in his letter – and he was quite right – that the girls never had a fair do."[9] In this respect Claude was fortunate in his marriage to Elsie; her character was as strong as his and she was his equal in intellect, understanding, and dedication to her profession. Financially she was the dominant partner. She understood money, was the better earner, and had her own private income. Claude respected her judgement as an administrator and as a painter, and she in turn appears never to have wavered in her belief in Claude's work. It was a marriage between two strong characters of equal weights and equal self-centredness. It cannot always have been easy. Claude was accustomed from early childhood to being the focus of a great deal of feminine love and admiration. If he did not get it from Elsie he found it elsewhere. While his loyalty to Elsie as his wife never wavered, he needed the affection of other women and he gave great affection in return.

During the phoney war Claude and Elsie spent much of the summer of 1939 at Rodwell, staying with Helen Anrep, and a company of others. They were there on September 3 when war was declared – "we were digging up a potato bed when the wireless declared war." Graham Bell was also there, acting as chief gardener, and he and Claude remained at Rodwell during much of the autumn, digging the garden and planting vegetables, and excavating a slit trench through solid chalk at the south end of the garden. They also did some painting. Others there at the time were Baba and Igor Anrep, Olivia Popham, Phoebe Pool and Sonia Brownell. Nobody knew what to do at first. Olivia Popham, Graham Bell's girlfriend at the time, remembered an occasion when the police appeared at Rodwell early one morning, before most of the household were dressed. They demanded to know what sort of an establishment Rodwell was, and were very suspicious. It turned out that Baba Anrep and Sonia Brownell had been talking to some soldiers in the local pub, and had been taken by them to be subversives. The police asked questions. Where did Claude come from? He replied Buenos Aires. Where was Elsie born? Jamaica. Sonia Brownell had just returned from Central Europe, Olivia Popham from Holland, and Helen Anrep was stateless. The police turned in their bewilderment to Count Benckendorff whose old German name they trusted at once.[10]

Avery Colebrook wrote from Eastbourne saying that he had let his flat in London to some of Michael Reynolds' BBC friends and asked "If I were to do a cycle trip sometime would Mrs Anrep put me up for a night . . . so that I could see you all? You will be feeling rich in experience of the English landscape. It is unusual for a painter to see it at close quarters and for so long a time. It cannot hurt you."[11] Colebrook was right in this, and in Claude's case it was most probably these long months in Suffolk that made him a committed painter of landscape.

The prospect of heavy bombing in London made it necessary to close down the Euston Road School. It was never to re-open. Coldstream and Pasmore remained in London, however, taking over Vanessa Bell's studio at 8 Fitzroy Street. Here they had one or two private students, some of whom came on from the School. Claude apparently had some students of his own at Rodwell among the evacuees, for an extract from the *Glasgow Citizen* of April 1940, while assuming the School was still in existence (news presumably travelled slowly to the north) refers to these: "London's art centre has been shifting away from Chelsea. One of its more prominent homes today is the humbler neighbourhood of the Euston Road. Here a new school was founded three years ago, with Mr Duncan Grant and others as instructors. The names of its young artists – Rogers, Coldstream, Pasmore, Graham Bell, Devas – are already associated with those of Cézanne, Monet, Renoir, Degas on the lips of the experts and collectors, and their pictures fetch good prices. But few of them have yet shown much of their work. The founder of the school,

Mr Claude Rogers, who has been painting for over ten years, has just opened his first one-man show at the Leicester Galleries, and in a few days has sold £500 worth of his pictures. Mr Rogers is burly, spectacled, roughly tweeded, friendly in manner. He used to live in the Norwegian Seamen's Mission at Gravesend. Now he is living in Suffolk, painting evacuees and initiating them into the mysteries of art. They complain that he does not put his paint on smoothly enough."[12]

When the Euston Road School closed it was evidently still in financial disarray, and owed money to, among others, Margery Fry. Amongst Claude's papers is the draft of a letter to her prodded out of him by Helen Anrep to whom Miss Fry had complained. Presumably the final version of the letter was sent and the matter resolved. "The Euston Road School feels so deeply grateful to you for lending us the money . . . and so so sorry the war made it difficult to repay you . . . Would you care to accept a painting from each of us instead? If the money would be more convenient I'm afraid that possibly I alone can pay my share at the moment since I've just been paid for some work. Victor is in the unfortunate position of being a conscientious objector whose appeal has been rejected. He can't get any job and he is not called up. His wife is having a child and he is not selling anything just now. The others are in the forces . . ."[13]

Claude wrote regularly to his mother in London: "I had to borrow a very small green pair of pants for bathing – with sensational results. Elsie and I have also bought bicycles. Mine cost 30/- second hand and is really rather swell with a three speed gear and so on . . . Graham Bell (helped occasionally by me) has been planting a lot of seeds in the vegetable garden. We occasionally go and look at a house – a long procession, on bicycles – more for the fun of seeing the houses than anything. Count Benckendorff is over, or we are over there quite a lot. He inspects the garden with Mrs Anrep and immediately all the landscape seems to be part of the Rodwell estate. We are going to pick his apples for 6/- a day, so I shall be earning a bit for a few weeks."[14] In late October Claude apologised to his mother. "I've not written I know, but I've been painting so hard – wet or fine – that I usually go to sleep if I sit down. In the rain I have a two umbrella system one for my palette and one for my canvas. I really love being in the country and painting landscape. Never been in it so long in my life. I have a few landscapes at the Leicester Galleries, one at Wildenstein's and shall have one at the Red Cross show at the Academy."[15]

Claude remained at Rodwell through the winter until February 1940. In November he reported to Ida that he was working hard, and kept her up to date on his paintings: "I have pictures at Oxford (two portraits), London Group (the colonel), Agnews (three small panels) and the Leicester Galleries (a landscape) at present. There aren't many reviews just now and at the moment nothing much is happening in the way of sales. A small show of pictures 9½ × 6 inches is coming off at the Leicester Galleries next month. £5 a time and one might sell a few. I have four nice ones so far. Then there is to be a large show at the RA for the Red Cross to which, as a member of the London Group, I shall be asked to send. Clark is getting us permission to paint pictures of military subjects; and altogether I'm pretty busy . . . People are beginning to say there is a chance we may all be able to get back to London but I don't know. I'm very happy painting here and am doing a lot of good work."[16]

In January 1940 not only did Baba Anrep catch measles, putting the whole house in quarantine, but Rodwell was buried in a very thick snowfall, causing the houseparty to be completely snowed in. Claude reported to his mother "by some miracle the pipes thawed and I spent a day getting them all covered with straw and stuff so that they shouldn't freeze again. You see for three weeks we've only had water from a pump in the village. But the pleasure it gave us all to see the taps running again – the fun it was to have a hot bath . . ."[17] Claude not only discovered a passion for painting landscape, but also landscapes under snow, and he painted at least two of these during the winter at Rodwell. Eventually, however, the isolation of Suffolk in winter combined with a wish to be part of the war effort, drove Claude back to London. Elsie was still teaching during term time at Southlands College which had been evacuated to Weston-super-Mare. Claude took up temporary quarters above the offices of Faber and Faber in Russell Square. He wanted to paint a picture for an exhibition entitled *England in Wartime* and he explained to Ida "I have been driven crazy trying to find a war picture to paint in Suffolk, trying to be friends with the military, in spite of loyalty, gallantry, pigheadedness and whatnot I could not find anything at all of a military nature to paint so I came to London . . . while there are lots of things to paint in Suffolk, as far as I'm concerned it's not at war. The only thing I could think of was St. Mary's Blood Transfusion. Especially when I saw people working hard in a group, with pretty coloured bottles about so I brought an easel and started. You know it's an extraordinary thing but between the time it takes me to look at that table and walk to the picture everyone vanishes on some job. Not only that they take all the pretty bottles and I am left with a fairly blank table top! However, in spite of this, with Keith's assistance, I really hope to get it done and it's going quite well!"[18] Claude's brother Keith was running the St. Mary's Hospital transfusion service during the first year of the war, and was able to help him with his subject. The result was Claude's first hospital painting, *Preparing Apparatus, Voluntary Transfusion Service.* This was a theme he was to return to later, and with an inside knowledge of the subject.

At the beginning of the war Claude had registered for military service, but had been rejected by the RAF, having applied for Balloon Barrage work. He volunteered to do Air Raid Patrol duty and in July 1940 was appointed to St. Pancras First Aid Post.

When in London that autumn Claude began going regularly to the National Gallery with William Coldstream for Air Raid Patrol practice. He later told a story which reflected his relationship with Coldstream. "It was a comic and curious business. One would go there on a Sunday morning and sort of mooch about, and then a bell trilled out and everything was ordered confusion. Certain pictures were assigned to each of us, and one had to take them down in a lift and see them down to the basement . . . I remember having a moment of extreme release with Bill on one of these occasions . . . One of his pet sort of pecking order things with me was to say 'Oh you are clumsy' or to indicate how clumsy I was, and I remember one day he and I were running along, each with our little picture, to the lift and suddenly Bill stumbled, and somehow his foot went through the picture he was carrying. He looked at me with horror in his eyes and I said 'Who's clumsy?' It was very satisfying."[19] This story must have reminded Claude of Sickert's story about Whistler. While printing in Whistler's presence Sickert dropped a copperplate. 'How like you,' said Whistler. Five minutes later the improbable happened. Whistler, who was never clumsy, dropped one himself. There was a pause. 'How unlike me!' Whistler said.[20]

Claude vividly described his life in London during these first wartime days. "During the early months of the blitz Graham Bell and Andy (Olivia) Popham were among those who came round very often to join us at night in the basement of 23 Russell Square. This basement was also the stockroom of Faber and Faber from whom we rented our flat. Apart from the shelving stacks, the ceiling was heavily reinforced by a scaffolding of timber . . . We used to play bridge, according to Mr Culbertson's system (handbook kindly loaned by Messrs Faber) or read some of the latest books when things were very noisy and bad. Elsie also learned to knit. One jumper had an arm about half the size of the other simply because it was done during a very bad raid and therefore with much more tension than in the knitting of the other arm. In the mornings after the raids there was a heady sense of release. There was a smell of burning, a crackle and sweeping up of tinkling mounds of glass. One had to get out, to see which bits of London one knew were gone; and how very very much that one knew and liked still remained. Graham and I would mount bicycles and set out to see. And one of our games was to discover buildings which had actually been 'improved' so we said by the bombing. One of our earliest discoveries in this category was the range of shops on the south side of Tavistock Place, between Gower Street and Malet Street. A bomb to the north of them . . . had scarred and chipped the gothic revival niches and fretwork and given the architecture a patina which in the normal way it would have taken centuries to acquire."[21]

Claude joined the emergency auxiliary fire service early in the war, and in July 1940 was appointed to St. Pancras First Aid Post. The first casualties occured there in August, and he described the situation in a letter to his mother. "We have had a fair number of casualties - nothing really to speak about. The noise of the barrage is deafening at night but rather encouraging in its way and much better than listening to the drone of planes coming and going and the occasional thud of bombs. I found a bit of shrapnel in the entrance to the decontamination room at the post . . . Bombs have dropped all over our area - scattered odd ones, in Brunswick, Mecklenburgh Squares, in Great Ormond Street, in the Euston Road, Howland Street, Maple Street and so on. Tussauds got a whopper and the Cinema's gone, but considering it weighed a ton the bomb didn't do such a lot. The facade stands but the whole back has gone; and it looks as if a naughty boy with a hammer had run round the adjacent flats and bust a pane or two in every other window. We haven't had much chance to get the flat straight yet but it's fairly comfortable anyway. The gas gets rather low at times so it's difficult at times to have a bath!! I'm rather enjoying myself. I've started a small painting - the first I've done for some time, though I've done some drawings . . ."[22] There is no doubt that, despite the hazards, these months in London were exciting, and that Claude enjoyed them. He did, however, suffer a severe shock when a bomb blast in the corridors of University College hospital blew the heavy swing doors open, killing the men walking on each side of him and tearing off most of his clothes.

When war broke out Ida gave up her flat in Maida Vale and moved with Beryl and Lily to a cottage in Sussex, rented for them by Keith. Beryl worked as a land girl at first, but eventually found a job teaching music at a private school in North Devon and took her mother with her there. Acute appendicitis took Ida into hospital in Brighton, and then recuperation in Weston-super-Mare, in a methodist boarding house found for her by Elsie who was teaching nearby. Ida returned to London for a further major operation, and then moved into her brother Arthur Rubinstein's flat in Broadhurst Gardens. This flat was bombed, and Claude reported to Elsie "Mama's flat has been blasted to blazes. The roof's in ribbons. Not a window left or door. Mama – she wasn't even scratched . . . what with running about for the old girl she has all sorts of little wants – and gas practices here, where we are working out techniques for handling casualties with the new doctor, I haven't done very much . . ."[23]

Elsie meanwhile went to teach at Langford Grove School in Herefordshire. This was an unusual school run by a Mrs Curtis on free-thinking lines. Elsie described it in her letters to Claude: "There are no punishments at all in this school as far as I can make out – it makes the children so nice and reasonable . . . My own childhood was spent in evading punishment with all manner of cunning, but perhaps it was good training for life – Baba Anrep and Lawrence Gowing as finished examples of the method of 'free' education tend rather to put one off . . . Most of the children have rather intellectual parents I gather. They are quite extraordinarily clever children. Priestley's children are rather interesting – most individual with a sort of dogged vitality – very Yorkshire . . ."[24] Clearly the war hardly infiltrated as far as Herefordshire, and Elsie's concerns remained very personal, enabling her to write about trivialities to Claude "it has been the most lovely autumn day and I feel so alert as the result of doing a little exercise. Really one ought to exercise oneself regularly – dreadful thought. Unfortunately it's so difficult to be strongminded about it . . ."[25] Elsie remained physically lazy all her life, possibly as a result of her cossetted upbringing in Jamaica, and possibly because of a thyroid problem; she never tried to lose weight and eventually became very fat.

The teachers from the Euston Road School, as the war took over their lives, found themselves in very different situations. Pasmore at first undertook River Patrol duty (in A P Herbert's craft) and Coldstream got a job teaching at Canford School in Dorset. Pasmore kept Claude in touch by letter, writing on September 23 1939: ". . . may I explain that I do my reading inside or in more nautical terms on the port bunk in the after cabin. When exposed to public view I wear a smart white cap with a gold braided badge and a dark blue jersey . . . I am still holding out at No 8 [Fitzroy Street] . . . Bill arrived yesterday and stayed the night – he says he's got a teaching job at Canford School . . . The Café Royal has become the centre of London . . ."[26] Graham Bell joined the RAF on the outbreak of war, and by October 1940 was "dressed like a bird man already", looking forward to being "posted to my training wing to start learning the death dealing business. I don't fancy I shall be good at it, but I think if anyone else can do it I can and I long to put an end to the presumptious and brutal enemy . . ."[27] He had time during training to organise the exhibition of the Euston Road painters at the Ashmolean Museum in Oxford, and many letters from him flew around the country on this mission. In April 1941 he wrote to Claude, wondering if there would come again a time "when we can go into Buhler's for a small black seems almost too good to be true – when shall we have spring and flowers untainted by war shall we be able to go to France or spend a morning lounging in the biscuit coloured sun. This is a boil this war which has collected all the poison of those years and left them innocent and gay in the memory . . ."[28] The time for drinking or lounging never came. Graham Bell was killed on a training flight on August 9 1943.

As Willy Townsend had indicated, most of his friends were filled with a surge of creativity during the early months of the war. This was true of Claude, whose excess energy was channelled into embarking on writing a History of Western Art. This was a personal and rather meandering history, which never saw publication but which nevertheless engaged Claude and some of his friends in a lot of time and thought. As a result of an admiring letter after Claude's 1940 exhibition, Quentin Bell, painter, writer and the son of Clive and Vanessa Bell, had become a friend, and he read Claude's manuscript, making many helpful suggestions. Graham Bell also read it, as did Helen Anrep and Count Benckendorff. Helen Anrep warned him against getting involved in "philosophy, metaphysics, psychology, sociology", adding that "it is so easy to generalise, and a mistaken interpretation vitiates your whole theory – so go very slow, be as tentative as you can and understate always – and stick as much as possible to your own subject . . . you very often draw conclusions from inadequate data."[29] Helen Anrep was, as always, generous in her help and wise in her advice – Claude's copious writings are usually lively but spread in ever-increasing circles far from the main point. Claude continued with this opus throughout the early part of the war, but the project seems to have been dropped by the end of the war, not before he and Quentin Bell had had a good deal of enjoyment testing their theories on each other.

After his one-man exhibition in April 1940 was over, Claude felt he was not doing enough to help the war effort and in June he registered for military service. He was not actually called up until 1942, when he joined the Royal Engineers. He had not unnaturally hoped to become an official war artist, and had applied to the War Artists Advisory

Committee to do so. This Committee was set up in November 1939 by Sir Kenneth Clark, then Director of the National Gallery, and by Frank Pick, Vice-Chairman of the London Passenger Transport Board, who was appointed Director General of the Ministry of Information in 1940. Its aims were several: to use the arts for moral good against the forces of evil, to boost morale and create propaganda, to record the effect of the war on the landscape and architecture of Britain, and also to support Britain's leading artists. The Advisory Committee was carefully selected to cover a wide range of styles but sculpture and abstract art were excluded. The annual budget was £5,000 and paintings were acquired for the nation in three ways: by paying artists a salary for all their work (these were the official war artists), by giving individual commissions, and by purchasing work submitted to the Committee. Contracted artists were paid £400 a year; they were vetted by MI5, given sketching permits and their work was sometimes censored. All painting materials, otherwise unobtainable, were provided by the Committee. Among the Euston Road circle, only Coldstream succeeded in being taken on as an official war artist. Claude pressed his case and clearly had a meeting with members of the Committee, for a letter from the Ministry of Information dated March 26 1942 let him know that the committee were "glad to have an opportunity to see your two pictures at their last meeting, have recommended that their War Office representative should do his best to secure facilities to enable you to draw and paint in your spare time after you have joined up. Would you therefore please write to me as soon as you have been posted to a unit where you are likely to remain for some time."[30] The procedure necessitated obtaining permission to draw or paint, explaining the subject of the work beforehand to the security officer, and producing the final work for him to approve its release. Claude managed to obtain only one commission from the committee, for a painting entitled *The Wiring Party.* This painting features in the records of the Imperial War Museum, but its present whereabouts are unknown.

Claude also tried to get into camouflage, the next best thing for an artist, and he pursued Kenneth Clark with this request, but received the rather discouraging reply from the National Gallery: "I have always found it very difficult to get people into camouflage – there seem to be so few vacancies – but I will of course write to Colonel Beddington and hope that something will happen." Colonel Beddington at the Inspectorate of Camouflage was no more helpful, although later in the war Claude was seconded for a short time to Western Command Camouflage School, near Chester, where he was given the dull, repetitive job of painting black stripes on rolls of hessian. He was also shut in a shed with a needle and scissors and a roll of sacking and told to make a camouflage suit. After cutting it out, Claude realised that the suit would not allow room for movement and spent several hours puzzling over the insertion of a gusset.

March 1942 saw Claude, therefore, not painting but arriving at Blacon Camp in Chester as Sapper Rogers CM No. 2158083 No 2 Section 75 Party A Company. A postcard fired off to Elsie is optimistic: "Everyone v. kind and helpful make Sapper of me in HM Army Food Good Air is balmy Chester is all old woodey. No clothes actually fit my tum but tailor to do things to uniform." He sounded similarly euphoric in a letter to Olivia Popham: "I am really very lucky being sent to this camp. There is hot water to wash in, lavatories with handles to pull, wash rooms with showers. I sleep on the floor (they hadn't got a bunk for me because I was a week later than the rest of the draft) but very comfortably and like a log. I enjoy the drill. It's really fun trying to put some swank in it."[31]

His first long letter to Elsie from the army is a little more subdued. "My tum being big is letting me out of work for the moment (no proper clothes) but I can see the next few weeks are going to be très tough. We get up at 6 but WE get up at about quarter to 6 otherwise endless wait for wash and late breakfast. Clean and tidy till 7. Breakfast 7. First parade quarter to 8. Parades and PT and lectures till lunch (12), parades, lectures till about 6 in evening. Parades mostly drill or rifle drill. One afternoon a week compulsory games. Sunday afternoon free. Me I'm not used to it so I shall have to work hard. This [first] 6 weeks at least . . . After that 8 weeks digging trenches building bridges. Then one doesn't know . . . The fucin foods fucin good but the fucin langwidge – oo – is fucin."[32]

Claude was not the material that soldiers are made of, but at first he seems to have been unaware of this. He took an interest in everything, even enjoying the strangeness of it all, and of course connecting it with his painting. He discovered other artists – perspective artists, landscape gardening artists – amongst the other sappers and told Elsie that he did not want to be back in London, because "it all seems so distant and this here seems much more fucking real . . . I would love to paint this . . . Funny how much I want to paint now. I seem connected with the war and so could do something really good I think."[33] He decided he would not want to become an officer, because he liked being an "ordinary chap". "I'm as jolly as a trivet" he wrote to Elsie. "Way I look at it is – I haven't had a holiday for 2 years and now His Majesty's giving me one free. Marvellous air, plenty to do, good food."[34] But this mood was not to last. "I haven't yet managed to open the paints and am a bit fed up about it . . . we are preparing for an all day route march tomorrow. Knowing how much I really hate walking you can guess how much I look forward to it. But I want to do it too: see if I can manage it somehow . . . I still have no idea what they are going to do with me . . ." And later "I hope to open up the paints this afternoon . . . The Army Education Corps Art Teaching job appeals to me more and more if I could get it – more than camouflage really – partly because one would have quite a bit of spare time to paint in and I feel I could really do some good work now I'm in the army – partly because I should be a Sergeant with quite decent sort of pay . . . and all found and none of the bothers and limitations of being an officer. I have an idea the way to paint the army is from the ranks."[35]

The first years of the war inevitably involved separation for Claude and Elsie. They had been married hardly three years when war began, and for the next three years they were apart most of the time. Although they wrote to each other often, each was going through different experiences and developing independently. Their relationship still contained degrees of uncertainty, to which Claude alluded in a letter to Elsie at Weston-super-Mare: "I wish I knew you better. It would be so lovely to have a holiday together alone . . . I so love watching your pretty movements. I so like talking to you . . . you are such a nice EQUAL person to be with and I enjoy that. I want to share things with you."[36] Claude needed that 'equality' on the feminine side, and he seems to have drawn strength from his friendships with creative women. But he also appears to have had difficulty with the emotional demands of those close to him, and his friendships flourished better if those demands were few. Claude needed appreciation and reassurance at all levels, and while his marriage acted as a 'safe house' to which he could always return, he did not always find his needs met within it. Claude attempted to explain some of this to Elsie in a letter. "About Alison. Yes, there's something in their 'common' gossip again, blast their bloody little barnacled backsides. As you know I got all stuck with you somehow in spite of loving you so much. It is odd. You give me all sorts of things no one else in the world can, and yet, in some ways, I always feel inferior and in others just don't work right – like any other chap. Please don't think I wasn't worried or unaware of the situation . . . It just happened; and as a matter of fact I got rather split in pieces . . . In the end I went to a psychologist . . . It was such a relief having a man to talk to – someone I felt would take an unprejudiced view . . . he is interested in painters –

dabbles a bit himself – and he helped me immensely in the short time I was with him. I began to understand all sorts of minor things and could laugh at myself about them – things like my attitude to Bill and the silly way I used to push pictures on after they obviously couldn't go further with advantage. But as luck would have it the blasted call-up came before I really got to the deeper things . . . I'm glad you know in a way but I wish it had happened nicely if that were possible. What would have been the nicest way? I wondered and wondered."[37]

Poor Claude. He had entered the army in something of an emotional turmoil and although he tried hard to fit in with army life, even believing that army discipline might do him good, he finally found himself unable to adapt to it. He was bored by the company in which he found himself, exhausted by the long hours of mindless physical labour, and frustrated in his need to paint. He was eager to help his country, and had no moral objections to fighting, but he was totally unfitted to become a soldier. He was no good at the drills and routines; fat, short-sighted and clumsy, he never really learnt to clean a rifle properly or even sew on a button which stayed on for more than two days. He went through a training course to become a non commissioned officer but failed to make the grade. In the army he had no authority. The authority that he undoubtedly displayed, before and after the war, in art was of the kind that is gained by excellent work and maintained by example. He was always unable to give orders or to operate *de haut en bas*. His inability to cut the sort of figure His Majesty's Service expected sapped his confidence, and made him worry about himself. In letters to Elsie he revealed his anxieties: "It's odd how odd I am. I don't like myself too much . . ." and "this blasted cadre course is not very nice to me. Truth is I'm not the NCO type, I don't like shouting at people much when I feel nothing. And another thing, I just don't know the stuff . . . Funny how clumsy I am at drill and knots and lashings and things."[38] He was quite realistic about his chances of promotion to NCO status: "I can't see any possible hope of getting a stripe out of this cadre class; and unless one gets a stripe for a bit one can't get a commission now . . . I can't understand why I'm so stupid at drill . . . I'm not really stupid I'm sure . . . Blast the army. I suppose it does its best but I wish it had some way of using chaps like me, who will never make proper engineers or soldiers in a useful way that let us feel alive a bit." He confided further: "I've been v. depressed indeed lately as a matter of fact. We blew some holes in a field as I told you and then, god help us, we filled them in to teach us digging. It was so pointless I could have wept." He worried about what would happen to him in the army and he told Elsie "I can see the same sort of thing driving Victor to desperation. Painters need some feeling of stability, or interest in something constructive (not destructive) to make life possible. And the constructive interest in my case seems to need brain work of sorts attached to it. Just lumping about bits of iron for a bridge is too bloody dull for words."[39]

Claude still thought about painting all the time. He had grandiose plans for a picture "to be called 'The Parade' or 'Before the Parade' . . . early morning light . . . 7 o'clock. It's a terrific subject really and if I could wangle the time I'll try it really big – say 6 × 4 or 12 × 8 ft and I'll bloody well ask Clark to let me do it in a room at the NG or the Tate and get 2 months at least . . ."[40] Presumably this picture never materialised in its full-sized version although a small version appears to have been produced before the War Artists Advisory Committee. Claude was eventually given permission to sketch or paint during non-duty hours, and he embarked on a study of barbed wire. "No 2158083 Sapper Rogers C of No 5 TBRE will be employed between 15 and 21 June [1942] on sketching a portion of the perimeter wiring of this HQ. During the latter part of this period he will have two or three sappers with him who will form a working party. He will hand a list of their names and numbers to the camp commandant each day they are here. He will himself report to the Camp Commandant on arrival each day . . ."[41] Too much planning and administration was involved and not enough looking and painting; it was enough to make any painter's work bog down. Despite having chosen this subject Claude must have wondered what on earth he was doing and he sent some plaintive doggerel to Elsie:

What a bore
Is a war
When your leg's feeling sore
And you want to draw well
A picture to sell
A picture of wire –
Why wire you enquire?
I'm blowed if I know –
Sort of struck me, and so
Here I sit in a field
While my blood is congealed
By the wind and the rain
And I say yet again
What a bore
Is a war
That's put me here
It's ber-luddy damn queer

I think.
And I probably stink
Just a tiny bit
As I sit
In the rain
On this strange terrain.[42]

His records show that he did some drawings and one oil painting of the subject, but, given the bureaucracy involved, little work resulted.

On September 12 1942 Elsie received the expected news: "Well, I didn't get a stripe out of the Cadre class. About 18 did . . . One day the war will end and then perhaps I shall be able to dive into painting."[43] Meanwhile Victor Pasmore, having originally registered as a Conscientious Objector, then enlisted in October 1941 and had a successful army career for a year, walked out of the army and returned to his studio in London, once again a Conscientious Objector. He was arrested and imprisoned, but released after a trial in which he was supported by Augustus John, Clive Bell and Kenneth Clark, who called him "one of the best painters in England". Claude was delighted by Pasmore's release and wrote to Elsie "It's v. good news about Victor the old ruffian. How I envy him in a way! Of course he'll be impossible from now on, having beaten the whole British Army . . ."[44]

Other friends fared differently, and tried to keep each other's spirits up. Ralph Nuttall-Smith, who had been at the Euston Road School with Claude, wrote on September 25 1942 saying "the Army must be a frightful waster of time to people who feel they have something to do. It got me before I had recovered from the dazed condition that school left me in and so I didn't really notice much difference. It was about the same level of meaningless boredom and mechanical activity . . . If I can do anything to make things more cheerful for yourself or any other soldiers etc. I should be very glad to . . ."[45] Helen Anrep's wartime correspondence to all her protégés was voluminous, and she wrote long and encouraging letters to Claude throughout his time in the army. She attempted to console him in his various troubles: "Remember the Army is not your Aunts no matter how alike they seem, you aren't a rebellious little boy . . . you are on the contrary an . . . intelligent ingenious man with exceptional powers of adapting yourself to circumstances and understanding and sympathising with people . . . when you don't turn them into your Aunts! . . . You are resisting and then get into a panic about it all. Relax. Don't worry about those two girls either. Everything will arrange itself. Everything is in the day's work, partings and meetings again and time arranges a lot of things . . ."[46]

Army leaves were rather poignant affairs. In a letter to Thelma Hulbert, Claude described one of his leaves in which he stayed with Elsie at Southlands College, in its wartime home at Weston-super-Mare. All his concerns - wife, mother and friends are in this letter. "It was an extremely odd sort of leave . . . I'm thinking of writing a short monograph to be called 'Married Life in a Girls' School'. My mama was hellishly mama-ish, because as luck would have it she came round to see Elsie the morning after I arrived - a rare thing for her to do - and ran slap bang into me. She took one look (I was still in uniform) made no comment but gripped my arm, led me outside and just dissolved into tears - all over Southlands and the pavement. I had to listen to an unending flow of grumble. We all three went to a café and it just went on and on . . . Apart from this it really was a very jolly time. Somehow I managed to eat very well. The staff were kind. The students giggly but pretty. I slept a lot. Did a bit of painting, and read nonsense. But really it was very odd of odd Miss Wood to have a man staying in the house . . . Really I'm not a military gentleman though I can endure. It seems I'll bloody well have to endure for some time doesn't it. Let's hope art is long and t'army's short . . . is there any news about Bombadier Vic Pasmore or Captain William Menzies Coldstream? It's really very lucky we aren't in the same mob. We would get so mournful and disconsolate together I think. It is necessary to keep up some sort of a front to the chaps. Course it's a bit of a strain at times but somehow it is done . . . up to the minimum necessary point."[47] The strain was eventually to prove too much.

In January 1943 Claude was still at Blacon Camp involved in much the same routine, and he was bored stiff. He joined the camp discussion group but found that he did not think in a suitably disciplined way. "One must have a philosophic belief of some sort - some standpoint from which to look at things. I simply haven't got one. At least I don't think so. It's awful." And the introspection which the army forced upon him continued: ". . . I have a lazy, busy, imaginative mind that loves wandering among hazy ideas. It likes facts but much rather plays with ideas."[48]

In February Claude was seconded to Western Command Camouflage School where he was made a corporal on a pay of 31/- a week instead of 19/-; and here he found a room in which to paint - an office in the Sugar Control. The job consisted mainly of dusting the models and filling the oil stoves, but it was here that he was taken up flying for the first time. He enjoyed the experience - "it's very nice but so remote and distant. Everything loses its human touch." He remained fascinated throughout his life with the look of the land or the clouds from aeroplanes, and when much later he was searching for new subject matter he returned to the theme of the aeroplane.

Despite these distractions from his own troubles, by April 1943 he was severely depressed, getting himself "wound up into states". While on leave he went back to see his psychiatrist, Dr. Ronald Macdonald, and appealed to Elsie in a letter ". . . The trap has snapped – and here I am. I must get out. The idea that I may burns brightly . . . a bright little flame. I ache to paint . . . The thought of leaving the army . . . makes me delirious. I can't hide any longer my feelings that it's nonsense as far as I'm concerned and the result is pretty odd as I snap at dear Major Lake and Sapper Bissett . . . let the poor barmy artist paint his pictures he isn't much good otherwise . . . Lord deliver me quick, quickee Lordee! and Dr. Macdonald wave the magic wand so that my rifle turns into a paint brush . . . they seem to want to issue me with one (a rifle) and I hate it. You should never have married a painter – especially if you wanted to paint too, quite crazy of you. I'm sure you need treatment perhaps they'll let you out of it . . . Darling Elsie, you are the nicest, dearest person and such fun . . . I must love you lots in my barmy way – your husband, Claude."[49]

Claude could no longer cope with army life. In June he found himself rather suddenly in Lancashire, in Southport Emergency Hospital, and he straight away let Elsie know. "You see where I've got to. I don't know much about it yet. I was told to bring some papers here as I was to have an interview with a neurologist." Southport Emergency Hospital in fact dealt with cases of nervous breakdown. Here Claude was treated with sympathy and understanding, and he reported a long discussion with the resident doctor, who said "I may as well tell you that you are not a neurotic, but you suffer from what's known as 'artistic temperament', and a very good thing: more people need it."[50]

Claude was given painting materials and allowed to paint and read as much as he wanted. He had his own room and enjoyed the privacy and quiet, comparing it favourably to university life. He also enjoyed the privileges that the hospital's blue uniform conferred on its inmates – free cinemas, buses, deck chairs, concert parties and bands, as well as a free distribution of ten cigarettes every other day. He painted a solemn self-portrait in hospital blue with red tie, and two small paintings of Southport front in which the curves of the distant switchback, seen above the intricate pattern of wrought iron balcony, have an unmistakeable *joie de vivre*. The tone of his letters to Elsie changed dramatically. ". . . It's so exciting painting again that I'm delirious with pleasure - and I'm reading and able to write a bit if I like! My word. You know if only one could arrange life something after this fashion in civvy street. One gets up because one is called and the curtains are drawn back. Goes to breakfast and leaves when one is finished. There is one's room - you tidy it, make the bed: read a bit: then up to the ward for the doctor's round and letters. Come back - it's only 9.10 at most. And then painting till lunch at twelve. Read a bit - more painting. Perhaps a bit of writing. Tea 4.30. Supper 7. Out 7-9. Wed[nesday] out at 1 if you like. No maids to bother about. No food to buy. NOTHING to bother about. Can't you get in here too?"[51]

Claude spent his time outside the hospital making friends with the troupe of visiting actors at the pier concert hall and wandering along the beaches collecting seashells. It was this growing collection of seashells spread out in his hospital room that apparently convinced the doctor that he was unsuitable for the army, "so I think we will get you out of it." By the end of June Claude was feeling so much himself again that he wrote to Elsie "I feel rather a fraud in this blue get up really. Damn it, here I am living buckshee, on the spam of the land, treated like a hero and doing practically as I wish . . . Am I enjoying it? My word I am. It's bloody lovely I assure you . . . The shells here will give you endless ideas for designs. My collection is becoming famous throughout the hospital."[52]

By July Claude was out of Southport hospital with advice from the psychiatrist to go and start a family as his war work. He admitted to rather liking the idea. Elsie came to collect him from Southport, and by August 1943 he was discharged from the army. His career as a soldier had lasted exactly eighteen months.

NOTES

1, 2 Claude Rogers Papers, Tate Gallery Archive.
3 *Apollo*, April 1940.
4 *The Times*, April 9 1940.
5 Mortimer, Raymond, *New Statesman and Nation*, April 6 1940.
6 Claude Rogers letters, collection Mr Crispin Rogers.
7, 8, 9 Claude Rogers Papers, Tate Gallery Archive.
10 Interview with Professor and Mrs Quentin Bell, January 8 1993.
11, 12, 13 Claude Rogers Papers, Tate Gallery Archive.
14, 15, 16, 17, 18 Claude Rogers letters, op. cit.
19 Claude Rogers Papers (Euston Road lecture), Tate Gallery Archive.
20 Sickert, Walter R, *A Free House*, Macmillan 1947.

21 Claude Rogers Papers, Tate Gallery Archive.
22, 23 Claude Rogers letters, op. cit.
24, 25 Elsie Rogers letters, collection Mr Crispin Rogers.
26, 27, 28, 29 Claude Rogers Papers, Tate Gallery Archive.
30 Claude Rogers letters, op. cit.
31 Claude Rogers undated letter to Olivia Popham, collection Mrs Quentin Bell.
32, 33, 34, 35, 36, 37, 38, 39, 40, 41, 42, 43, 44 Claude Rogers letters, op. cit.
45, 46 Claude Rogers Papers, Tate Gallery Archive.
47 Claude Rogers undated letter to Thelma Hulbert, collection Miss Thelma Hulbert.
48, 49, 50, 51, 52 Claude Rogers letters, op. cit.

Contours like steel

"'None of us enjoyed the real war at all . . . At a cocktail party which I went to very early on in the war, I remember Leigh Ashton [a friend and patron] who was a real wit, being approached by a sort of delicate young man who asked him what the first world war was like (Leigh had been in the infantry in the first war). Leigh sipped meditatively at his drink and turned to him and said 'My dear it was TERRIBLE. The NOISE . . . And the PEOPLE . . .!' "[1] Despite his own miserable experiences, Claude was later able to tell this story with relish.

In the summer of 1943, with the war still going on, Claude found himself suddenly back in 'civvy street'. A letter from the Ministry of Labour and National Service headed Resettlement of Disabled Persons, required him to state whether he was employed; if not, he was asked to call at the office for efforts to be made to place him in suitable employment. Claude was fully employed, doing what he was trained to do – painting pictures. Release from the army acted on him like a runner on a starting block. He began to paint steadily and consistently, breaking new ground. "When at the end of 1943 I was invalided out of the army I started painting again mainly on a couple of Still Lifes at Taviton Street – *Still Life with Cast* and *Cast over the Mantelpiece*, and also picked up the painting of the *Boys at Lunch at Raynes Park School*, which under the title of *Glasses*, had been exhibited in 1937 at Agnews Coronation exhibition and the Carnegie International. The whole time I had been in the army I had been wondering about a letter which Augustus John had written, to my surprise, after he had been to my Leicester Gallery show in 1940. In this he said that he couldn't help wondering why, in my painting, I made so little use of 'contour' – ie the defined, linear, bounding edge. Thinking of my painting I realised that most of it WAS pretty fuzzy, partly because of the influence of Bonnard but also a hangover from the teaching of painting when I was at the Slade, where one had started with a tonal pudding in the middle of the figure, or form, and worked tentatively outwards towards the boundary, though one was always told 'do not be in too great a hurry to pin down the contour'. As this was difficult to do in any case it was only too easy never really to come to grips with the contours at all. The two Still Lifes depended much more on edges if not contour than my earlier work. And my object in taking up the *Glasses* painting again was somehow to give it more precision (by close inspection of the drawings I had done and from memory) while not losing the colour."[2]

Another painting done soon after leaving the army was *The Cottage Bedroom*, a study of Elsie in bed seen through the bars at the foot of a great brass bedstead. It was painted at Great Kingshill in Bucks where they were staying, done fairly rapidly directly from the motif. Claude couldn't find a good place to draw from in the little room and one day began to draw Elsie through the obstructions of the bedrails . . . "I started by drawing the bedrails as accurately as I could, then drew Elsie's head to scale and the rest followed."[3] In its conception this painting directly relates to those he made of Southport, where the focus of the picture – landscape or figure – is seen through a patterned screen. The horizontal waves of the bedstead across the picture plane echo the curving 'switchback' shapes of the Southport paintings. In his notes he jotted down "Problem. Something seen through a screen . . . (Southport front) landscapes seen through screens of trees at edge of wood." Not only was he setting himself interesting new design problems, in dealing with patterning and compressed space, but he was attempting to be firmer both in the handling of the paint and in the delineation of the subject. This painting is more linear than, for example, *Elsie in a Black Cape* of 1939. Claude noted the difficulty of getting the structure of the figure under the bedcover, and became aware of the essential balance needed between relatively blank areas and complex passages in composition. It is one of the first of his paintings which can be said to be composed firmly from edge to edge; the design is not concentrated in the centre of the canvas, growing looser towards the edges. Frustrated by his inability to paint in the army, his mind had been active, developing ideas and pondering especially on Augustus John's remarks about his avoidance of the contour line in his work. He now started to treat the contour much more firmly, and in a series of remarkable still life paintings the 'stroked' areas of paint are surrounded by an unequivocal line. His notes again referred to "blank areas and complex passages", and an attempt to achieve a "simpler, harder realisation of shapes", even insisting on the silhouette. He noted the difficulty of drawing really straight lines which still have character, and he tries to make the objects as real as possible, stating: "I draw by the shapes; I think of areas and mass, but I draw by the contours . . . I try to paint as I draw, by the shapes, sometimes starting with the big shapes, not in a general way, but trying to get their character from the first and thinking also of their relationship one to the other. In drawing these the constituent parts – the little shapes – are kept in mind, with eye-testing all the time to see if there is ample room for them . . . I like each painting to be a statement of clear shapes, forms that offer resistance to the eye . . . The simplest rule for what is called composition that I know is to decide on the shapes that interest you, and to see that anyone who bothers to look at your painting notices them straight away."[4]

Claude was beginning to reject the restraints of Euston Road painting and to look for a more personal means of expression. The trouble with Euston Road procedures was that the results tended to look the same. Looking at the subject objectively produced an all-over view of it which tended to deny both depth and human engagement – it was how the eye saw, but not how the brain saw. Claude's approach to painting was naturally more physical and emotional than intellectual, and the conflict between his own nature and the intellectually held tenets of the Euston Road produced an awkwardness which is almost the hallmark of his work. By the 1940s this was evident to others, and Francis Hoyland, a post-war student of Claude's, was aware of his difficulties. "Claude was into revolt from the time that he first taught me in the late '40s, since I think it was about then that he painted the cast hanging on the wall with the open drawer; and a bit later, the blowpipe, which I heard him describe in a lecture as a 'fine masculine shape'. The drawing remained measured but local colour was rolling over from the 'tone ladder' and the paint was assuming the unattractive, uncompromising, clay-like matière which it was to keep from then on."[5] Claude further diverged from Euston Road ideas in his approach to subject matter. In Euston Road painting anything was possible as a subject provided it could be observed at leisure. The decision to paint something – the act of choice – was enough to give the most unpromising material importance. Claude came increasingly to feel that the subject was important as a symbol of those things which interested him in his life.

The objects which figure in Claude's post-war pictures are important, and full of personal meaning. He began to concentrate on their definitive shape, and to give them edges as well as a tactile solidity. Claude had no difficulty finding still life subjects to paint, noting how useful it was to capitalise on his general untidiness – "I often find that the objects which casually arrive among the drifts of papers that collect on tables in my room provoke my interest." He haunted junk shops and bought a motley collection of items for their shape, colour or texture. The *Still Life with Cast*, painted over the years 1943–6, was partly a found still life, and partly arranged. He saw the lamp in a junk shop one day and it reminded him of the lamp his family had had when he was a child.

The apples got there one day when he was unpacking some shopping and it was their addition to the scene that made him want to paint the picture. Several generations of apples were involved, and the painted apples were taken out, scraped down and repainted many times.

During this fertile period Claude also painted two snow scenes direct, in about ten sessions, from two different windows of his flat. He became interested in the way a dull view was transformed, and the geometry of the buildings emphasised, by the falling snow. He did drawings to work out what he actually could see, and tried to paint the snowflakes to scale, the nearer ones being much larger than the more distant. He was developing an interest in representing movement in paint, and came to the conclusion that for him the best way of doing it was to observe all the various positions of the objects in motion and make a deliberate selection of the ones he wanted for his picture. The snow scenes, while harking back to Slade painting in their low tonality, are nevertheless solidly constructed and painted in clean slabs of paint. The late 1940s were a crucial transitional phase in Claude's work, and he was gradually to develop a more solid and personal style.

Among other paintings at this time, Claude worked on the little *Eclipse at Blandford*, now in the Tate. It was, as he put it, a "picture that had to be painted" - of an eclipse of the moon that he had seen in 1940, and of which he had jotted down some notes, and drawn the landscape in daylight. The central 'idea' for the painting was the "copper-coloured glowing lump surrounded by a slate violet" of the eclipse, with the "necklace of Blandford lights trailing off into star clusters." In this beautiful small painting Claude attempted to paint the 'unpaintable' and his interest in unusual phenomena as subjects for painting is first revealed.

In 1947 Claude and Elsie had moved into the top three floors of Taviton House, 13 Taviton Street, a building which belonged to London University and which they were to occupy until it was pulled down in the 1960s. Claude had a painting room on the first floor of this building, and they lived in the rooms above. He taught part-time at St. Martin's and at Hammersmith College of Art, while working on his own paintings. Their son Crispin was born in 1944, and when Elsie returned to teaching after a year Catherine (Reny) Higgins joined the Rogers family to help with Crispin and run the house. It turned out that she had a baby boy, Martin, almost the same age as Crispin, whom she had left in a mother-and-baby home. Elsie insisted that Martin should be rescued from the home and brought up as a member of their family. They were now five in all; Claude was now a paterfamilias and he needed a regular job.

"I had a class at St. Martin's at this time on Saturday and Sunday morning, mainly of professionals or Sunday painters with a lot of experience. There was a model but some of them brought along paintings which they discussed with me and worked at during the class. I saw Victor a lot at Hammersmith Terrace. He was running a painting class at Camberwell and had an idea that William Johnstone, the head of the school, might get me there too if the numbers increased a little. The Camberwell students were obviously a younger bunch than those in my St. Martin's classes, and the thought of working together again pleased both of us I think."[6]

Claude embarked at this time on a series of portraits: of the actress Sonia Dresdel, of Lorna Humphries and her husband Dr John Humphries (both unfinished), of Count Benckendorff's daughter Nathalie (Mrs Humphrey Brooke), and of his sister-in-law Margerie Few. The first four portraits are handled very much in the Euston Road style. John Rothenstein praised the portrait of Nathalie Brooke, and Claude observed "It's a good likeness. I had a real idea for the design, if only she had been able to sit a bit more and the room had remained. I wonder if I could have made more of it? I always want to resolve bits of it when I see it."[7]

The portrait of Margerie Few breaks new ground. In it Claude showed a new concern for 'painting flat', for respecting the flat surface of the canvas and letting the shapes, while suggesting all the volume and subtlety of the figure, create the flat design. His sister-in-law agreed to give him as many sittings as he needed (it took about 40 sittings, often four hours each), so he was able to relax about the outcome of the picture and no special expectations were forced upon him. As this was to be a portrait of a pianist the main interest was the relationship of the figure to the music and the keyboard, and the implied movement of the figure against the static piano. Claude started by doing lots of drawings to select the pose, finally choosing the pose after listening to her play one evening and seeing her turn round to talk to someone. He allowed himself to think in terms of a play of silhouettes for the design of the picture. The red background was chosen to act as a foil for the cool whites of the piano music and the lace dress. His notes recorded that he had constantly to redraw and simplify the head, which in its final version has an almost icon-like quality. He was fascinated by the 'butterfly effect' of the hands, and both the hands and the bulge of the shoulder over the back of the chair are beautifully seen. This picture was tightly composed from edge to edge, and the skirting board has a vital compositional importance. It was the first of Claude's great 'skirting board' pictures, and later pictures used the device with even more panache.

Claude now had the time to think deeply about his painting. He explored the possibilities of flattening and abstracting shapes, but was rigorous in his efforts not to generalise. He noted that "I know things are going wrong if I can only identify the course of a line - a contour - in a general way, and cannot recognise the particular inflections. As the boundaries of my shapes slowly appear - and I use plenty of measurement to fix them - I try to place them in space by painting each side of them. I like to try and hit as near as possible to the full strength of colour and tone at once. I repaint each surface several times in practice, because I gradually develop the shapes, and this seems the only way to get something of the weight and modulations of which I am so often conscious."[8]

In another notebook he further described his methods - "I like Corot's idea of going for the values straight away and I try to get the full range of colour and tone from the first . . . If the painting is started in middle tones and muted colour with the intention of expanding the range in subsequent paintings, in my experience one actually sees and paints with less resolution and attention as though at the back of one's mind there was an escape clause of some kind . . . The first slow covering of the canvas, which has perhaps the most beautiful of all qualities, cannot have the density which is obtained by means of subsequent and judicious touches."[9]

As a dedicated realist painter Claude always investigated the lessons of abstraction, finding out how they applied to him. It is revealing to find in his lecture notes about this time the following handwritten scrawl: "the reason why artists paint in different ways - why some paint abstract pictures and others try to represent what they see or feel - is because, by doing so, each is painting the most REAL thing he can. All painters are trying to be REALISTS - that is to say they want their [paintings] to be as real as possible. Your abstract painter today finds a greater reality in ordering geometrical shapes than in the imitation of nature. It is the reverse with the contemporary painter of landscape . . ."[10]

The business of art was going on despite the war. Claude was elected a member of the New English Art Club in 1943, and in 1945 took part in an exhibition of British painting at Wildenstein's gallery. This exhibition consisted chiefly of Euston Road painting, and Claude was picked out for special mention by Eric Newton, reviewing the show in the *Sunday Times* on January 28 1945. "Claude Rogers, whose position is the exact centre of the group . . . has painted the only memorable picture in the show – a still life. Here, for once, is a picture that illuminates and transforms a fragment of life instead of gently appreciating it and charmingly translating it into paint. Here, for once, the shapes and inter-relationships of shape have a vividness of their own."[11] Claude's efforts to think in terms of shape were followed with interest.

Victor Pasmore's plan to include Claude among the teaching staff at Camberwell was realised. As young people were released from the forces they began to pour into the art schools, mingling with the new school leavers, and more staff were needed to cope with the influx. Several of the Euston Road painters were taken on, and Claude started teaching at Camberwell in the autumn of 1944. He found himself amongst old friends – William Coldstream, John Dodgson, Lawrence Gowing, Sam Carter and Michael Salaman, as well as Edward Ardizzone, John Minton, Tom Monnington, Vivian Pitchforth and Keith Vaughan. It was a fertile mixture, and the presence of the Euston Road group attracted a special group of students. Although the Euston Road painters were beginning to diverge in their ideas, Camberwell still maintained the spirit of unprejudiced enquiry into the philosophy of painting the visible world. It was a remarkable time and it produced a remarkable generation of painters.

At that time Camberwell had about 70 full-time students in the painting school. They shared four studios. One of these was the 'antique' room containing plaster casts, and one end of this was used for a head model. There was a large life drawing room and another large room, once the gymnasium, used for composition. Four or five models posed each day and the number of students working from a model could be anything up to 35. This often meant having a poor view and using very small canvases. Camberwell was seen as the leading school of figurative painting and, with this post-war burst of creativity, it achieved a reputation second to none. The list of distinguished painters who were a product of those years is long – Euan Uglow, Patrick George, Patrick Symons, Anthony Eyton, Robert Hurdle, Richard Lee, Earl Haig, Howard Hodgkin, Gillian Ayres, Francis Hoyland, Terry Frost, Adrian Heath, were a few of them. They benefited enormously by the general determination to get on with painting after the wasted years of the war, despite the difficult conditions and shortage of materials. As Patrick George remembered, the conditions made it a bit of a jungle – overcrowded with a hotchpotch of students, school leavers mixed up with war veterans, some with limbs missing, all wearing old ragged clothes and bits of worn-out uniform. Many of the windows had no glass in them and the place was cold and dirty. The walls had acquired a very fine grey-green sludge colour, and Patrick Symons remembered Pasmore causing some regrets by having one room painted white. Everything was covered in paint, and the rather good plaster casts were daubed in paint and extremely battered - the horse had no legs or protuberances of any sort. Students had to fight for easels, painting stools and space in the life rooms. The teaching was relaxed and informal, done mainly at the easel, and there was a feeling of equality between the staff and the students, who were treated as mature artists from the beginning. This feeling helped to create a close network of friends who all helped and encouraged each other in their work. Claude as a teacher was especially encouraging, and was able to get the students to relax, making it possible for them to paint in an unforced way. He would reassure them by saying that if they confronted the object to be painted and looked hard enough at it they would inevitably have something genuine and personal to say about it. He felt it important to have an idea for the picture to be painted, but an idea which was based on observation: "you can't start a painting from what you don't see." He encouraged students to trust their eyes, and not to rely only on measuring - which created a system of dots and dashes - known as 'Dot-and-Carry' or 'Camberwell easy' - and to draw by the contour. This reflected his own development as a painter - he had come a long way from the Slade teaching methods. He was also keen on exuberant colour, in contrast to most of his colleagues, who were still somewhat addicted to 'Slade mud'. Camberwell colour tended to be drab, but this probably reflected the environment which was drab in those post-war years. He frequently drew or painted on students' work and was refreshingly down-to-earth; Patrick Symons remembered him saying "if a thing looks wrong, it IS wrong. Look harder." And he thought the idea of the 'psychological portrait' rubbish - if you confronted the subject and painted what you saw the portrait was bound to be 'psychological'. Patrick George remembered a memorable lesson from Claude when he was painting the model's hair with 'hairy' strokes and Claude told him to look at the 'shape of the hair'. He also remembered a mature student, Mrs Buxton, who was painting a rather hesitant rendering of the head of a model. Claude came to look at her efforts and at the tiny amount of paint laid out on the palette. Taking a brush, he mixed up masses of paint and spread it liberally all over her canvas. His first attempt was not right and he kept putting on more paint until her canvas was completely covered and the original painting buried; she was left completely helpless as a result. Patrick Symons remembered a student who always saved the best bits of his painting until last. He had on his easel "a life painting virtually complete except for the tits. Claude came along and painted the tits in, beautifully!"

His students remembered Claude with admiration and affection. Earl Haig thought him one of the straightest people he had ever met. "I first saw Claude Rogers in 1945 when he came aboard a no. 36 bus and sat down in front of me en route for Camberwell. The general impression was of warm benevolence beneath a wellworn tweed pork pie hat. Gradually as I came to know him I realised his sensitivity and kindness and sense of humour. He was never able to push on his own behalf. He was very much loved by those of us who were lucky enough to be his friends." Anthony Eyton recalled that "at Camberwell Claude was very endearing. His relish and down-to-earth responses to models, still-lives etc was infectious and very welcome. There was a rumbustious quality about him. His face was ruddy, his shoulders broad so that they seemed to graze against the door post or easel as he strode into the room. Once an easel became a bone of contention with Norah Langley, a student, who was painting in the corridor. Claude insisted that the easel was needed in the life room and a tug-of-war resulted. Both became heated and there were angry words. Claude was very much the painter, and compared to the rest of the staff, his approach was very direct. He was able to acknowledge the difficulties as well as the delights of getting things right. I remember him drawing a model's thigh by way of demonstration. 'Draw the contour like steel' he said and proceeded to do a very beautiful drawing. It was a sensitive piece of direct observation about the contour and volume of the leg, concise and true."[12]

Francis Hoyland also remembered Claude's lessons in drawing. "Claude would concentrate on a small part of the model. He used to work his way out from a central point by an additive process of shapes governed by proportion. Most of the other staff at Camberwell taught in the same way but Claude's example had two distinctive features. The first was the frequency with which he used the word 'interesting' (he used to pronounce it 'intwEsting'); and the second was the way that at least once he really kicked over the traces and had a full-bodied, rhythmic swing at the whole pose. This was, for a moment, almost total revolt. Claude's interest was both genuine and infectious – the way things were always brought him delight and it was on this that he focused his intellect. He liked facts and he liked to see them straight. One was expected to share his ardour and he took it for granted that one would make the necessary effort to share his experience."[13]

Christopher Pinsent came to Camberwell after working for some

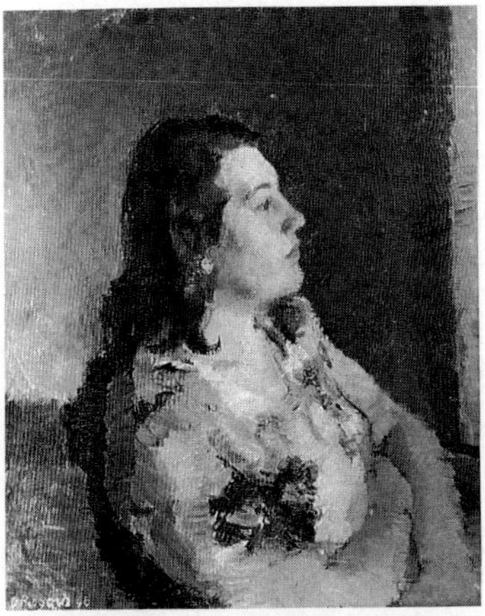

36. *Mrs Humphrey Brooke*, 1946.

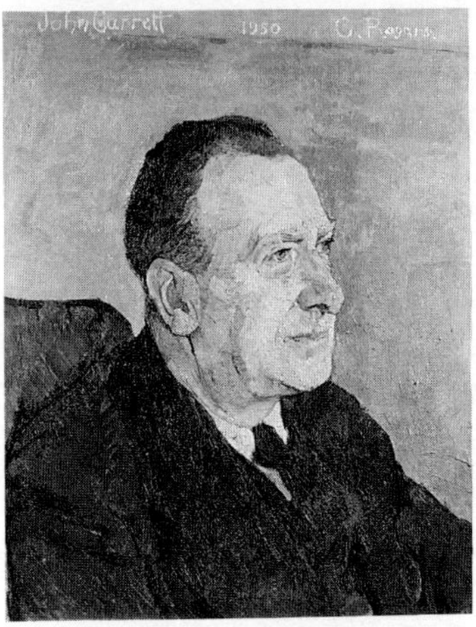

37. *John Garrett*, 1949–50.

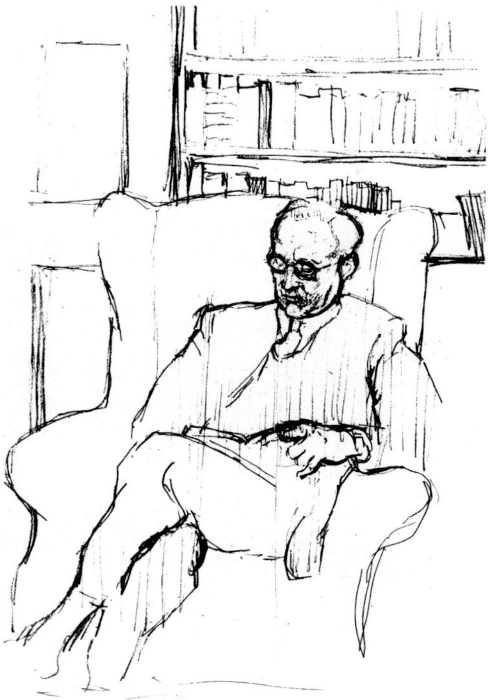

38. Drawing for portrait of Thorold Coade, 1950.

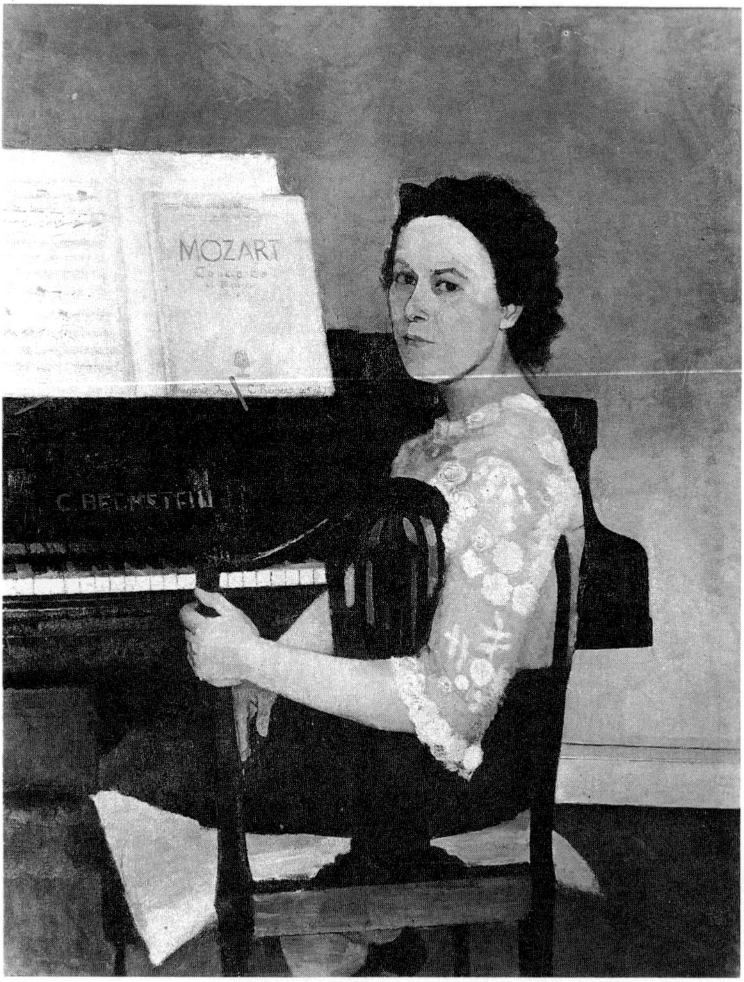

39. *Margerie Few*, 1945–47.

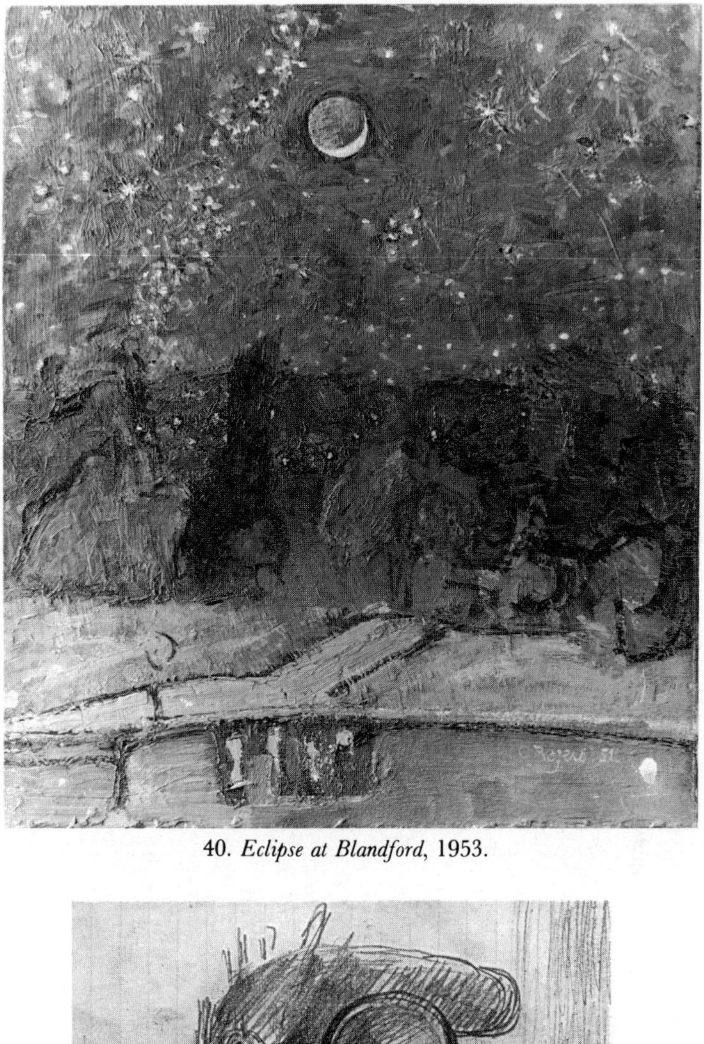

40. *Eclipse at Blandford*, 1953.

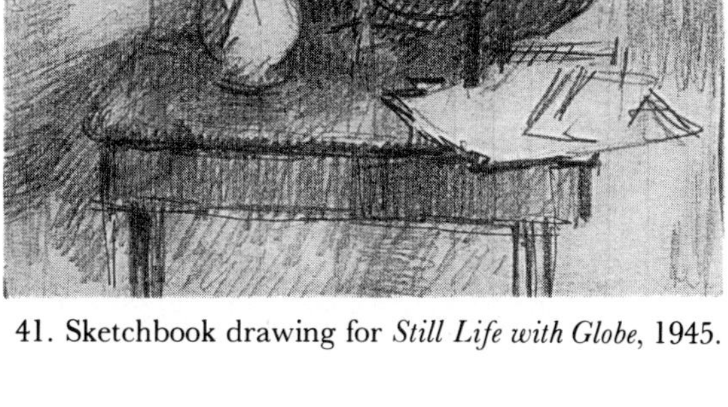

41. Sketchbook drawing for *Still Life with Globe*, 1945.

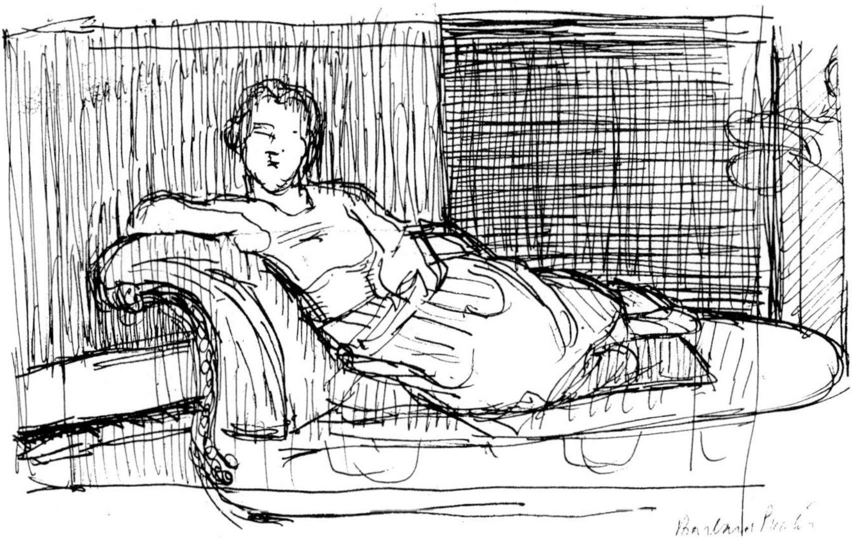

42. Drawing for portrait.

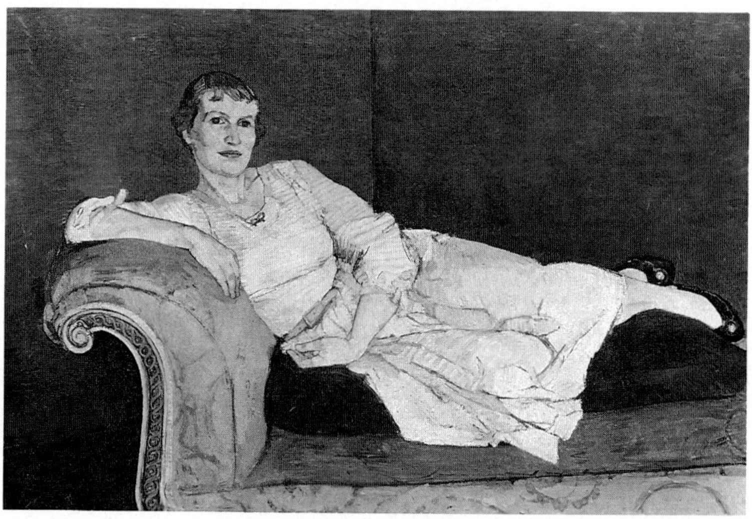

43. *Barbara Proctor*, 1956.

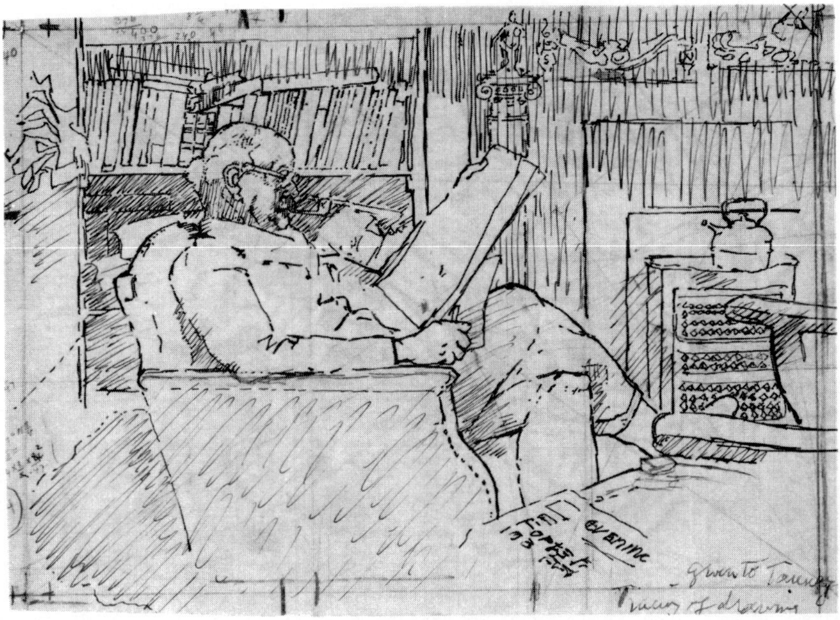

44. Drawing for portrait of Professor Tawney, 1952.

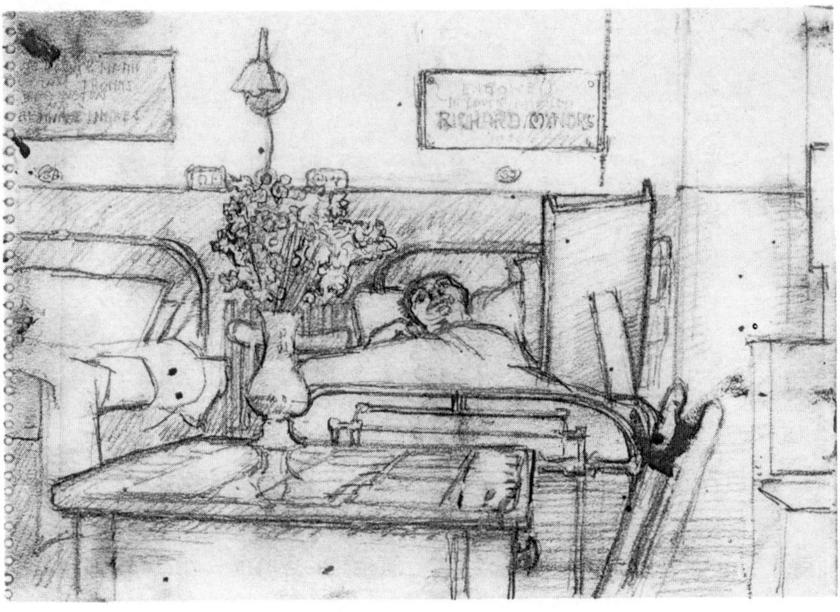

45. Drawing for *The Patient Opposite*, 1952.

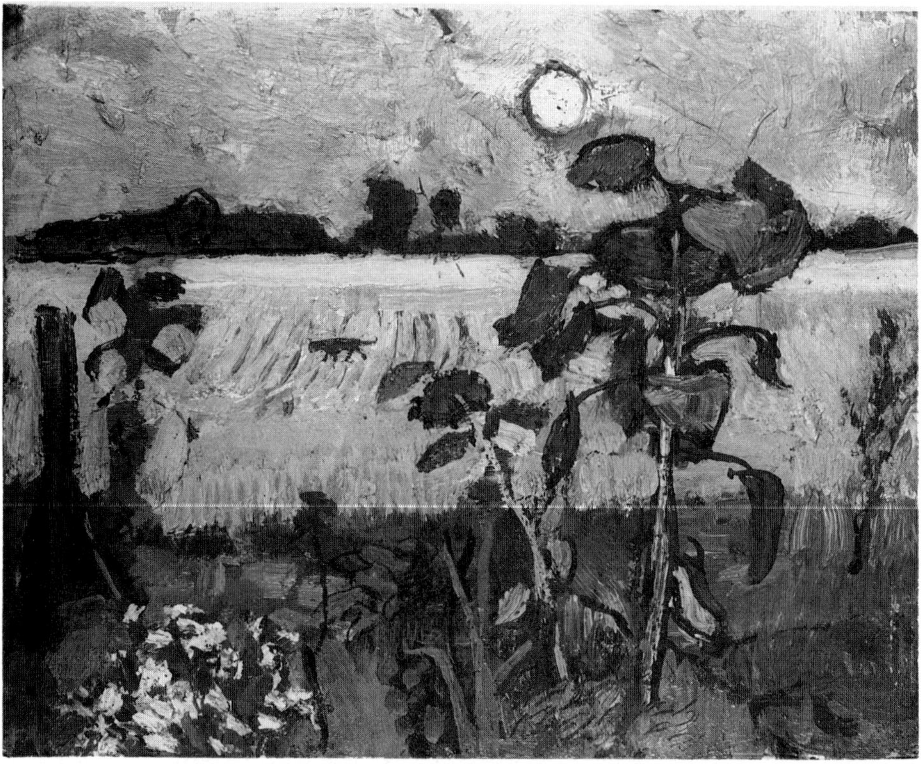

46. *The Hunting Cat*, 1950.

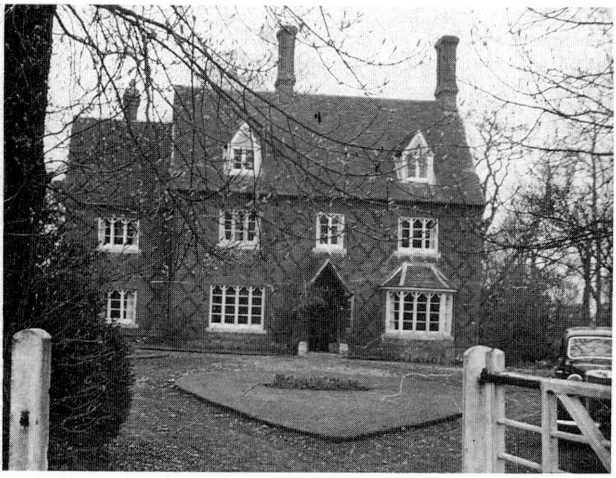

47. The Old Rectory, Somerton.

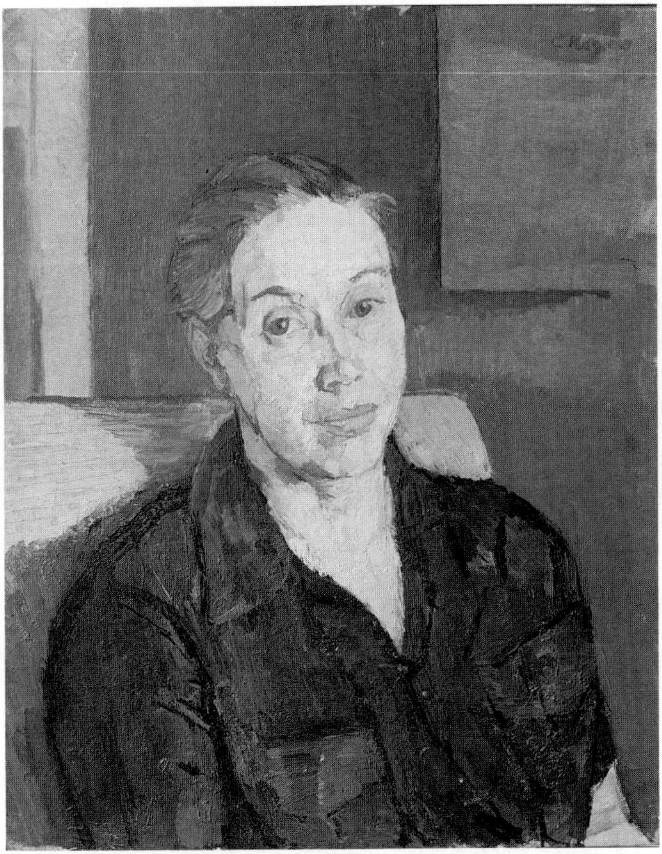

48. *Mrs Jacobsen*, 1954.

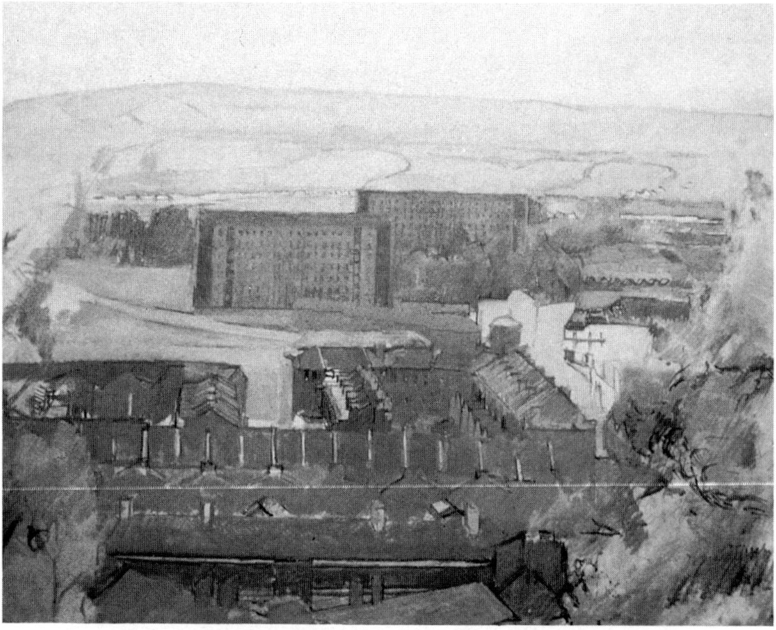

49. *Bonding Warehouses, Bristol*, 1949.

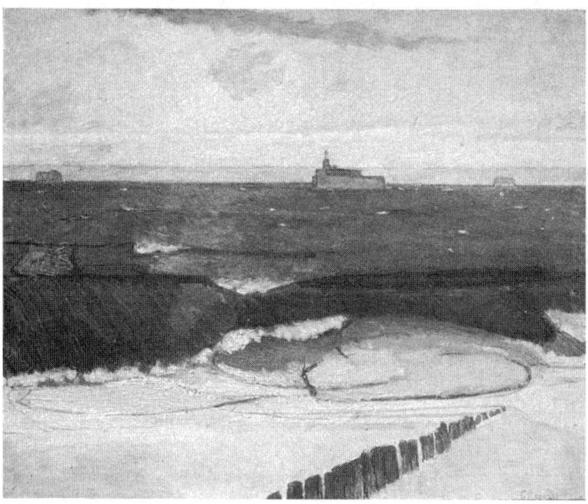

50. *Spithead Forts*, 1953.

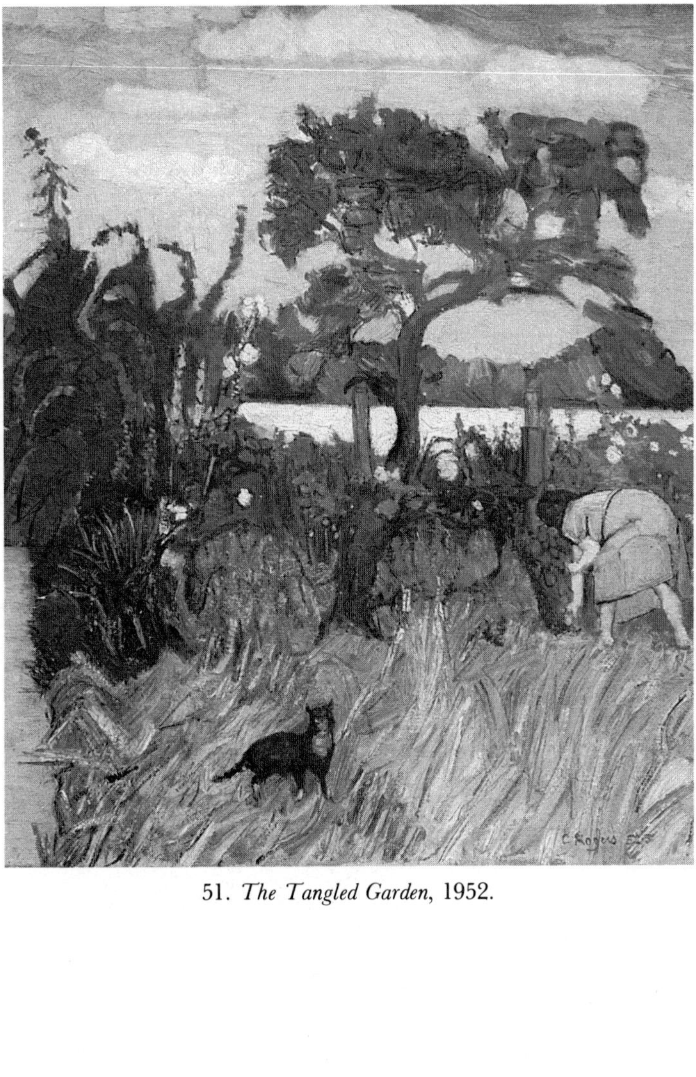

51. *The Tangled Garden*, 1952.

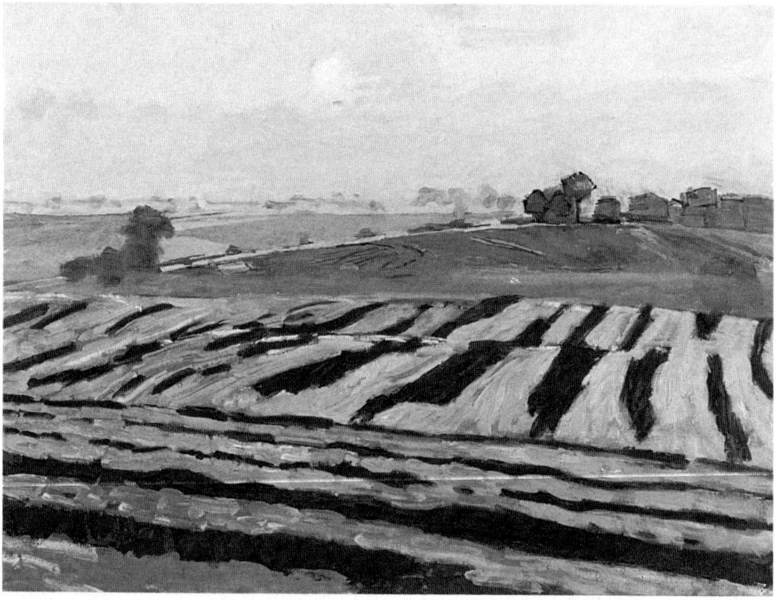

52. *Sunrise over Burnt Field*, 1977–78.

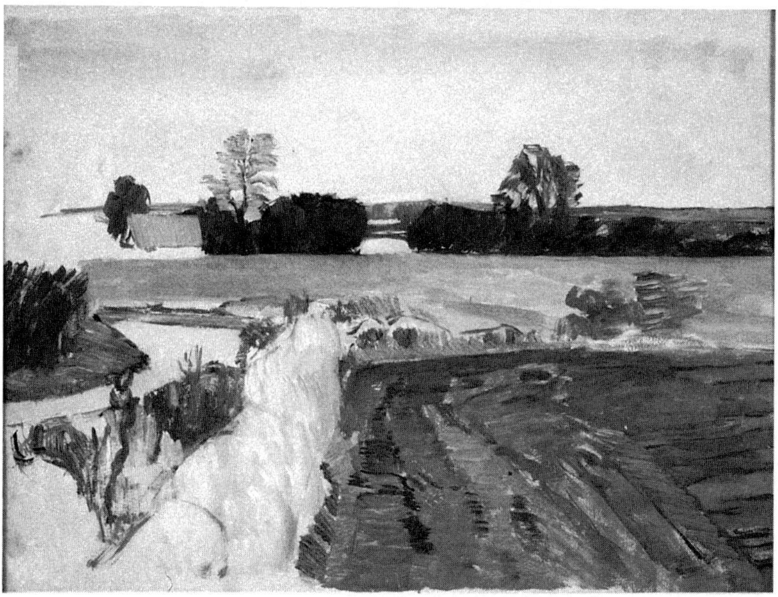

53. *Winter Landscape, Frosty Fields*, 1956.

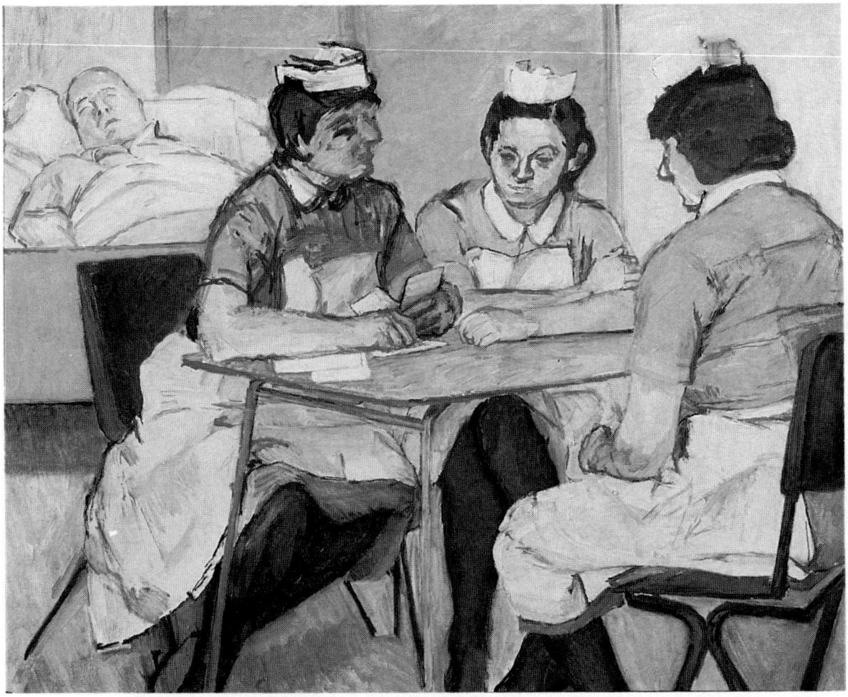

54. *Three Nurses*, 1977.

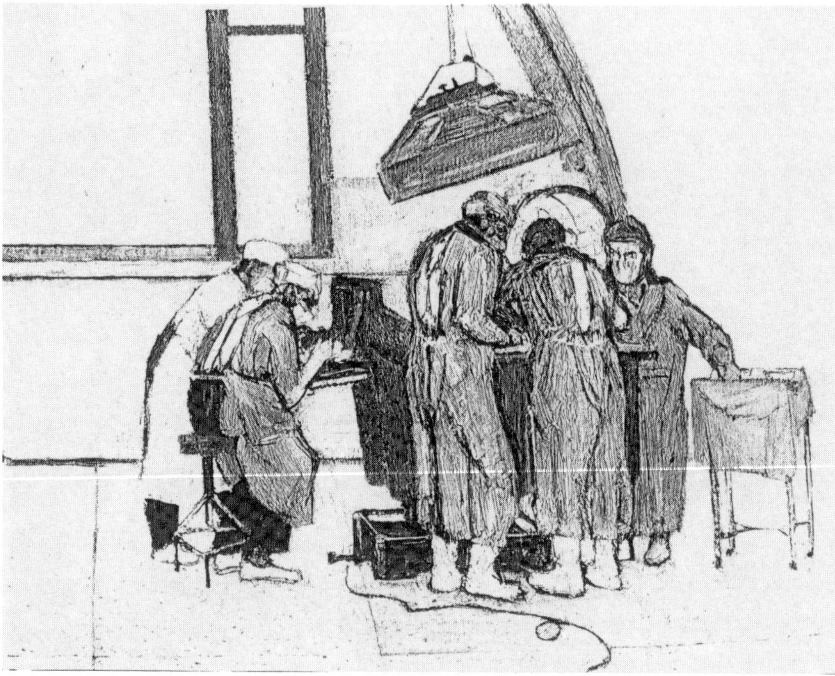

55. *Operation in Progress*, 1954.

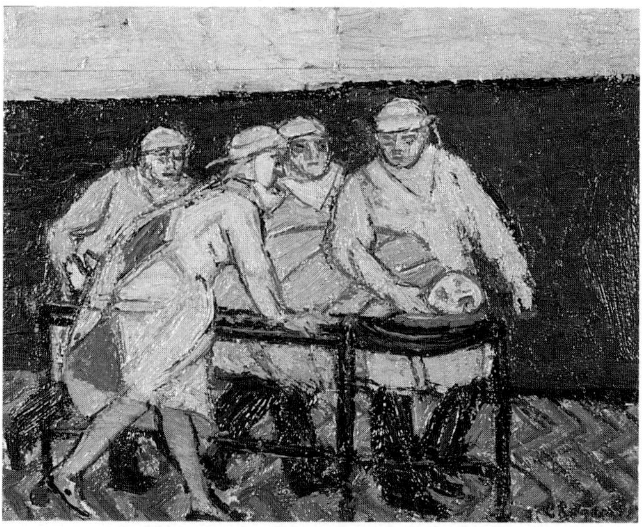

56. Sketch for *The Theatre Trolley*, 1952.

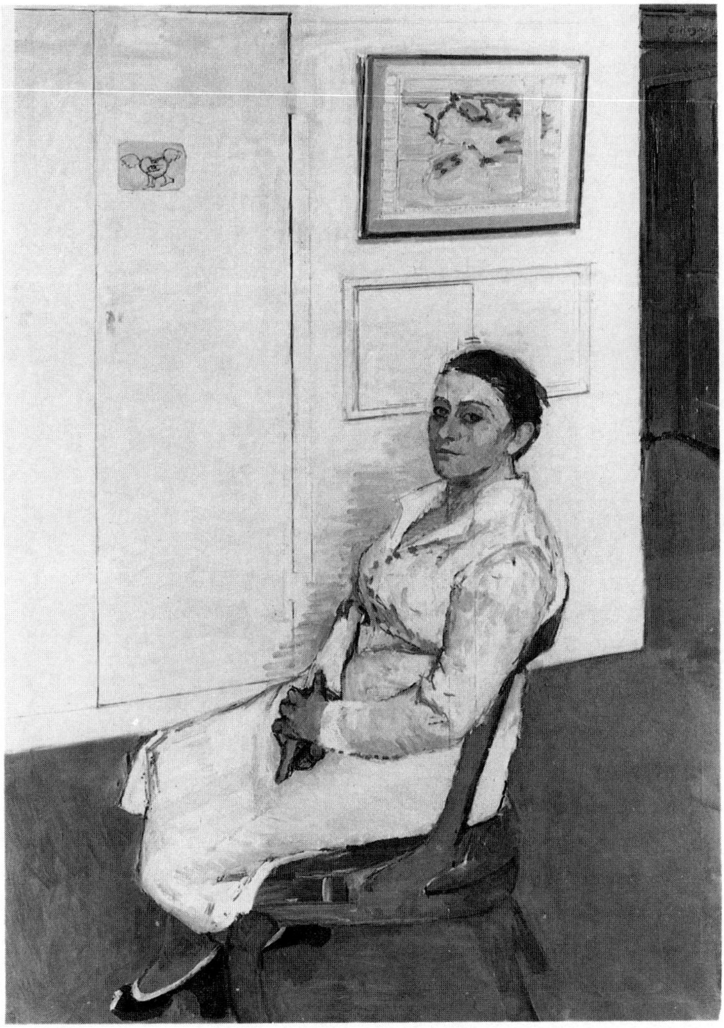

57. *Dr Anna Frenkiel*, 1974–77.

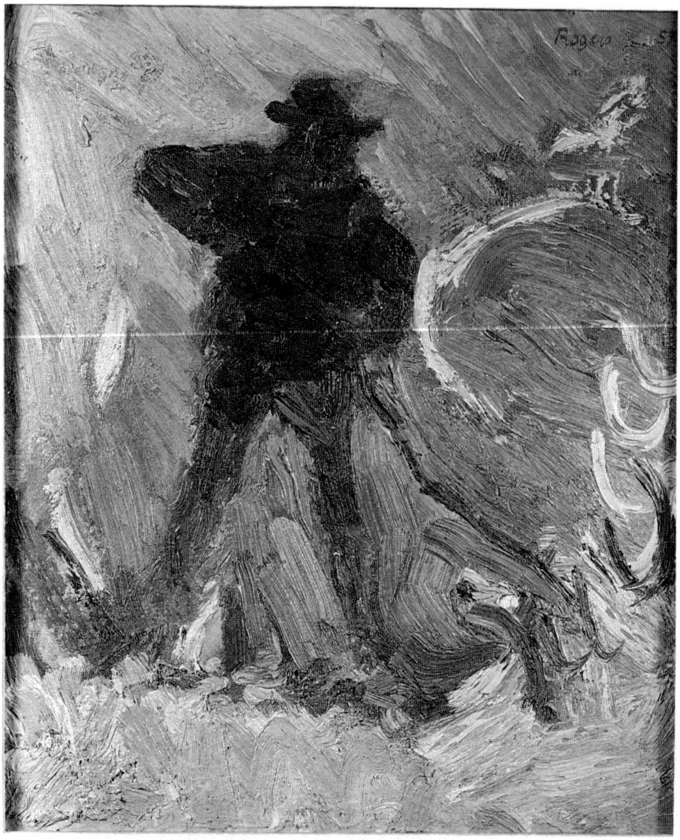

58. *Farmer, Smoke, Flame*, 1959.

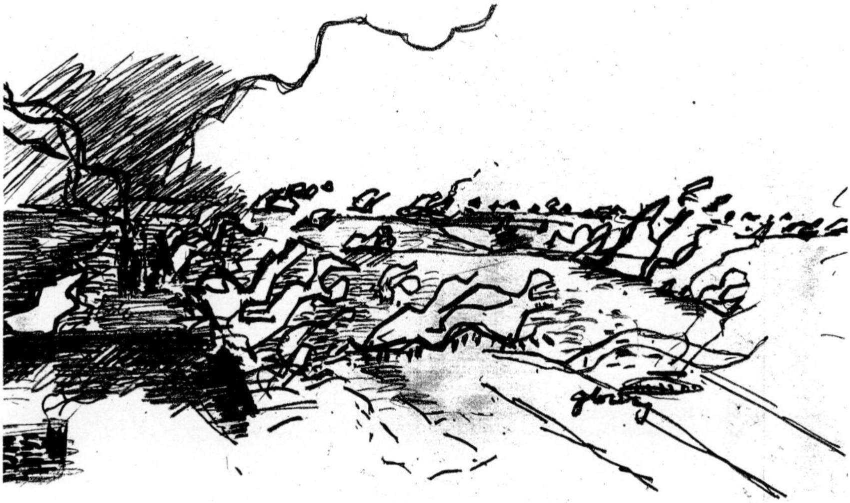

59. Drawing of burning stubble, 1966.

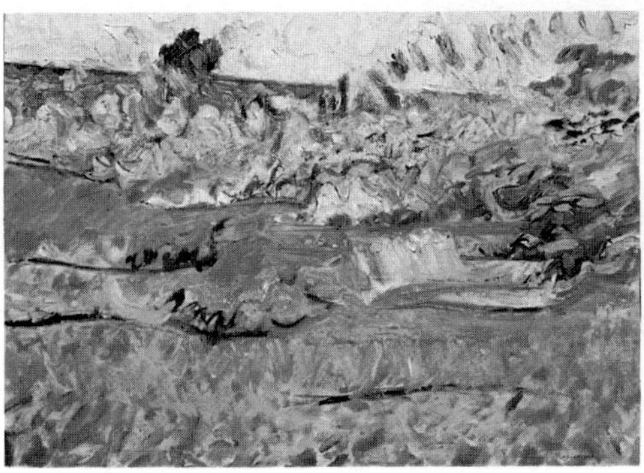

60. *Field Afire*, 1958–59.

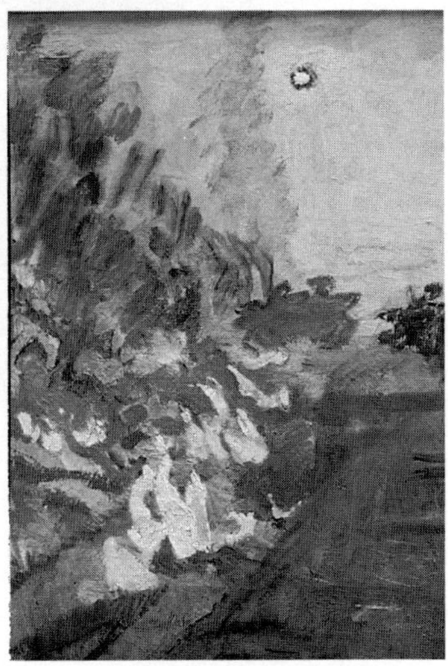

61. *Sun and Burning Stubble Field*, 1977–78.

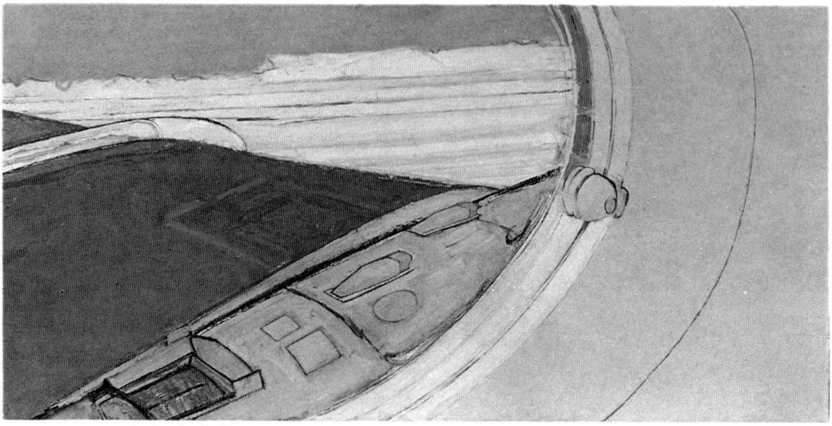

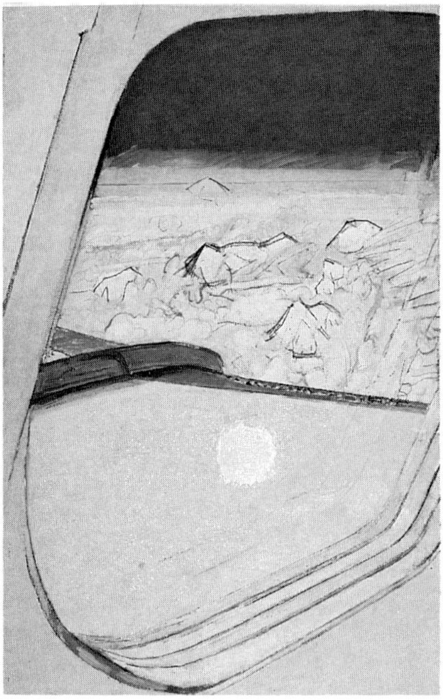

62. *Wing of Aeroplane*, 1970.

63. *The French Alps I*, 1969.

weeks in Coldstream's studio at 12 Fitzroy Street, and had been present at the last of the Euston Road classes at 10 Fitzroy Street. There he had met Claude. He was delighted to see him again at Camberwell. "No one I suppose could meet Claude again without being immensely cheered and warmed. However, I was conscious of being a little inhibited by his direct and unintellectual approach to painting. Only now, 45 years later, do I realise how much I learnt from him in an almost subliminal manner about the act and the fundamental nature of painting. The essence of this was his aptitude for the special physical immediacy involved in painting. To see him at work was like watching a star performer. Unlike other teachers he would take up the palette and brushes of a student who had got stuck, and with a few mixings and placings of solid clear colours propel the painting forward . . . The teaching at this time was dedicated and disciplined. The staff of the painting department were serious artists with various and personal but mature aesthetic standards. In retrospect it seems to me that those who were students there then were exceptionally fortunate, and that seldom in any art school occurs such a concentrated devotion to searching out the nature of what is being undertaken. Claude was assiduously professional in his teaching in the painting studios. Unflagging too in his interest and personal advice was that original painter John Dodgson. He and Claude were often in the trenches, so to speak, dealing ad hoc with the difficulties in individual students' paintings.

"A characteristic of Camberwell at this time was the discrepancy of ethos between the painting department and most of the rest of the school which was being conducted according to the official curriculum of the National Diploma in Design. Many of the painting students had returned from the war and had chosen to come because they expected to find either a continuation of Euston Road devoted entirely to drawing and painting, or something like a large atelier, or a sort of continuation of a Tonks-like Slade. They were not interested in the variety of separately named subjects that were part of the official course. Nor were Coldstream, Pasmore, Rogers and Gowing. Occasionally orders were issued from elsewhere in the school for painters' attendance at a class in design, there would be a rumpus and confusion, and then things would continue as before. Then Coldstream was evidently told by the principal that he must run a class in 'composition'. Coldstream turned to Rogers and said 'Claude, you're the only one of us who can do this, you will have to do it'. Claude in fact was extremely conscious of and articulate about the design of his own pictures. However, I think honesty prevented him from cooking up a formula for conducting this class. After a few meetings this class must have quietly evaporated without trace. Weeks later, however, we were all engaged in painting giant cartoons to illustrate the theme of the Christmas Dance, 'The Naughty Nineties'. Claude seemed very happy walking around and giving off the cuff advice. 'We can't get this black black enough' I said. 'Put some white in it' he replied. Then he and Coldstream went round together to appraise the completed scheme, and stopped before a charming cartoon by Barbara Harris, which much pleased them. 'She's our best person at placing' said Coldstream. Not composition. Placing. 'Placing' is a word of Coldstreamian modesty implying that the design of a drawing or painting is to be found concurrently with looking at the subject, and thereafter is unfolded by the exacting ritual of getting positions and colours on to the canvas. In looking at a work by Coldstream one is aware of a meticulous ritual being unfolded in time. Not quite so in a Rogers, for these intellectually definable considerations were submerged by his sheer love of painting. He was not only a master but the openness of his talent made him also the leading STUDENT of the Euston Road, as if he had already composted some of its showings into a tilth in which other artists could grow . . .

"When the great evening of the Naughty Nineties party arrived, Humphrey Lyttleton's band set itself up in the largest studio, and the room began to fill with sea-captains, jack-tars, jack-the-rippers, gym-mistresses in tunics, Oscar Wildes, whores shrouded in feathers, Sherlock Holmeses and Watsons, Alma-Tadema goddesses etc. Whirling joyously into this rather gawky and stuffy assembly suddenly burst the rotund figure of Claude, in fireman's uniform with a great brass helmet. In a few minutes the whole occasion was transformed into the great wedding party of King Babar and Queen Celeste of the Elephants, with trousered legs and great boots, white calves and slender slippers all showing a myriad of ankles beneath the lurching and bouncing and fluffetting of cloths and stuffs and buttons, beneath the bobbing of suffused faces, none more noticeable than the entranced, perspiring, careering rosy visage of Claude."[14]

Christopher Pemberton, a student who arrived at Camberwell via Oxford and the RNVR, added to the vivid accounts of those days. He had chosen Camberwell because he had been excited by seeing the work of Pasmore, Coldstream, Rogers and Gowing.

"The exciting new vision of these painters helped me to make a decision. I took a tram to Camberwell, where as I discovered, they taught. Too uncertain of myself to make enquiries at the door I walked straight down a corridor and into a Life Room. It was break, and two spectacled figures in grey suits, one short and fat, the other tall and gangling, were exchanging some witticism at the far end of the room, perhaps at my expense . . . On joining the school that autumn (September 1948) I found the short one was Claude Rogers, on acquaintance not at all formidable, though his first appraising glance was alarming: penetrating and short-sighted at the same time.

"Small round eyes glinted through thick-lensed gold-rimmed glasses beneath a fringe of dark hair, with matching beard. With his short-sighted round face and snub nose he looked a bit like Socrates or Mr Pickwick. One came to love his exuberantly high-pitched voice and his emphatic way of underlining his words, pronouncing his r's as w's as he passed round the class. One became aware of his neat square hands at work, well tended like a doctor's. In moments of abstraction he would stick these into the pockets of his smart baggy trousers, legs astride, in a slightly jaunty fashion. He was full of zest. "Yes, not BAD," in a high nasal voice, "that bald head, but Rembrandt would have made it as round and hard as a CANNON ball." He was the kind of teacher who taught by demonstration, not hesitating to draw the model on the corner of your paper and sometimes taking your brush. His pencil would move from contour to contour (a favourite word of his) bringing out the fullness of the model whose proportions, although scrupulously examined, always seemed to end up in sympathy with his own. The drawing would be small, compact, enviably firm, and recognisably a Rogers . . . It was he who recommended me for my first job filling a sudden vacancy at Bryanston, an act of faith which started me off as a teacher. He came down that summer (1951) to work on his portrait of Thorold Coade, then at an advanced stage. It was May and behind the blue coated figure of the headmaster, in the thickly painted glimpse of fields and buttercups, he was adding another lot of tiny contented looking cows."[15]

Claude's years at Camberwell were fertile ones for him. He was working hard, and more importantly, he was among friends again and would often have supper after teaching with the others and discuss both painting and teaching. A diary entry gives an idea of his life at this time: "Sept 29 – Got on with still life at Camberwell. Not much time though . . . Palette for still life: naples cad, cad orange, bit of ochre, b. sienna, aliz, l. red, viridian, cob, ultra, f white (at present) aliz for towel, naples for drawings, v little medium starting with thin pastes, firm paint. Sept 30 – did a touch or two to the Clover Fields and improved it. Olivia came. Victor dropped in and seemed to like Clover Fields quite a bit. Igor came too. Thur . . . Went back to tea with Pat George, Pinsent and Andrew Forge. Tony Fry there too. They talked about teaching . . .

George felt that teaching was 'unreal' - always dealing with less mature minds . . . I told them my views on teaching - real teaching, that the teacher learnt, that it was not the overwhelming imposition of a more mature personality . . ."[16] It was this point of view that made Claude such a gifted teacher. Earl Haig gave evidence of this, remarking that Coldstream and Gowing especially were apt to dominate their students. Claude never did.

In an address given to Camberwell students when opening the annual exhibition of students' work in July 1947 Claude tried to give some guidelines, aware that the students, like the staff, were facing choices in the direction of their work.

"Don't bother about style but look at nature, and try to set things down simply and with conviction . . . I do not pretend that objective painting, such as I believe in, is the only approach. It is simply one way of painting. Indeed, today, objective painters are in the minority. This kind of work has been under a cloud since the beginning of the century - and for a very simple reason - it had, before this, evolved its own clichés. Those of us who are interested in it are only too aware that our work is experimental. Many of you may be, by temperament, subjective painters. There is this great division in painting today - more marked than at any other time in history. In fact, if we look backwards, we see that hitherto painting has been predominantly one or the other - either subjective or objective. Yet, today, both kinds of painting exist side by side: and both are producing vital work. You must make your own choice in the long run. But which ever kind naturally attracts you, remember this: never make up anything haphazard, or try to make your picture look - well, too much like a picture you have seen. Try to decide exactly what interests you - what you want to express - and try to see the shapes you want to put down clearly, either in your mind or in nature. You can learn the principles of your art by studying the great masters, living or dead. They are the friendliest of guides. But their mannerisms and peculiarities are not to be imitated. In their hands these mannerisms are original. We admire them. But imitation leads to a dull pictorial formula."[17]

Claude also lectured at St. Paul's School, where he had organised an exhibition of modern British painting. He was forced to clarify his thoughts for these talks, and his notes are revealing about his attitude to abstract painting. "I have always been drawn to Mondrian, admiring the extraordinary painted-out quality of the white background, brought slap up to the resisting and undeviating line, relishing the sparing but primitive colour and the simple variation, the unusual cut. I shall always remember a Mondrian I saw at an exhibition at Burlington House, the *Ecole de Paris.* It was in a room of recent non-figurative work and it sang out like a bell. It was small but tough and it made every picture within sight look feeble and slight."[18]

Claude had an informed eye and was widely appreciative of all sorts of painting; by this time, although he never had a firm theoretical position, he knew where he stood in relation to 'modern art'. His own art was able to coexist quite happily alongside it. It was not until later in the 1960s that the rivalry between abstraction and figuration was to become so intense. Claude was able to discuss work with his friends, seeing them almost every day. The whole group had a detailed knowledge of each other's activities. His diaries contain remarks such as "Lawrence said he painted 18 pictures this summer . . . 'I took your tip of taking the picture back next year and do you know it was easy. Why, I finished one I had been struggling with for months last year in 25 minutes.' . . . Victor said he found it difficult to finish and even small canvases were v. much retouched in order to get unity. He said I was the great realist of the group in his joking way . . ."[19]

At about this time Claude was also consolidating his ideas by working on a history of the Euston Road School. This manuscript presumably replaced that of the History of Western Art, and Claude reworked it from time to time during the rest of his life, although it was never completed. Despite the fact that his work was changing, he became the chief spokesman for the Euston Road; Pasmore and Coldstream were never so eager to promote it, and when the idea of another Euston Road exhibition in 1947 was mooted they were doubtful. According to Claude "their line is an exhibition and book is making too much of us – too pushing I suppose and not quite gent. My line is that if we believe in our kind of painting – and we must, surely – it is necessary to fight for it. . ."

Pasmore's belief in Euston Road painting was already wavering, for by 1950 he had become an abstract painter. Coldstream had become the Slade Professor and was building up the Slade on a wholly different system. An exhibition did result, however, showing at the Wakefield City Art Gallery in May and June 1948. Claude showed seventeen pieces of work.

In June 1947 Claude had a second one-man exhibition of his paintings at the Leicester Galleries. He appears to have shown about 60 paintings, including the three major post-war still lifes, the portrait of Margerie Few and several major landscapes including the *Clover Fields near Toppersfield Church* and the *Landscape with Quarry*, then known as *The Sandpit.* The *Times* critic wrote perceptively: "Mr Claude Rogers is perhaps the most conscientious of all the group of English painters whose conscientiousness led them to realism; he has always designed his pictures methodically and with evident forethought, patiently setting out all the facts needed to give each form its full solidity and weight. The obvious danger of such an approach is an academic dryness, and it is all the more welcome to find in his recent paintings at the Leicester Galleries an increased vitality of touch and delicacy of perception. His compositions are still very deliberate and he is clearly a slow painter, stalking his effects from a great distance, but in such works as *Girl at a Table* or *Perks Lane* the final result has many of the qualities of a scene that has been sharply perceived and swiftly recorded."[20]

The Leicester Galleries were shared with some of Edward Burra's watercolours, and the two painters made an odd combination. William Townsend went to the private view and noted in his journals that "Burra's pictures stared and clamoured from the walls but Burra himself did not appear; Claude with beard neatly trimmed and a huge rose on his chest gave an effortless display of an extrovert painter enjoying himself. His pictures look very well, unshakeably constructed and worked through to the end and no difficulties shirked. Nothing seems to deflect him from his concentration on the small ordered piece of world in front of him, he rarely seems to want either to alter or add to it, but he looks until he really sees a great deal about it. Of all the painters of talent today he must be the most convinced and happy realist."[21]

During the 1940s, the Euston Road painters were having a mild flirtation with the Royal Academy. The Academy was, of course, the main showplace of contemporary British painting, but both the Slade School and the London Group were totally opposed to everything it stood for, although the Academy was the venue for one of the London Group exhibitions during the war. A letter to Claude from Victor Pasmore dated May 15 1943 discusses Coldstream's resignation from the RA and adds "I think it would be a pity for the Euston Road School to get mixed up with the Academy. I feel that all we know about painting has been learnt in an anti-Academy school. It would mean a considerable loss of faith if we suddenly turn over to the Academy."[22] In 1946 Claude apparently failed to be elected ARA, and according to Townsend "Victor was delighted to think he had been kept out - not at all through any jealousy but because of his contempt for the idea that the Academy can be reformed from within, that it can do anything but corrupt a good painter . . ."[23] Tom Monnington, who met Claude at Camberwell and later became President of the RA, tried to persuade him to join. Claude's response was negative, and Monnington replied "I am sorry about your decision in regard to the RA but I cannot quarrel with you – the RA is a good theory but rather horrible in practice, and I can well sympathise with anyone for wishing to keep out of it."[24]

At the end of the 1940s Claude embarked on two commissioned portraits, the first in the series of about seventeen academic portraits for which he became well known. These were of John Garrett, who had been his headmaster at Raynes Park School and was now at Bristol Grammar School; and Thorold Coade, the headmaster of Bryanston School. For the latter he charged 200 guineas; it involved many visits to the school and many sittings, and the painting suffered some vicissitudes. Claude wrote to Elsie from Bryanston in 1949, "I have felt most uneasy about the picture . . . I don't feel I've quite got the control I had. Anyway I shall just plug away. It's a marvellous subject. You know, these big planned pictures are awfully like a game of chess. There's the opening which is usually interesting and exciting; and then there's the long hammer and tongs of the middle game; it's that that exercises you. The finishing, the end game, entirely depends on it."[25]

The portrait of John Garrett is a simple head and shoulders, sympathetically treated and chunkily painted in thick, closely laid strokes of paint. Claude managed to catch in paint his expectant, quizzical look and his 'debauched eyes'. He described him in a letter to a close friend, Susan Jacobsen: "He's got an interestingly shaped head with a lot of character and is an amusing old boy – a tremendous exhibitionist, much more interested in the stage than in headmastering really; and with an immensely complicated private life . . ." Claude's diaries give evidence of the very slow progress of this picture and notes the colours he was using: "Remember – left corner of mouth gathers in. Reconsider back of head with contours of forehead; also left temporal region. Palette – naples, light indian, vermilion, b sienna, cobalt (ultra) viridian cadmium orange f white."[26] Fixing up the sittings probably had caused difficulties, and a poem dated January 15 1949 survives amongst Claude's papers.

Lines written while thinking of J. Garrett
Does it matter if Thursday or Friday
Or Wednesday's the twenty first?
No one of them now is MY day
And my poor little heart will burst . . .
From a quarter to one in the morning
Till three in the afternoon
John and Sir John will be yarning
And plying a knife fork and spoon;

The afternoon light will flicker
The afternoon shadows will grow
As they quaff their elegant liquor
And savour each low bon-mot . . .
Aye! half a term will have gone
'Ere I look again on The Face
To decide each delicate tone,
To give each feature a place.
From the twenty sixth of the second
To the twenty eighth of the same
(By the Julian calendar reckoned
If that is the Calendar's name)
I'll expect you then, John, with a lector
To prevent you from getting bored:
He shall read from the Great Detector.
Yours ever, the painter, Claude.[27]

NOTES

1, 2, 3, 4 Claude Rogers Papers, Tate Gallery Archive.
5 Hoyland, Francis, letter to J Pery December 12 1992.
6, 7, 8, 9, 10 Claude Rogers Papers, Tate Gallery Archive.
11 Newton, Eric, *Sunday Times* January 28 1945.
12 Eyton, Anthony, letter to J Pery December 23 1992.
13 Hoyland, Francis, op. cit.
14 Pinsent, Christopher, letter to J Pery November 30 1992.
15 Pemberton, Christopher, letter to J Pery October 19 1992.
16 Claude Rogers Papers, Tate Gallery Archive.
17 Claude Rogers, Address given when opening Annual Exhibition of Students' Work July 4 1947, collection Mr Patrick Symons.
18, 19 Claude Rogers Papers, Tate Gallery Archive.
20 *The Times*, June 1947.
21 Townsend, William, *Journals*, Tate Gallery 1976.
22 Claude Rogers Papers, Tate Gallery Archive.
23 Townsend, William, op. cit.
24 Claude Rogers Papers, Tate Gallery Archive.
25 Claude Rogers letters, collection Mr Crispin Rogers.
26 Claude Rogers letters, collection Mrs Susan Jacobsen.
27 Claude Rogers Papers, Tate Gallery Archive.

The middle game

In 1949, when William Coldstream moved to the Slade School of Art, Claude went with him. Coldstream was fulfilling his friend W H Auden's prophecy when he was appointed Slade Professor ("and the Slade School I choose for William Coldstream to leave his mark upon"[1]). On his appointment he demanded, and was given, a full-time Secretary (Ian Tregarthen Jenkin), six permanent new members of the teaching staff (William Townsend, B A R (Sam) Carter, Thomas Monnington, Patrick George, John Aldridge and Lucian Freud), and six Visiting Teachers (Victor Pasmore, Claude Rogers, Henry Moore, Graham Sutherland, John Piper and David Jones). When Coldstream arrived, the staff consisted of virtually the same people who had been there when he was a student. All staff were part-time and all were practising artists; the only full-time appointments were the Slade Professor and his Secretary. Although it was difficult to obtain money from the University for new appointments, Coldstream managed to bring in new blood, without shedding old blood. In his new appointments he deliberately varied the disciplines covered by the teaching staff, and presumably Claude was appointed to cover realistic and figurative painting.

For his first session at the Slade, 1949–50, Claude as a visiting teacher was required to make three visits each term for a fee of eight guineas per visit. During that first academic year he actually made five visits to the Slade, and the following session he became a Fine Arts Assistant, which involved him in two days' teaching a week at an annual salary of £435. Later he became a Grade IIA lecturer within the university salary structure; and much later, in 1961, he was recognised as a Teacher of the University in the Faculty of Arts.

The Slade comprised about 250 students (painting and sculpture). There were six painting and drawing studios. There was often a total of 17 models posing each day, three to a room. The number of students painting from the model was never more than ten, and the places were carefully worked out by putting easels, with canvases on them, around the model.

Teaching at the Slade was a more disciplined affair than at Camberwell. Every student was allotted a tutor and set tutorials were held in private between tutor and student three times a term. Reports on each student were submitted by their tutors to the Slade Professor at the end of every term. An effort was made as far as possible to match tutors to the sort of work their students were doing; if the gulf between tutor and student became too wide it was possible to change, although tutors tended to stay with their own students throughout their time at the Slade. Claude enjoyed teaching, and was an excellent tutor - accessible, reasonable, understanding and sympathetic, although he suffered meretriciousness badly, and used praise sparingly. He was particularly averse to flashy or slick work, and in his thoughtfully handwritten reports he would pull no punches if he identified such work in his own students. A letter he wrote to his friend George Sweet (then head of painting at the West of England College of Art) discussing students' work, revealed his overriding aim - to make not good students, but good painters. "It seems to me immaterial HOW a candidate passes (whether he's a B+ B B- or even A- really) because all that will ever be known is that he passed or failed . . . what I have been most concerned about is to keep anybody who shows merit, but little skill or wobbly accomplishment - in a word those who are 'a bit of an artist' - in the running . . . I am absolutely sure the real toppers (the As and A-) are just brilliant students who will never really make it. They show no evidence of struggle - they are TOO ruddy good."[2] He was prepared to take endless trouble over those students whom he felt had genuine talent, finding out about their circumstances and the state of their health, and doing what he could to help them. A particular example was Gillian Turral, a gifted figurative painter whom Claude tried to help. Her work at the Slade was excellent and she won a Rome Scholarship. When in Rome she disappeared for a while, causing a great deal of concern. Claude was consulted about her, and took her under his wing. He persuaded his friend Rosemary Pearce, who had the ground floor flat in Taviton House, to take her in as a lodger so that he could keep an eye on her. Claude found her a job with Lionel Penrose at University College illustrating Penrose's experiments. Penrose's secretary also took an interest in Gillian, but both her interest and Claude's efforts were not enough to prevent her eventual suicide. Claude, however, had done everything he could for her.

Claude's teaching methods were practical and realistic. He believed in teaching by example and where possible put this belief into practice. Robert Organ, a former student of his at the Slade, has given a valuable first-hand account of a lesson from Claude which he received at the West of England College of Art, before he went to the Slade (Claude was acting as a visiting tutor there at the invitation of George Sweet). Organ recalled: "We painted in the rooms of a Victorian house, the annexe, in ordinary rooms with light from the windows modified where needed with muslin sheets – a perfect preparation for the sort of environments in which we would attempt to carry on painting in the world later on. I was absolutely new to painting and I found a little room in which I set up a still life. I found a case with a stuffed barn owl in it. This seemed to me the sort of object one should have in a still life, vaguely antique and picturesque, and besides I was quite passionate about ornithology and it was a beautiful owl. I assembled with it some other respectable seeming objects, cloths and apples I expect. I had been working on a canvas for a week or so and was in a hopeless muddle with nothing in the correct position on the canvas, my owl overdeveloped at the expense of what was around it in an indulgent and non-pictorial way and me quite unable to make radical decisions and corrections.

"Claude had been stomping about the studios. He had developed a great passion for a lively and sensual girl called Thelma on one of his previous visits and was pursuing her with the sort of unashamed zeal I had only previously seen in Harpo Marx – he actually chased her up the stairs crying out 'give us a kiss Thelma' and then minutes later back down again with the same entreaties. I was most impressed by this off-stage drama, it was I felt what real artists did. Suddenly he exploded into my little room, seeming to me huge and tweedy and pungent with tobacco. After eyeing my efforts, he told me to stand aside and sat down on my chair – made me clean off my palette and then rearranged it in a warm-cool sequence, blues to the left, through greens, yellows, earth browns to the reds on the right – an order to which I have adhered ever since. Then he cleaned off my picture down to a smudgy underpainting and set to reorganising it while I stood and looked over his shoulder. He explained what he was doing as he began to redraw the composition. Until then I had understood from the rigorous drawing teaching we had, how interrelationships between objects could be established, the model related to her or his space and the things around, screens, floor, walls and so on, the way that Sickert had advocated and the Euston Road had carried on, but I had not had to deal with fixing these relationships within the predetermined rectangle of a canvas. In drawing, the paper seemed a more expansive and flexible field, and of course one of the objects of drawing for a subsequent picture is to discover just where those boundaries to a composition should be. He showed me with great clarity how measured observations of the objects before him could be translated into shapes and lines on the canvas which constructed a firm pictorial pattern in which nothing pertinent seemed excluded and no surplus baggage was included.

"The shape of the owl found its correct position within the rectangle of the canvas in such a way that the shapes it made with its case were also determined along with those the case itself made with the wall and the table top and everything else. In other words he created a coherent abstraction in which every element counted, and he did this without any compromising of his perception – no generalising or arty bending of the facts. It was a marvellous lesson for me – I saw quite suddenly how an eager scrutiny of the visual world could become inseparable from a rigorous sense of the picture; in my own case the two had been quite antagonistic until then – the one always precluding the other. When he got up, after a couple of hours work, he explained again why and what he had done and told me to carry on . . . Minutes later, after he had left the room, I again heard from the landing above his squeaky entreaties 'where are you Thelma – how about just a little kiss?' "[3]

Claude's teaching was always clear and practical, and he avoided the type of obfuscating remarks which became prevalent in art schools later on. Contrary to his own experience as a student, Claude advised his students that they should be attracted in some way to their subjects – "there must be a tickle of some sort, even an unpleasant one" – and that they need not look far afield for subjects. He told them to keep their ideas simple – "many pictures have enough material in them for a one-man show" – and he insisted upon the importance of drawing as being 'the bones' of a picture. Above all he stressed the value of work, quoting Sickert: "Talent is not infrequent, but the cultivation of it, year-in, year-out with sequence (suite) through a lifetime is not common . . . Art can only be extracted from us – as any labour from any workman – by the same means as oil is got from a nut – by pressure – incessant, cruel, regular, grinding, unintermittent, painful pressure."[4] Claude's students at the Slade remembered his extreme affability and genuine interest. He would give a direct, independent, non-institutional view of the work in progress, and his comments were always useful. His advice was worth having as students were aware that he was exhibiting frequently at that time; they could see for themselves his own standpoint on art. Stephen Chaplin, the Slade archivist, remembered an occasion when he needed one more figure painting for his diploma. When he came to paint the allocated pose the model, a peroxide blonde with red lipstick, was draped in a shocking pink stole. He complained to Claude, who robustly exclaimed "Damn the Diploma. Just look at those colours." John Wonnacott remembered Claude watching him paint when he was heavily under the influence of Frank Auerbach. Claude said "Johnny, all you chaps don't paint with your wrist any more, you paint with your whole damn body. How can you draw like that?" At the Slade he gave talks to groups of students on pictures, and David's *Madame Recamier* was the subject of one such talk. Robert Organ found that this talk made an indelible impression: "I can never see even a postcard of that picture without again seeing what he pointed out, the inversion of the top of Madame R's shape which is made by her falling skirt - the humming harmonies between the warms and cools - intense colour made from the most muted means."[5]

Claude loved teaching at the Slade, and it became something of a second home to him. Wednesdays, Thursdays and Fridays were his usual teaching days, and this arrangement left him with a four day chunk of the week in which to work on his own paintings. His home in Taviton Street was conveniently close to the Slade, and he was able to combine portrait sittings or other work on his paintings with his teaching. He could return home when he forgot his pipe or matches; even at this time he was notoriously vague and would sometimes forget to reappear in the Slade. Living so close to his work, however, he was able to make up for the 'lost' hours at the Slade by giving his tutorial students extra attention. He often had his students round to tea at his house, and was able to take a personal, almost fatherly, interest in them. Euan Uglow, a student who had followed Claude from Camberwell to the Slade, remembered the delightful family atmosphere of the flat at Taviton Street, and Elsie presiding over the proceedings, being "very severe and intelligent".

The Slade years proved a fertile time for Claude's own painting. Under Coldstream's wide-ranging and catholic régime there collected a heady mixture of talent amongst the teaching staff, and a brilliant new batch of students were emerging. The Slade seemed a central part of the London art world, and the traditional rivalry between it and the Royal College of Art only added spice to the mixture. Claude, with his usual curiosity, benefitted from the ideas he came across in his teaching and from the discussions with friends and colleagues in the pubs and restaurants after work. His home life was in satisfactory order. Elsie, having stopped teaching for a year after the birth of Crispin, was back at work, as principal of the Art Department at Gipsy Hill Training College. Reny Higgins was running the house and looking after the two boys Crispin and Martin. Claude worked in his painting room on the second floor of Taviton House, overlooking Taviton Street; and in the holidays the family decamped to Essex, where Claude and Elsie had bought Hawkshall Cottage, between Wethersfield and Sible Hedingham.

The cottage was situated near the then derelict Wethersfield aerodrome.

It was in the middle of arable farming country, not so far from Rodwell and the East Anglian haunts that Claude knew from the years before the war, and the type of man-made, intensively farmed countryside that Claude knew well. The Rogers' neighbours were the Grimwoods, who farmed the land around the cottage. Crispin and Martin spent a great deal of time on the farm during the holidays and Claude, essentially a Londoner, was necessarily involved in some of the farm's activities, becoming aware of the management of the land at first hand. The big field at the back of the cottage became a stage on which different events took place, giving him many ideas for paintings. Some of his most personal and considered landscapes, such as *The Tangled Garden* and *The Combine*, were painted from Hawkshall Cottage, both featuring different aspects of the field. *The Combine* was painted from an upstairs window, and started in the summer of 1952. Claude did not think much of the painting, and left it behind when he returned to London. In the summer of 1954 he had another look at it, saw its pictorial possibilities, scraped the picture to the bone with a scalpel, started work on it again and completed it in five or six days.

During the 1950s Claude was at the height of his powers as a painter. He was shaking off the 'fuzziness' of Euston Road painting, and his handling of paint was becoming firmer, his designs of interlocking shapes more rigorously observed and structured. He was more concerned with respecting the flat of the canvas, and with recreating the effects of light in terms of flat, local colour. His colours now made little concession to distance or atmosphere, but were put on as purely as possible to achieve maximum intensity. He began to think of the flat face of the picture plane as an element in the dramatic tension in the composition, with depth and recession indicated by the drawing and the contour, rather than by modelling or by tonal changes.

For him part of the excitement of painting was created by the attempt to reconcile flat shapes with very particular indications of their volume and position in space, an objective virtually denied to non-figurative painters. By painting in this way Claude was giving himself painting problems which had all the detective interest of the sleuth stories that he loved, and he pursued his aim with a Holmesian zeal. His pre-war paintings, with their modelling in tone, still create a 'window' of the canvas, where the forms are seen as it were behind the picture plane. In the post-war paintings the forms are laid flat on the picture plane, but their character and their distance from the eye of the beholder are indicated to the brain by means other than modelling, and chiefly by the meticulous drawing of the contours. The painting of Margerie Few gives the first indications of this shift in his approach, and by the early 1950s many of his paintings showed a flattening of carefully observed shapes painted in areas of local colour, the most extreme example being *The Hornby Train*, on which he worked from 1951–53. The change in his attitude was noted by discerning critics. Alan Clutton-Brock pondered over this, and wrote "Rogers himself would describe or explain this complete change of style as having come about because in the old days he was interested principally in the effects of atmosphere, which inevitably led to vagueness in the definition of contours, but now he is concerned to get the form of each separate object exactly right. He wants to do this without much modelling, to rely on the outline to suggest the solidity of things."[6] Claude's effort was to establish objects within his paintings without distorting the facts of their appearance, working with these facts until the picture achieved a completely firm and unified entity, an entity as real and solid as the motif from which he was working.

The main drama of his life was now more than ever tied up in his paintings: the search for subjects which were both part of his life and therefore satisfied his requirement to make art out of his actual experience; and the struggle to transform this experience into a satisfying visual composition, with its particularity intact. The battleground was the studio and the weapons canvas, paints and brushes. There is no doubt that Claude often regarded painting as a battle, equivalent to a game of chess or to one of Wellington's battles, which he knew by heart. Painting became for Claude a way of dealing with reality, while the realities he encountered in his life served as a visual vocabulary for his paintings.

With the need to flatten the design of his painting came an equal need to construct the picture firmly from edge to edge. Claude's designs hung on watertight construction and sharpness of drawing. A *Times* reviewer picked up Claude's new assurance: "There is no doubt that there has been a marked advance in his power of realising forms . . . His landscapes with flat fields of corn or stubble have a firmness of construction which is very remarkable; from the foreground to the horizon, even when there is no obvious feature on which the painter can seize to mark the recession, there is never the slightest break in the continuity of what really amounts to modelling."[7]

In an introduction to Claude's exhibition at the Hatton Gallery in 1955 Quentin Bell wrote: "There are painters whose virtues must be explained, who must, so to speak, be 'sold' to the public – painters who make use of an oracular language which stands in need of translation. Claude Rogers makes no such secret of his intentions; no one who is at all acquainted with the pictorial idiom of our century will find him, in this sense, difficult. In his case the task of an introduction is rather to persuade the visitor to accept a manner of painting whose very straightforwardness is sometimes at first sight uncomfortable. Veracity is Rogers' aim, and while every painter has his own vision, to which he is more or less faithful, Rogers' truth is of a self-evident kind and he clings to it with heroic tenacity. However elusive, however tenuous the logic of the natural forms before him, Rogers puts his finger firmly on it. He insists; the characteristic shapes of his art are made square and stubby by the pressure of his insistence on their reality. Reality is a passion with him; the force with which he places colour against colour is the force of a deep and humane feeling for real, physical things . . . To enjoy these pictures it is therefore necessary to share in the painter's passion for fact-finding, his joy in the rigorous, unequivocal establishment of shapes, his delight in the discipline of measurement. The rest is easy, for within the framework of his austere method Claude Rogers is a gay and sensuous artist, a master of harmonious intervals, of limpid aeriality and of positive colour . . ."[8]

In 1950 Claude had embarked on the third of his portraits of academics, a picture of the economist Professor R H Tawney, commissioned by the London School of Economics. Tawney lived in Mecklenburgh Square, and Claude did his preliminary drawings there, using the drawings to search for the most telling pose in the same way that he had worked on Margerie Few. He finally opted for a side view of Tawney working on a paper, planning the design with the single large curve of the figure contrasting with the horizontals and verticals of the bookshelves and the skirtingboard. The detailed areas - head against books, pipe against papers - are balanced by the large plain area of wall, in which the energetically braced black foot against the orange skirting strikes an organic, idiosyncratic note. Negative shapes such as that beneath the lower leg provide strong leads into the centre of the picture. The warm colour harmonies were dictated by Tawney's orange tweed suit, which must have been a garment after Claude's own heart. This portrait involved Tawney in a great many sittings, probably about forty, and when he moved house, Claude reconstructed the furniture of the painting - books and papers, bookcase and chair - in his own studio. The result far surpasses the usual run of academic portraiture - a warm, affectionate rendering of a particular thinking, active human being.

The portrait of Professor Haldane is equally impressive both in the discovery and organisation of shapes and colours and in the empathy which imbues the rendering of his head and hands.

At the same time as starting on Professor Tawney, Claude was invited by the Arts Council to contribute a painting for an exhibition planned for the Festival of Britain in 1951. The Arts Council was then only five years old, and this exhibition was to be its major contribution to Festival Year, designed to reinvigorate the artistic scene in post-war Britain. The Arts Council commissioned sixty pieces of work from contemporary British artists in a bid to represent the current state of British art. All sixty paintings were to be exhibited together in London, and then to tour to the regions. Canvas, which was still difficult to obtain after the war, was to be supplied free of charge to each artist, and the only stipulation was that each painting should be large, ie not less than 45 × 60 inches. This stipulation must have come as something of a release after the inevitable restrictions of wartime Britain, promoting a sense of optimism about the future and a desire to get away from small easel paintings designed to go into drawing rooms via dealer galleries. Philip James, whose initial idea the exhibition was, had two aims: to give living artists an opportunity to produce works which would be a contribution to posterity; and to encourage public bodies to realise their responsibilities as art patrons to the welfare state. Ten sculptors received commissions for major pieces of work, and sixty painters were chosen out of a total of 145 names put forward. It was also announced that the Arts Council would buy five of these paintings for £500 each without regard to their current market value. The judges for the selection of these five paintings were Jonkheer Sandberg, Director of the Stedelijk Museum in Amsterdam, A J McDonnell, Advisor to the Felton Bequest, National Gallery of Victoria, and Alan Clutton-Brock, the art critic of *The Times*.

Claude was naturally delighted to be included in the sixty painters, and he thought long and hard about his painting, turning over in his mind what his current interests were which would be suitable for a large picture. Although he had had ideas for very large paintings during the war, this was to be the largest picture he had painted to date. His original idea was to paint a nude, and he wrote to Gabriel White at the Arts Council saying that he had seen the very model at Camberwell and requesting financial assistance: "the thing I really want to paint is a nude . . . not any nude, but a particular model who has recently turned up in the art schools. She has the purest forms and the most exacting drawing I have ever seen - a sort of living Ingres - Praxiteles - Raphael - with a little snub-nosed English-Degas face. I know more or less how I want to paint her but simply couldn't afford to have her enough. I reckon it would cost between £50 and £60 . . . is there any way, on the security of the picture, in which the Arts Council could lend me £60 in order to pay for the sittings I require?"[9] The model's name was Rita Wheatly, and Claude made several drawings of her to decide the pose and the size of the canvas. The Arts Council did not agree to pay for sittings, but Claude's friend and colleague Edward Le Bas helped with financing the model's fees, contributing £100 with no strings attached. Among Claude's papers is a letter (dated June 4 1950) reporting progress to him: "I have started to do drawings for the picture of Rita Wheatly, and have practically decided the size and shape of the canvas, so that if you can let me have the loan of that money I would be very much obliged. She really is a charming little creature, gay and natural and pretty as a picture. Much prettier I'm afraid than my picture will be."[10] Eventually, however, Claude was forced to cancel her sittings. A draft of a letter to her dated June 17 1950 revealed him working out how to do so. "Dear Rita Wheatly, I'm very sorry but I'm afraid that I shall have to cancel the rest of the sittings that we arranged. You see, I must get on with the picture and you have neither come for the last two sittings nor written, telephoned or got one of your friends to telephone for you. I was warned that you were unreliable but saw no reason to believe this. Alas! it seems to be true. It's a pity, I should have enjoyed painting you. With regrets, Yours sincerely, CR."[11] (Given the triumphant conclusion of the painting Claude finally achieved, it would be interesting to know if Rita Wheatly ever regretted her unreliability.)

At Camberwell Claude had recently passed a junk shop with a white chaise longue inside. It had struck him that Rita Wheatly would look rather fine on it with the brown wall of his painting room at Taviton House behind. He bought the chaise longue for £3 and reputedly carried it home from Camberwell to Bloomsbury on his back. He had in mind a picture possibly based on Manet's *Olympia*: small sketches done at the time with a cat at the feet of the model show that he was thinking of this picture. When Miss Wheatly failed him he thought of another girl he had drawn at Chelsea, Anne Lynn, who turned out to be "more interesting than the other girl, if not so arty". When he saw Anne Lynn nude on the sofa in his painting room he felt uneasy; "somehow or other she just looked silly." In notes he wrote towards the end of his life for Sheffield City Art Galleries, Claude vividly described the excitement of the project and the progress of the painting: "I don't think any of us thought in terms of a major work but the idea of trying one's hand at a larger painting than usual was exhilarating. It was an austere period. In my own case a 30 × 40 inch canvas was large: 3 × 4 ft was exceptional . . . The problem of the pose was settled at the third sitting, just as Anne was about to leave. She had dressed and, looking at her standing there in her candy striped skirt and dark waistcoat I suddenly thought how much more real she looked in her clothes in the environment of my painting room. There was something artificial, I realised, so far as I was concerned, with this particular girl and in the particular situation of the painting, in representing her stripped off. Not that I don't like naked girls. I do. But somehow this wasn't a naked girl painting and certainly not a nude. So she sat down again straight away and I did a very quick drawing. This I knew was it. I made no alteration to her choice of dress or ornament. The bangle, blouse and skirt which are represented are just what she happened to have chosen to wear that day. The bare feet came about partly because she was more comfortable lying there without her shoes - sandals I think. When she next sat I did a small painting. The next day I was teaching at the Slade. Tom Monnington and I went over to coffee, and . . . I told him about the idea of Miss Lynn and my hesitations about starting. He got me to make a small drawing of the settee and the pose and the setting . . . 'Well, what's bothering you? Why hesitate? You're funking diving into the water, that's all' said Tom, and, of course, he was right.

"Anyway, I still had to get the canvas from the Arts Council, but, deciding to do the figure a little under life size, I rang them up that day and ordered a 40 × 70 inch canvas from them, working out this size from one of the drawings I had done to show Tom. It seemed big when it arrived. My painting room at Taviton Street was on the second floor of a substantial early Victorian house now pulled down - the original gatehouse to Gordon Square. It was one of the better bedrooms, perhaps 20 × 16 feet or a bit less, high enough to get a good light with two windows facing east by north. I thought I might as well get something from the very small drawings I had done with Tom Monnington, so squared one up and very lightly indicated the important positions and cuts in it on my canvas. But I was determined to work in my usual way, from observation and measurement; so that these markings were notional only and subject to reconsideration and change in the light of what I discovered when faced with the actual subject. In the event I was surprised because some important lines and positions only required a measure of adjustment; but where any conflict occurred it was always the positions on the canvas determined by observation and measurement that prevailed. In other words, essentially I was not thinking in terms of a 'picture' but trying to discover what Miss Lynn really looked like in the situation of my room and from my viewpoint. My standards of measurement were related to the length and width of the various divisions of Miss Lynn's head. The actual painting of it plodded forward pretty steadily and undramatically and I do not remember anything of it until Victor Pasmore arrived one day, about halfway through. We were long accustomed to show works to one another and I had seen the genesis and the way his *Snowstorm* [also in the Arts Council exhibition] was developing. At this time he was very interested in the geometry of the canvas. Many of his paintings of this period were built up on – or, in the process of painting, presently subjected to – geometrical constructions – root proportions or the golden section. On the occasion of this visit to see *Miss Lynn*, after looking at it for a bit his interest quickened. 'Have you a longish bit of string, Claude?' said he of a sudden. When I had supplied this he proceeded to perform with it stretched out over the surface of my canvas in certain directions. 'Why' said he in surprise, 'I didn't know you used geometry. It's entirely on the golden section isn't it? And you're doing just what I do – find the right mark and then make your cut just that little bit off it to make it more real.'

"I disclaimed any such brilliance or intention . . . But I was vastly intrigued and after he left, reconstructed his experiments with string on the canvas, and by geometrical construction on one of the little drawings. And bless me, he was right. The only other event I remember connected with the painting was that sometime in mid-November I think, I received a telegram from Anne . . . which read something like this: 'Am Fourth Twinkly Fairy in Leeds panto. Will sit again as soon as engagement ends. Love Anne.' Anne was the niece of Ralph Lynn, the funny man of the Aldwich Farces. Her mother and aunts and other relations were all stage people and all her own ambitions were centred in the stage. So thunderstruck and dismayed as I was, I did understand – up to a point. The weeks rolled by, well beyond the New Year, and still the fairy twinkled, far away in Leeds. I was sick of seeing my unfinished canvas – and it took up so much room. I was working at other things of course, but my real interest remained in the Miss Lynn painting and I wondered more and more whether the delay would prevent me from finishing it. I took the precaution of getting hold of Philip James and telling him what had happened, and asking what the very last day could be for sending it in. He agreed to let me send it in a little later than the advertised date if that should prove necessary. And then, in February I think or maybe early March, Miss Lynn wrote and herself appeared for sittings, very professional about Leeds and the pantomime and with some stories that made me laugh. I needed part of the extra time allowed by Philip James but got the painting off, still wet in two parts (I remember telling the vanman not to rub the feet); and with no idea, really, what it was like though I kept a stiff upper lip among my friends, and especially at the Slade . . ."[12]

Miss Lynn was effectively the last of Claude's paintings of nudes – or Nudes that Never Were. Although he still did drawings of nude models in the various art schools at which he taught and sometimes of friends, he appears never to have completed a painting of a nude. Euan Uglow remembered seeing a painted nude torso on his easel, and Crispin remembered this painting as being vaguely offensive to him at the time. But it is not known what became of it. With his love of women, the nude would seem to be Claude's natural subject. It is a real loss to painting that there are no luscious females painted by Claude. But possibly he regarded the posed nude as too artificial a subject, or too abstracted and symbolic a concept. He was interested in reality. His paintings were to be about life; when painting people Claude painted portraits, making them as particular and as real as possible. *Miss Lynn* is a portrait from fingernail to toenail. A fifties rock-and-roll girl in the clothes and ponytail of the period, the impact of her physical presence puts her firmly in her time and yet is immediate and up to date. She is 'real' enough to get off the sofa, stretch, shake down her skirt, put on her sandals and whirl about the room. Claude started the painting with a thin sable brush, but the final surface is a dense mat of interlocking brushstrokes in wonderful colour harmonies, painted edge to edge with no loose passages anywhere. *Miss Lynn* is a triumph of sustained painting.

Although Claude had had no time to look at his painting of Miss Lynn before it was collected for the exhibition, he clearly felt he had done some of his best work, and was anxious as to how it would fare in the company of fifty or so of Britain's best painters. He described the outcome to Susan Jacobsen, who had helped him by sitting for the feet and the legs of the sofa when Miss Lynn had been away. ". . . The moment drew nearer for sending in my big picture . . . I got it done a day before I had arranged for it to be collected and immediately put up a bigger canvas on the easel . . . The varnishing day at the New Burlington was great fun – a Sunday, and all the artists looking at the other work and actually retouching and putting on varnish! I did neither. I liked the look of my painting, thought it one of the better ones there to be frank, but on consideration didn't think I had a hope as it looked quite different from anything else and not in the least 'ismic' or 'modernistic'. There were good pictures by Freud, M. Smith, Eleanor Bellingham Smith, William Scott, a Scotch painter called Maxwell, Minton, Victor, Nicholson, Medley, and Ceri Richards – no order, just as I remember them on the wall. Out of these I was sure the judges . . . would find five pictures without mine . . . The pictures were to be judged next day but the result was not to be announced till the Wednesday afternoon – a nerve-racking wait. I dropped in early on Wednesday, with no one there, and had a quiet look round alone. I still felt my picture looked well but somehow felt pretty despondent. I was teaching at the Slade. The girl at the desk said: 'Well, at four o'clock I have to stick the labels on the pictures chosen for the Arts Council.' 'Good God!' I said 'You don't mean to say you know now, do you?' 'Yes I do,' she giggled. 'Well,' said I. 'For heaven's sake, whatever the result, ring me at the Slade at 4 and let me know' . . . So at four I was in the office and Willy [Townsend] said 'Let's go to tea'. 'I'll just wait for that call,' I told him and at that moment it came through – Golly! Just like a *Boys Own Paper* School Story, last instalment – my picture had been bought together with Freud, Hitchens, Medley and William Gear . . . I rushed out to Charlotte St and got some drink and back to the Slade where we drank out of thimbles and tumblers. I took a bottle of champagne home for Crispin and Elsie . . . As you can guess I'm wildly excited. I really CAN go to Italy at last. I'd quite given up hope of ever seeing the pictures there. Neither Elsie or I have been abroad since 1938 so you can guess how tête élevée I'm inclined to be . . . With any luck it really may do me some good as far as reputation goes too. You see, I've always felt somehow that (as far as I was concerned) it was best to try and build a reputation on pictures rather than personality and contacts – not that I despised the latter, but felt it made it SO difficult if your reputation outran your painting, as so often happens to English artists. Also 'contacts' are so difficult to get on with and 'personality' is such a bore to switch on and so horrid to watch being switched."[13]

The exhibition attracted a great deal of interest. Almost all the paintings were figurative, and the *Autumn Landscape* by William Gear, one of the 'prizewinners' and one of the few abstract works, provoked a storm of protest from an indignant public, matched only, more recently, by the Tate bricks affair. This however was the only painting that the Dutch judge liked, and he would have nothing to do with the others, in particular disliking 'the old fashioned realism' of Claude Rogers. The other judges presumably saw in Miss Lynn a realism that would not date.

This exhibition and the prize gave Claude's confidence, often wavering, a tremendous boost. The critics were universally full of praise for the painting, as were Claude's friends. William Townsend wrote in his journal "Claude took me in the lunch hour to the New Burlington

Galleries to see the sixty pictures painted at the invitation of the Arts Council. They hang there for the press to see before their first showing in Manchester. The first impression is that the idea has been fully justified by the fact that at least a third of the artists have produced very good examples of their work that might otherwise never have been painted. Claude's picture is surprisingly successful. Far from looking the laborious and worthy essay of a dowdy painter that it might have seemed it holds the wall in its sophisticated company with great confidence; the design seems quite majestic if academic, the colour quite noble . . . the downfall of most of our respected elders is sadly apparent – Matthew Smith and Ben Nicholson are the exceptions."[14]

The Grand Tour of Italy took place during the summer of 1951, and was a success. Claude had travelled abroad far less than his contemporaries, and was basically xenophobic, regarding Abroad as a highly dangerous place where one could not drink the water. Despite his early knowledge of Spanish, he was no good at languages, admitting to Susan Jacobsen "I wish I was a hand at languages. I never shall be. My brain addles and my tongue swells into a solid lump and then freezes as soon as I am faced with any foreign human being."[15] She often wondered if his insularity stemmed from fear of travelling or from fear of flying, and if his later fascination with the visual aspects of flight may have been a way of dealing with this fear. The lure of the paintings in Italy, however, was strong enough to overcome worries about language and water. On this trip and on future trips abroad Claude kept notebooks on what he saw, mostly technical notes with scribbled drawings of compositions for his own private use, but which are interesting for the freshness of his response when he looked at familiar works of art for the first time in the original. The Sistine Chapel elicited the following remarks: "who ever painted in the draperies over the cocks – 17th century I think – did the painting with considerable understanding and discretion. It is said that there isn't a statue with a cock in the whole Vatican and certainly the plaster fig leaves aren't very well done. Beneath them the stigmata of our sex has been hammered off I understand." He found "The Canovas very cold, insipid. Extraordinary that so much strong emotion should make so little effect. Bernini's *Santa Theresa* is a very different cup of tea. Here at any rate, if the spectator doesn't entirely respond, he can respect the orgasm he observes." Leonardo's *Annunciation* filled him with fresh admiration: "A corker! What a design! and what clean drawing. One can really see the spaces between the grasses as though one was laying on one's stomach and pushing into the miniature jungle which grasses and weeds make."[16]

Italy refreshed his appetite for painting and from 1951 Claude seemed on high ground. He was 44 years old and painting well. He was acknowledged as one of Britain's leading painters. He was broadening his knowledge of the world and of the art it had to offer. Unfortunately his body started to play up. Later that year a small, non-cancerous lesion was found in his bladder, and he was treated for this at St. Mary's Hospital, Paddington. The treatment required him to be admitted at regular intervals, and during one of his visits a routine check-up showed that he was a diabetic. His diabetes was to give him trouble for the rest of his life. His doctor put him on a diet which dramatically altered his rotund shape and, having stabilised his blood sugar, operated on his bladder. Claude treated this operation with characteristic good humour and reported his condition to Susan Jacobsen on March 12 1952: "I seem to have about three navels which may be difficult to explain; and will tend to transform me into a legendary Hindu-ish character . . . Beautiful girls, in their busy way, perform acts on me that would cost pounds in the best brothels of Europe . . ."[17] Some subsequent investigations into diabetes suggested that it was sometimes triggered off by shock. Even if this were the case, it appeared that there was diabetes in the family and that Claude's love of sweet things had triggered his own complaint, and that he had probably had it for some time. However, Claude did tell Susan Jacobsen that the biggest shock he had ever had was winning the prize for *Miss Lynn.*

One of Claude's talents was the ability to turn negative to positive. The spell in hospital renewed his interest in hospital scenes as subjects for paintings, and his medical background gave him confidence to carry these out. He liked to know a good deal about the subjects he painted, and he found that having been a patient gave him the necessary experience to make painting the subject possible. The superb small painting of *The Patient Opposite* was done from drawings made in the ward, and developed into a painting done at home while convalescing from his operation. The colours are cheerful, taking their key from the bunch of daffodils on the bedside chest. Claude's interest in the compressed space of the bed seen end on and the shape of the man in it is evident; this is a similar drawing problem to that tackled in *The Cottage Bedroom*, and in this condensed little picture it is solved with panache. The patient is enclosed in his narrow convalescent world between the bedrails, the flowers and the boxlike splint, while the chest acts as a repoussoir, leading the eye into the heart of the picture. Claude took note of every detail. "The patient opposite, a Greek with an import business in Covent Garden had sepsis of the thumb and hand. The splint shown, a special contraption, was ordered by the house surgeon in order to immobilise the hand and forearm . . . the surgeon in charge of this bed took pleasure in pointing out, loudly and clearly, to the house surgeon and to a group of students, that this splint was entirely useless in this context. However, it seemed useful in the picture."[18] Not only does it lead the eye in, but counteracts the equivalent movement on the other side created by the elbow and bedding of the man next door.

While Claude worked on this painting he thought of other scenes at the hospital, and especially of a man having his dressings changed in the neighbouring bed within a sort of cave made by surrounding screens. The problem was to put the figure in the limited space within the screens, and to reconcile the strong reds and greens of screen and wall. He started the painting with no notes at all, and was surprised on returning to the hospital to find the actual scene very different and all the colours changed. He had two possibilities - to start again with careful drawings, or to go on with his original conception, working by trial and error. In the painting *The Dressing* he compromised. He made drawings of details - masks, nurses, sheets - but stuck to his original colour ideas. He noted that he had great difficulty with the heads and the flesh colours against the whites and reds. The result is a potent small picture, tightly painted in a way which suggests the hermetic, ritual quality of the subject.

A third painting which resulted from these hospital visits was *The Theatre Trolley*. Claude noted that the familiar scene of an unconscious patient between moving figures gave him the same excitement as Giotto's *Death of St. Francis*. His own painting was conceived as a group of verticals around a horizontal, but Claude hoped to incorporate an element of time in capturing the urgency of the movement. Movement and the suggestion of time passing became concerns which he was to tackle in later paintings, his choice of transient subjects achieving a particular tension resulting from his slow methods of execution. For this picture he had difficulty in quarrying enough information because of the necessity for speed, and the narrow field of action. He received permission to draw in the operating theatre, but finally chose the moment when the patient was just leaving the theatre.

The resulting picture, with its flurry of white against strong reds and greens, has all the impact of immediate reportage while maintaining a tightly controlled design, and succeeds in freezing the movement. These paintings reveal Claude's interest in human 'stance' - the positions people take up when working or playing - an interest awakened in his rugger-playing schooldays. The sporting analogy is apt, as Claude often thought in sporting terms. When his brother arranged for him to draw in an operating theatre, he wrote to Arthur Porritt, the surgeon in charge: "What I like about the subject when I see it is that it is entirely unlike the films . . . what impressed me was the loose discipline of the whole business which, oddly enough, brought to mind of all things, the kind of thing one sees and expects to see in cricket of Test standard."[19]

The hospital visits seem to have acted as a spur to Claude's painting. He had found a relatively unexploited subject which suited his particular brand of realism. He was constantly on the lookout for unusual subjects, but they had to be something that he himself experienced, that caught his eye or took him by surprise, and which contained both the germ of a design idea and the awkwardness of real life. He found another subject by chance in the playroom at home. The big canvas which he had put on his easel as soon as *Miss Lynn* was taken off for exhibition was probably destined for the painting of *The Hornby Train*. His interest was fired by seeing the two boys playing within the rails of the train set, and he envisaged a circle containing a vertical and horizontal figure. He wanted to capture the rapt attention of the children against the 'jungle fantasy' of the patterned carpet and the relative boredom of the adult. He made dozens of drawings of the boys, the train, the rails, the carpet, of Elsie and the cat (he was thinking of Hogarth's cat), but noted that he did not use drawings very much when actually doing the painting but worked from the image in mind, made positive in the process of doing the drawings. The impossibility of using the actual perspective in the small room presented him with a problem which he solved by tipping up and flattening out the floor in the painting, creating a decorative field on which to place the figures. This device causes the standing boy's feet to float, but he is firmly anchored in space by his head against the red sofa. Claude started the painting early in 1952, putting it away for long periods, and finally finishing it early in 1954. The picture implies multiple viewpoints, from looking straight downwards to straight across, all bound into a tightly controlled pattern of shapes. Claude created in this work an extreme of tension between the flat of the canvas and the suggestion of space and depth, and with its fully saturated colour it has a strong impact. However, he may have regarded it as untrue to experience, for he never again resorted to such perspectival distortion or sacrificed so much to decorative effect.

During the 1950s Claude undertook commissions for more academic portraits, including one of Sir Robert Wood, Vice-Chancellor of Southampton University. This commission presumably came about because *Miss Lynn* had been presented by the Arts Council to Southampton City Art Gallery. Others were R L James, the High Master of St. Paul's School, Dr Janet Vaughan, Principal of Somerville College, Oxford, the scientist Professor Haldane, Lord Justice Birkett and Professor Maurice Ginsburg. Both Dr Janet Vaughan and Mr James' portraits gave him trouble and he confessed to not much liking either of them at the time. Janet Vaughan was apparently horrified when Claude announced the number of sittings he would like, and then she replied "I understand, Mr Rogers - I too have done research." Claude recorded his reactions to his commission. "When I painted the Principal of Somerville, Dr Vaughan, she said one day that she would like to be painted in her robes as a doctor of medicine. 'All right' I said. 'Anyway, let's see them. Bring them along for the first drawings.' As a matter of fact, when I actually saw her in them I was staggered. She looked splendid. But how was I going to make the picture focus on her head when I had to deal with . . . a pretty fierce alizarin crimson silk, with large patches of vermilion flannel sewn all over them. I thought about this while drawing. And I kept on thinking about it afterwards. And then I got an idea. If I had a red wall behind her - this was perfectly feasible - so that I had three reds to deal with, that would be exciting in itself and would fit in with the general idea I was beginning to get. Moreover, I should have a RED picture. Any other colours - her black coat and skirt, whitish blouse and the flesh colours - particularly the flesh colours - were bound to tell against it. Better still, with all those tremendous reds I would be able to make even hot flesh tints quite creamy. And so it proved."[20]

In this statuesque portrait every shape tells - the pale central column of shirt and head gleaming against the dark green, black and red and the white sections of skirting board underlining and stabilising the solid dark shapes. It is the most 'fully frontal' of all Claude's portraits; hating the idea of a formula for portraits, he never repeated a pose.

Miss Lynn was responsible for obtaining another portrait commission for Claude. This was of Barbara Proctor, the wife of Dennis Proctor, then Chairman of the Tate Gallery's Board of Trustees. The Proctors married in 1953, and they put their wedding present money (£375) towards a full length portrait. Claude painted Barbara Proctor reclining on a vaguely eighteenth century chaise longue, borrowed from a mutual friend. He sent his sitter out to buy a new dress of pink striped cotton, and arranged her on the sofa. The painting took over a hundred sittings, and was finally finished on July 24 1956. Claude described it in a letter to Susan Jacobsen; "I am now stuck into Barbara. Well, that reads in a decidedly curious way I see: these technical terms . . . are disconcerting. I should say perhaps that I am wholly concentrating on Barbara . . . I'm beginning to know what I'm about, to think around the canvas, and to see what the drawing must be. The head is pretty funny. She may have a sillyish pretty face, but it's not as daft and silly as I have achieved. On the other hand the body is beginning to come and the hands, and I am beginning to get the sofa and the space . . ."[21] Claude worked hard, but this picture for all its bold curves and edge-to-edge completeness, still has an air of unease. The classical overtones of the sofa and the pose, with the truncation of the figure caused by the foreshortening of the legs, do not quite seem to come off. He evidently had difficulty deciding on the size of the canvas, and his drawings showed him deliberating as to where the right hand edge should be. The paint surface shows signs of struggle, and a more ample curve of the hip, probably necessary to the general design, was painted out at Dennis Proctor's request. Claude must have struggled with it as it took him even more sittings than usual; there is some beautiful painting in the hands and the folds of the dress, with their subtle colour changes, but it does not have the immaculate 'rightness' of *Miss Lynn*.

An article by David Wolfers in *The Tatler* discusses Claude's portraiture in a lighthearted way, but is interesting about his working methods. "Claude Rogers would hate to be a portrait painter to the exclusion of all else. He does, however, like the distinct limitations a portrait imposes. The definition of objective is a welcome counterpart to the relative freedom of landscape painting. He begins by making a few preliminary drawings or sketches – but, unlike many portrait painters, he never touches the canvas when his sitter is not there. These drawings enable him to think about the positioning of the sitter and the balance of the composition. He prefers to paint people just under or preferably just over life-size. Life-size portraits, he believes, hung high up in huge halls as they so often are, produce a curious off-key effect. The alteration of scale helps to right the balance. Having begun, he will not start on another commission until the one in hand is over."[22]

By the mid 1950s Claude had become something of a public figure in the art world. He and Elsie were invited to Buckingham Palace garden parties and Claude relished the occasions for dressing up in fancy clothes. In 1952 Claude was elected as president of the London Group. He had been a regularly exhibiting member for fourteen years and knew its workings intimately. He accepted the presidency with relish, and guided its activities with avuncular tolerance for the next thirteen years.

By the time Claude became president, the London Group had lost some of its importance as an exhibiting society. The proliferation of new dealer galleries made it easier for artists to show their work elsewhere. Nevertheless, it brought Claude into contact with all the leading painters of the day and his correspondence became voluminous. He enjoyed the work and took great trouble over it, getting involved in many other related activities as a result.

The London Group still represented the experimental face of British art. Nevile Wallis, in a review of a London Group exhibition, bemoaned "the frustrating prejudices in the art world which makes it unthinkable for such artists to enter or raise the prestige of the Academy, or, on the other hand, to become known abroad under British Council auspices. Their refuge is the London Group, home of austere non-conformity . . . allied to intensely serious purpose approved by fellow martinets."[23]

As president, Claude attempted to attract important artists to the group, and to encourage coming young painters to apply for membership. His circle of acquaintances widened and he even undertook visits to other painters. His visit to Lowry in June 1958 was such a one. He was teaching at a weekend school on Teeside at the invitation of Kenneth Gribble, then principal of Heginbottam Art School, who arranged the trip to Lowry's house and drove him over in his old Ford 8. The two painters got on well, and the visit was memorable chiefly for Claude's attempts to buy one of Lowry's drawings. They repaired to the local pub where they haggled interminably over a price, eventually striking a bargain to much mutual satisfaction.[24]

Claude entered into correspondence with Bomberg who, at the end of his life, was thinking of writing a history of the Group, of which he had been a founder member, but with which he had since become embittered. A letter from Fred Uhlmann dated July 11 1953 requests help from Claude. "A few days ago I had a drink with David Bomberg and he started to talk about the history of the London Group (as you know he is one of the foundation members and he knew Sickert, Ginner and the whole Camden Town Group). He mentioned that he would very much like to write a history of the Group, and I encouraged him, because I feel that it is very important that the few remaining foundation members should write down their experience before it is too late. There is only one point. Bomberg who, rightly or wrongly, feels completely neglected by the Group (he kept on repeating 'I am like a stranger in my father's house') wants to be invited. Would you - or better the Committee fulfil this - what seems to me - modest wish? After all it would give the old man great pleasure and would cheer him up considerably."[25] Bomberg died in 1957, presumably without the history being written, but it is likely that Claude would have been encouraging.

Claude also tried to bring talent from outside into the Group. He invited Peter Lanyon to become a member, but without success, receiving the following reply, sent on April 16 1952 from The Attic Studio, St. Ives. "The arts (a small a) seem to be more concerned at present with being either ancient or modern than with being alive. I cannot accept divisions among artists on the excuse that one 'side' doesn't understand the other . . . my relationship to society . . . must be a local one. You see, I'm a Cornishman and that is not an encouragement to be pleasant in foreign countries like England and particularly to some of the foreigners who inhabit this outpost. Perhaps a little of this hatred (of which I am immensely proud) would percolate into the London Group were I to come face to face with 'Art Politics Inc'."[26] St Ives was then a hotbed of artistic intrigue and Lanyon was clearly not aware of the broad and tolerant embrace that the London Group offered.

Outside his teaching and his painting, Claude's activities in the art world were various. He was asked by Duncan Grant to help with the selection of pictures for Grant's retrospective exhibition at the Tate. Grant's painting had had a strong influence on Claude's generation, and his weighty, classical treatment of figures had been unusual in their time; but now Claude was moved to irreverence. "I'm devoted to Duncan and really the early work is extraordinarily interesting and good. There's a lot of it, from his studio mainly, now collected together in the Tate cellars. They haven't much later work yet, and, wickedly, as I went back in the train last time, after drawing P James and seeing what work of Duncan's there was, I found the wheels humming:

Dear Duncan, I've looked at your pictures
I'm not much concerned with the style
But the COLOURS you choose
And the MIXTURES you use
Are indescribably vile!"[27]

One of Claude's visits to the Tate propelled him into more verse. He saw that the sculpture by Frank Dobson on the lawns of the Tate had been replaced by a Henry Moore, and sent the following piece of outrage to a friend:

Henry Moore is on the lawn,
His statue's made the grade,
It's Henry gets the pigeon-droppings now.
While Dobby's statue's gone

Poor Dobby's in the shade,
Poor Dobby can't do 'living art' nohow!
(chorus: for artists over 40)
It's funny how it happens - aint half a bleeding shame
A poor deserving artist's lost his perishing good name,
Can scarcely earn the dough to blow to satisfy his need,
At a word from Kenneth Clark or a wink from Herbert Read.[28]

At this time Claude was mixing with many luminaries of the art world. He described an evening he spent with the painter Matthew Smith. "Matthew Smith had asked me to dine with him at 7.45. My watch said 7.55. I ran to the phone, said I'd been delayed and wouldn't be long and dashed out of the house. I needn't really have worried. He was as bothered and agitated as I was and very grateful that I was late. We dined at an Italian restaurant I never dreamed existed, near S. Kensington Station, and excellently. For once the drink worked and made me relaxed and fluent. He's charming. He talked about the Slade - Tonks, Steer, Russell - and what a breath of fresh air it was to get to Paris, this circa 1908. He must have been quite old by then as students go as he had been first in a Bradford textile business 'cotton or wool, I forget' and then, when the owner, a friend of his father's, said he would never make a businessman, in papa's business. Ill health 'luckily' as he said, eventually persuaded papa to let him go to Manchester School of Art, though only to the design and commercial courses there. Then the Slade; and, after two years, to Paris. Everyone was talking about Matisse, who at that time, was almost unknown to England . . . as Matisse at this time was running a studio in Paris MS joined it. It was the usual thing. A German massier, Matisse going the rounds every Saturday morning. 'If you wanted a criticism you left your canvas on the easel. I was too shy to do that, but I followed round with the rest to listen in spite of the fact that I hardly spoke French at all . . .' Modigliani was about at that time, always drawing in cafés, everywhere, and irritably kicking up a fuss if anyone else in sight also attempted to draw . . . And Soutine. People were talking about Derain . . . Picasso was hardly known in MS's circle. Later he had a show and Macdonald (afterwards at London Lefevre) invited MS who couldn't go because he didn't have a dinner suit in Paris and didn't like to borrow one."[29]

Claude reported on other visits to painters. "I met Ethel Sands one evening last week. An extraordinary frail old body - must be about 80 - with thin white hair perfectly permed and an expensive black frou-frou dress on body like a - a - well, I'd say a broomstick but it isn't aristocratic enough, nor quite flexible enough. She's one of those aristocratic painters - not half a bad artist, but without the necessity to exert herself and with too many distractions. She was able to keep up a queer clucking noise - equal to a laugh in anyone else - throughout the conversation. It represented appreciative encouragement of wit, but made me wonder if by any chance an egg would appear on the floor."[30]

Claude was by now working for his 1954 exhibition at the Leicester Galleries. The galleries were shared with Vivian Pitchforth and Albert de Belleroche. Claude showed 33 paintings: 9 landscapes painted from Hawkshall Cottage including one with an aeroplane hangar (a foretaste of paintings to come), five seaside paintings conceived when on holiday in the Isle of Wight, two paintings of Italy, six hospital paintings, three portraits including *Miss Lynn*, and a mixture of other pictures including *The Hornby Train*. In one painting, a still life entitled *The Blow Lamp*, the painted objects achieved such a presence that they take on the dramatic character of actors in some mute and surreal performance. Claude's notes about this painting mentioned working for his show and hankering after a still life. He came across a drawing he had done at Hawkshall of the blowlamp he had used to strip down the cottage doors. He had liked its fine aggressive shape. He took the drawing and reconstructed the subject in his studio, emphasising the silhouettes to create a design of solids and voids, empty and full surfaces. The painting was done direct from the motif over about thirty sittings. The result is a masterpiece with a long lasting resonance.

The 1954 exhibition showed the breadth and depth of Claude's art at its best. The critics were enthusiastic. A review in *The Studio* points out "his matured confidence in handling a variety of themes: hospital scenes, landscape, portraiture, in which local colour dominates his composition to the detriment of atmosphere . . . But if atmosphere is missing, Mr Rogers in its place imposes a solidity of structure that is impressive in its strength and its matt texture of paint. In *The Blow Lamp* the flatness of the placing and the drabness of the colour take on the palpable attributes of an established style."[31]

The Times printed a long review entitled 'An Adventurous Realist'. "The courage, amounting to audacity, which Mr Claude Rogers now shows in his choice of subjects is a comparatively recent development and is certainly one, though only one, of the interesting aspects at the Leicester Galleries. If a quick, hit-or-miss, impressionist painter had taken on an eclipse of the moon, a highly coloured sunrise, a scarlet combine harvester in a cornfield, a large interior with children playing trains, and a number of animated scenes in a hospital, it would not be very surprising, but Mr Rogers is, of course, a slow, grave, absolutely

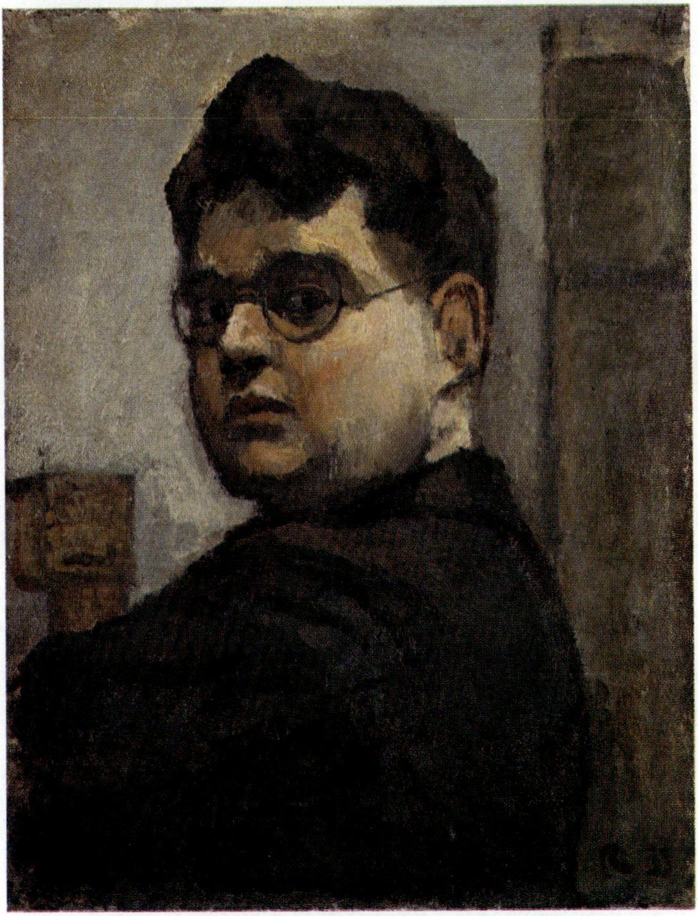

Self Portrait, 1933

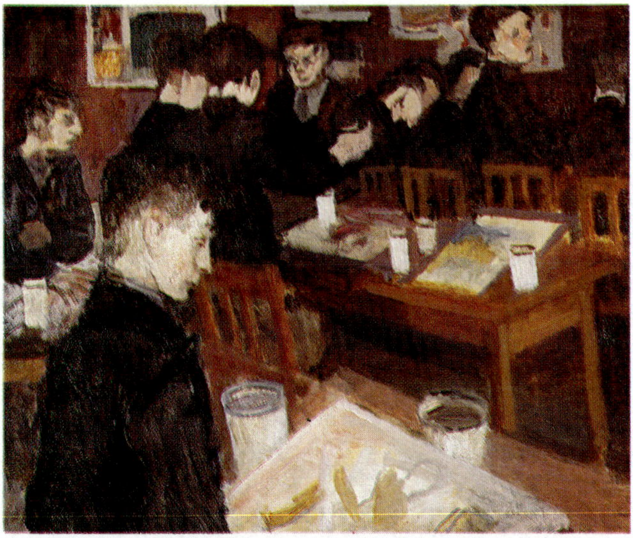

The Painting Lesson, Raynes Park, 1936

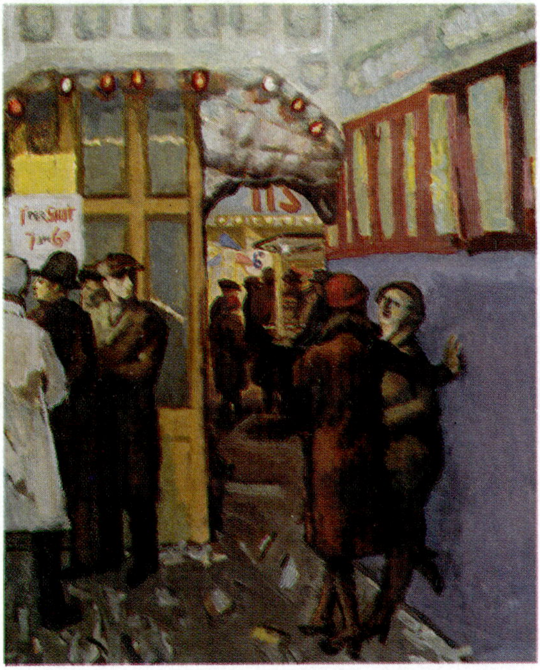

Hannibal's, 1933

II–III

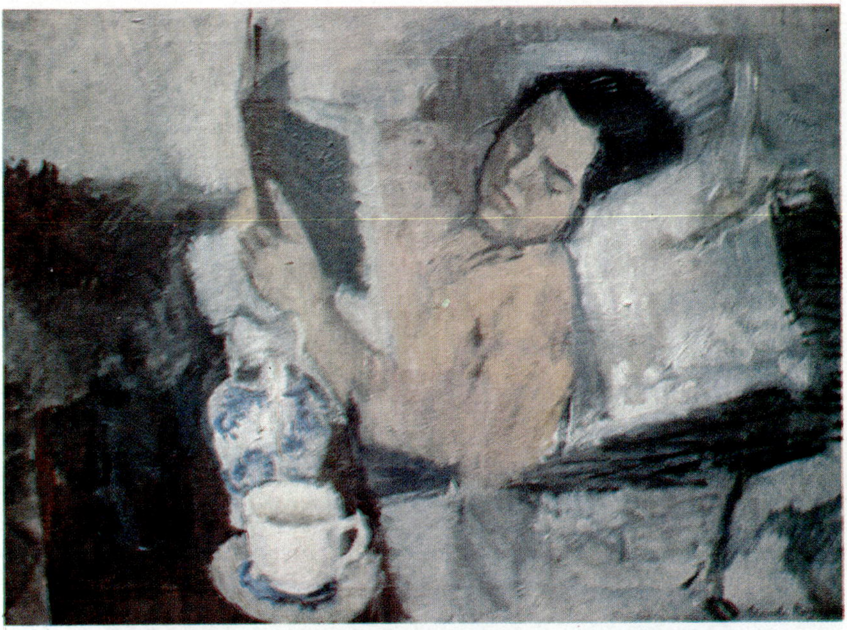

Breakfast in Bed, 1937

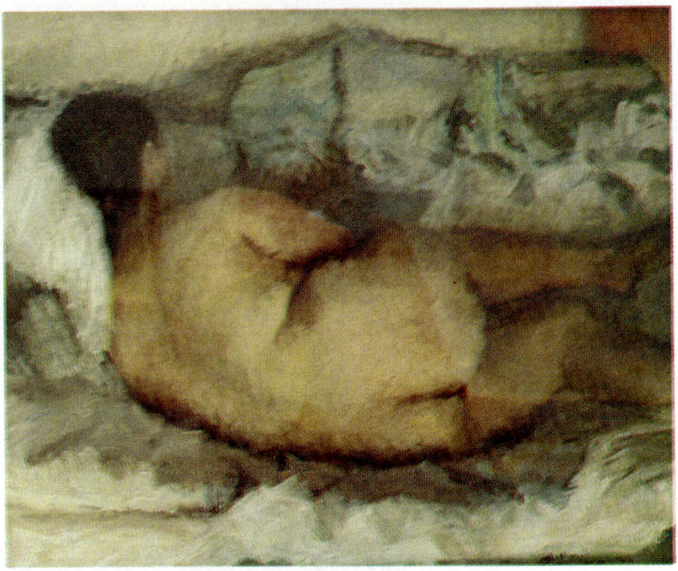

Nude, 1938

IV–V

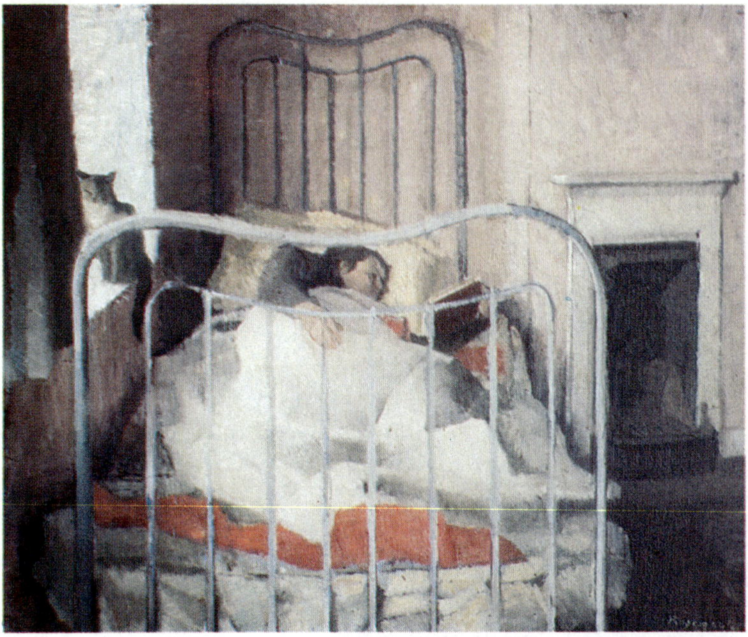

The Cottage Bedroom, 1944

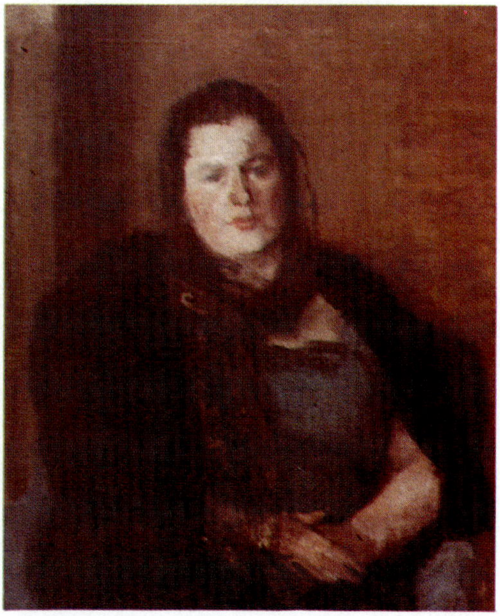

Elsie in a Black Cape, 1939

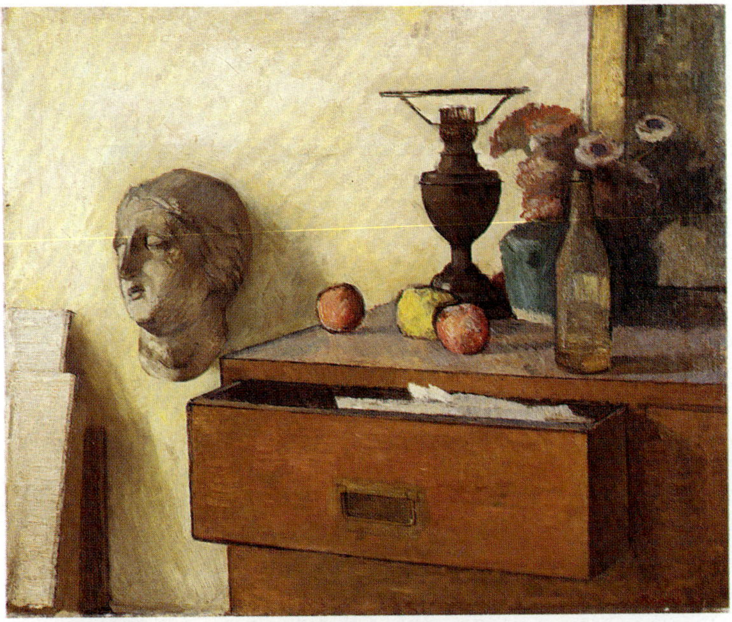

Still Life with Cast, 1943–46

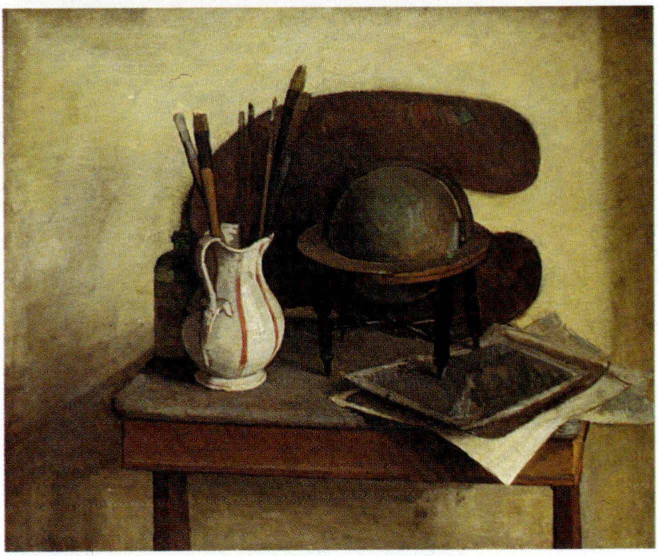

Still Life with Globe, 1945

VIII–IX

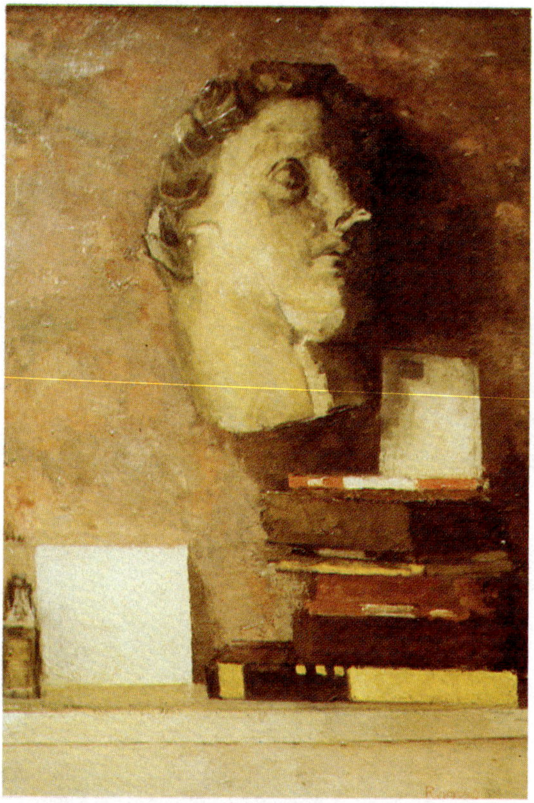

Cast over the Mantelpiece,
1943–46

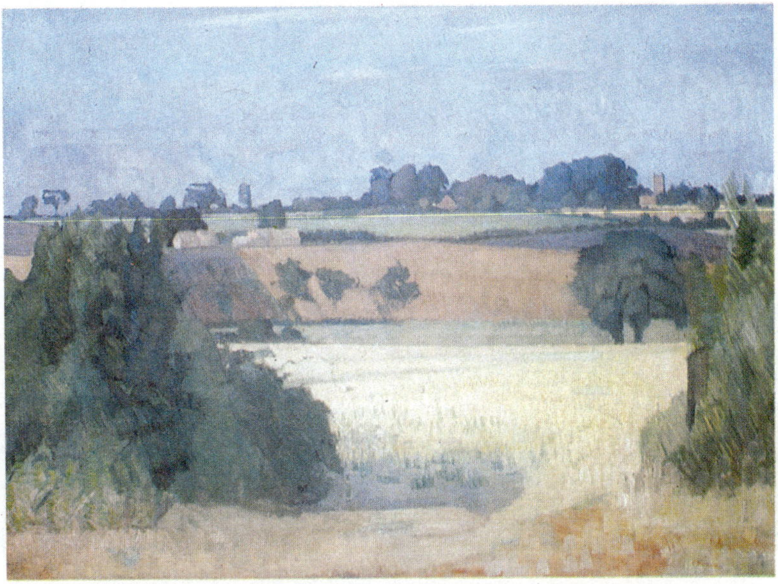

Clover Fields near Toppersfield Church, 1947

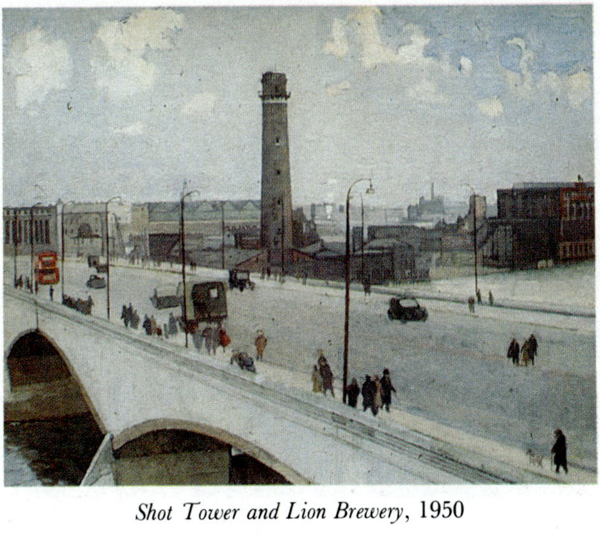

Shot Tower and Lion Brewery, 1950

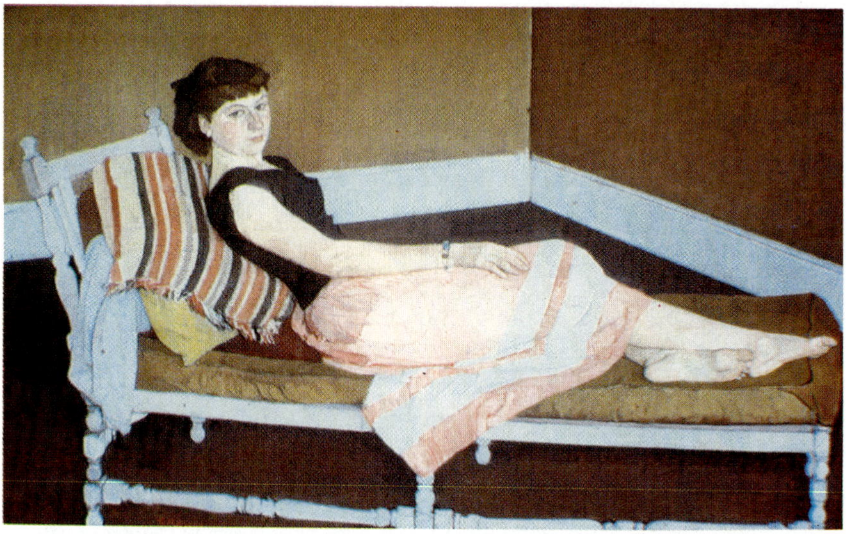

Miss Lynn, 1950–51

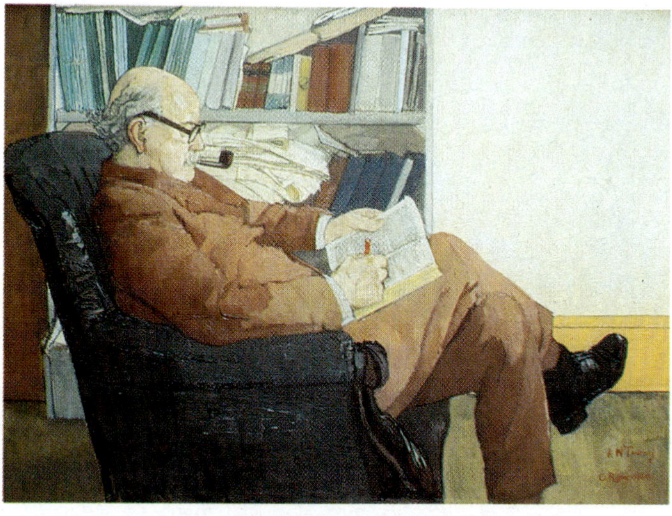

Professor Tawney, 1952

XIII-XIV

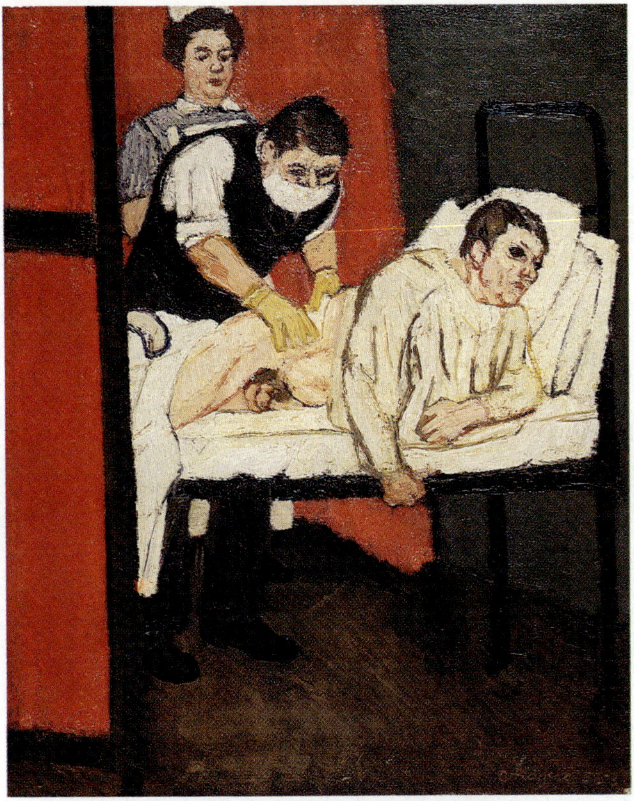

The Dressing, 1952–53

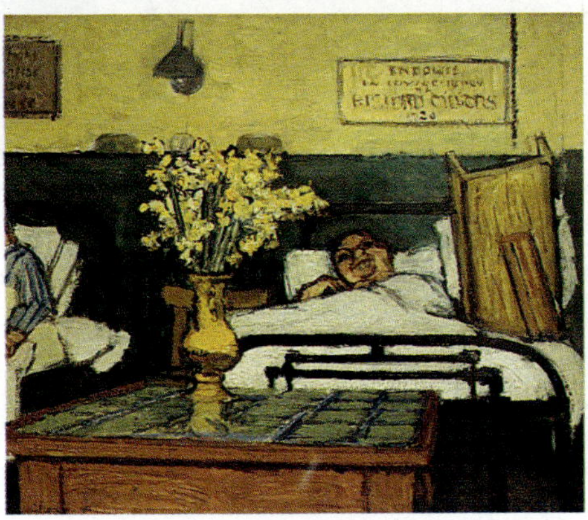

The Patient Opposite, 1952

XV-XVI

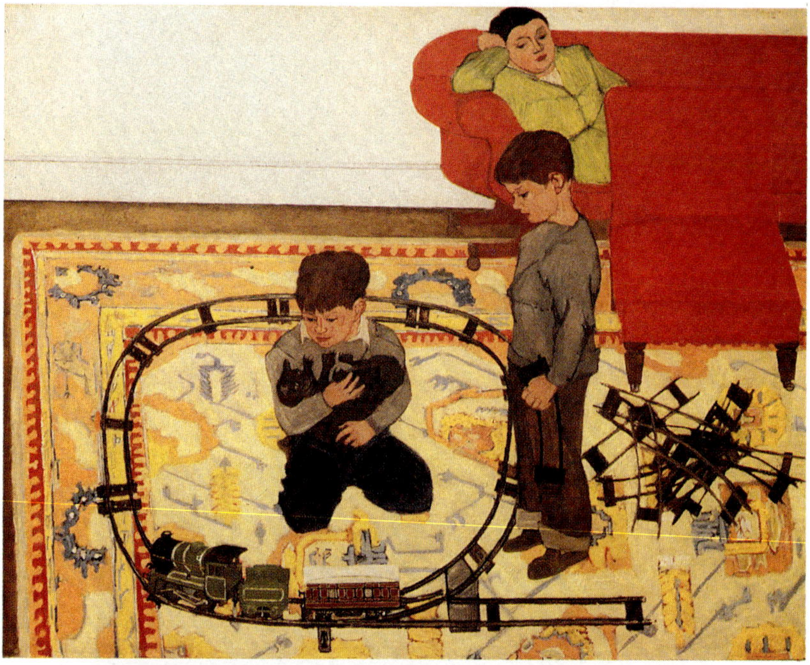

The Hornby Train, 1951–53

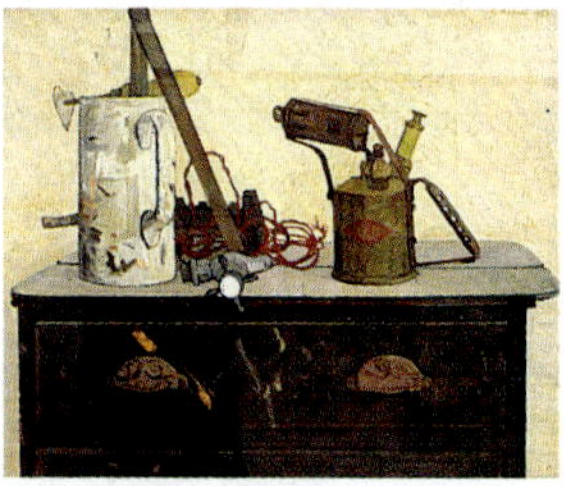

The Blow Lamp, 1953–54

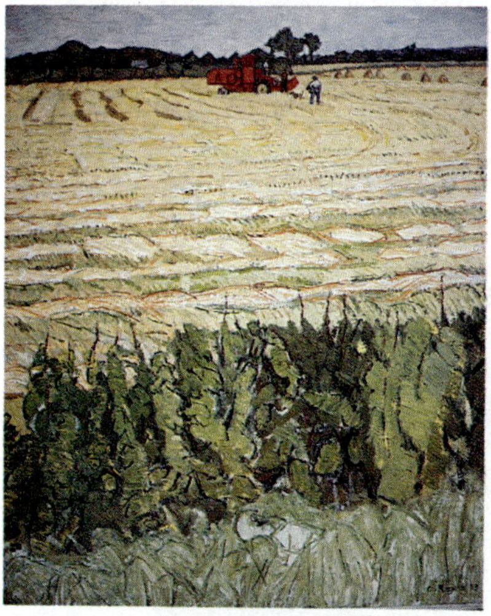

The Combine, 1953

XVII–XIX

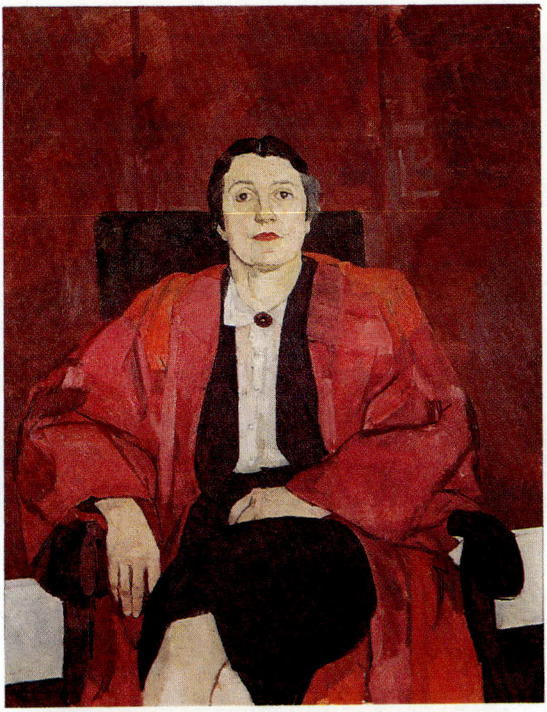

Dr Janet Vaughan, Somerville College, 1956

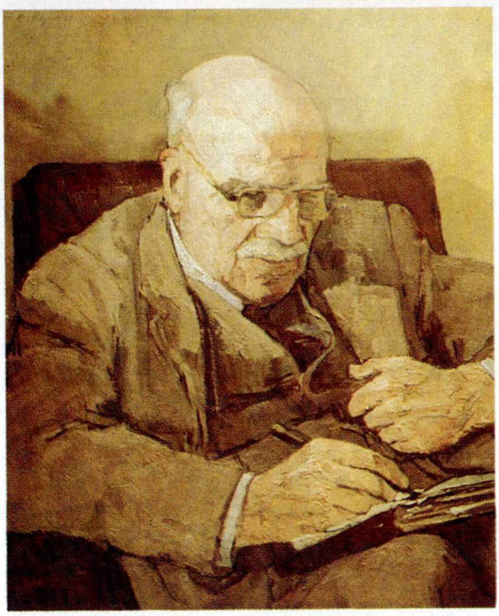

Professor Haldane, 1957

XX–XXI

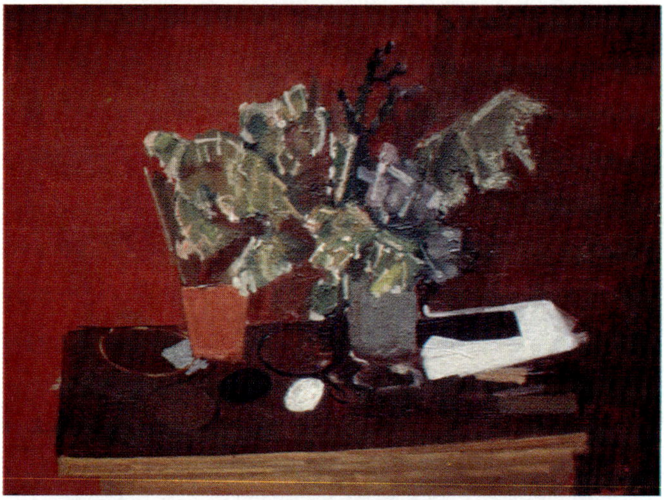

Red Still Life, 1958–59

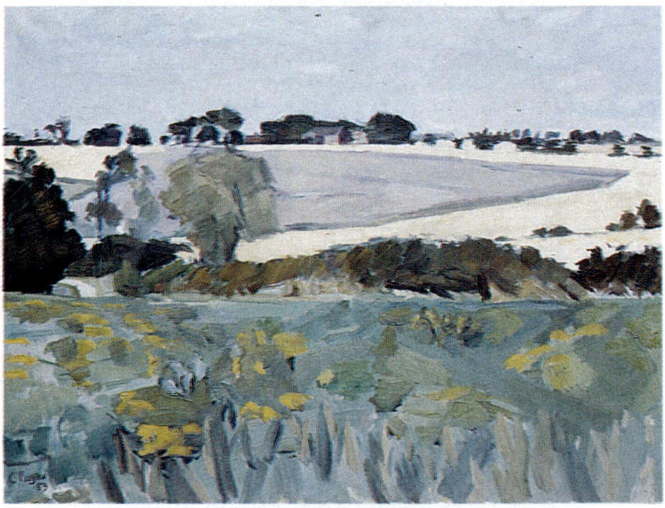

The Clover Field, 1958–59

XXII–XXIII

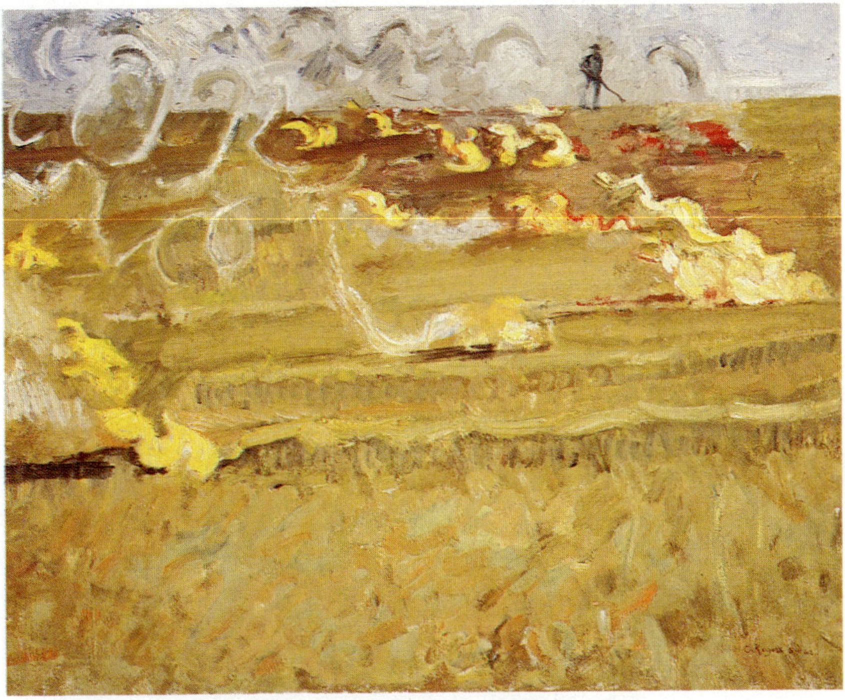

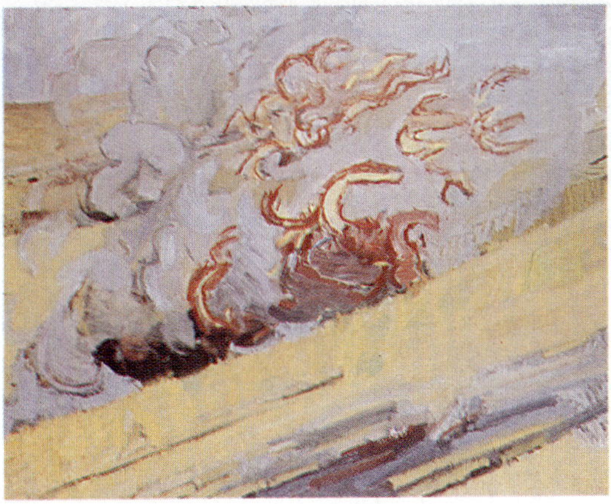

Burning Field,
1958–60

Stubble Burning,
1958–72

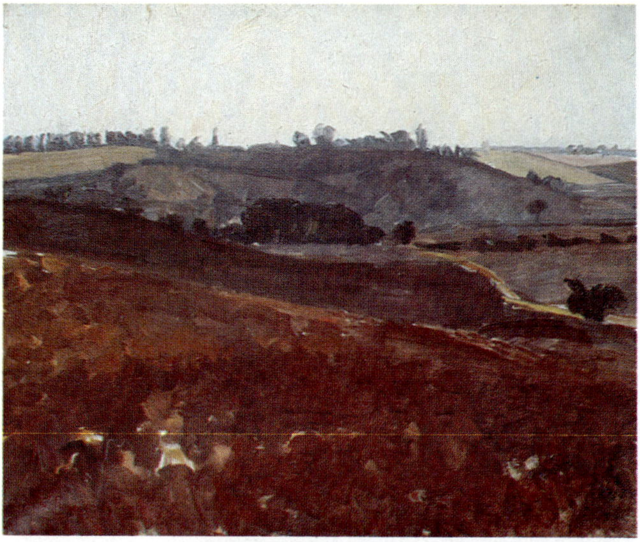

Plough into the Sun, 1960

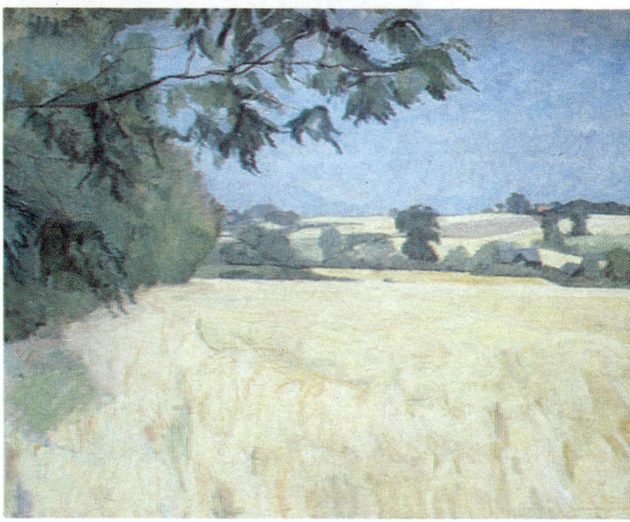

Cornfields at Somerton, 1961

XXVI-XXVII

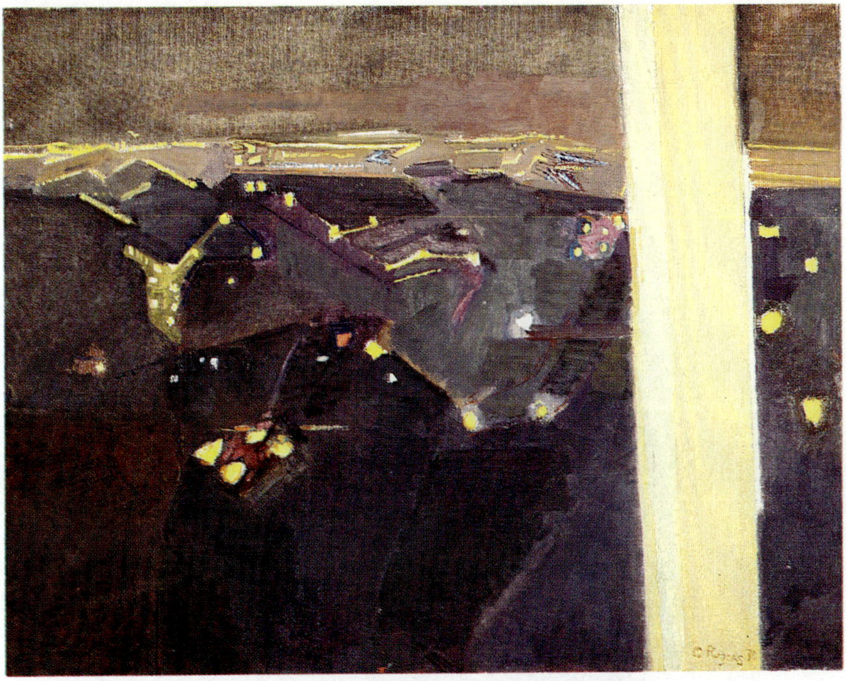

City at Night I, 1970

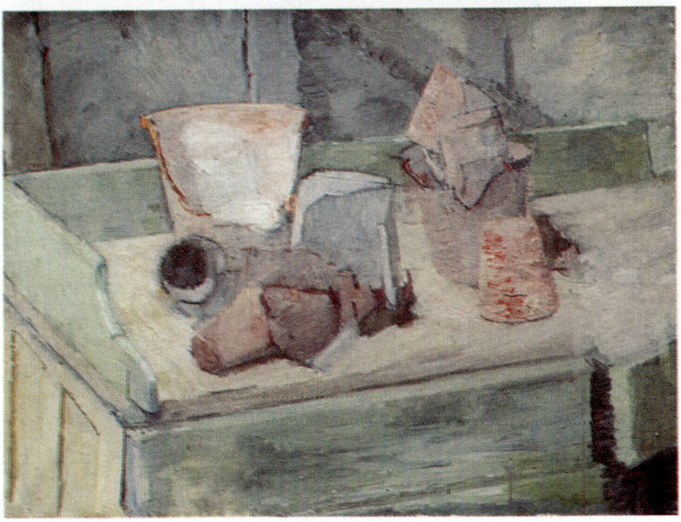

The Potting Shed, 1962

XXVIII–XXIX

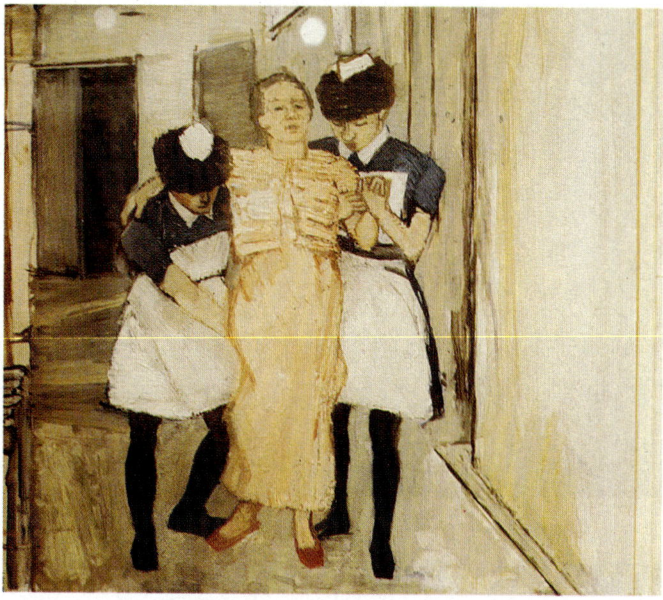

The Paraplegic, 1970–71

conscientious painter; one would naturally expect such an artist to confine himself to still life, portraits without embellishment, and unromantic landscapes."[32] It seemed that Claude was deliberately pitting himself against subjects of an ephemeral nature as a way of guarding himself against a too-easy vision and as a way of forcing himself to sift the essential from the non-essential. He probably relished the difficulties and excitements involved in wringing pictures out of transient raw material, and the battle to do so increased the power and excitement of the paintings.

This exhibition showed Claude at the peak of his powers – brave in his choice of motifs to attempt to pin down on the flat of the canvas, unyielding in his resolve to make his designs only on the basis of factual evidence. It was also a financial success; almost half the paintings were sold for a total value of £560. This sum, on top of his salary from the Slade and the excellent rates for his commissioned portraits, must have made him feel for once financially fairly comfortable.

In the mid 1950s the Rogers family received notice that the United States Air Force was planning to recommission Wethersfield aerodrome, and that Hawkshall Cottage was in the direct path of the proposed runway. The cottage was requisitioned and the Rogers were offered generous compensation, with which they were, in July 1957, able to buy another house not far away, the Old Rectory at Somerton, south west of Bury St Edmunds. Claude and Elsie mourned the loss of Hawkshall; they had had a permanent painting centre in East Anglia since the war, and Claude was becoming quite well known for his East Anglian landscapes, so the acquisition of another house was important. The Old Rectory was much more of an establishment, a Victorian Gothic Revival vicarage with a fair amount of land and some outbuildings. There was a pond and a croquet lawn and Claude had a good dry studio in one of the barns.

Claude clearly enjoyed exploring his new property and working on it, and a letter to Susan Jacobsen gives some idea of his efforts: "Apart from painting I've been busy with Improvements, in both the 20th and 18th century sense. I have erected Statues at the end of Vistas in the Ornamental Grounds; and made a start at putting draught excluders round some doors . . . the barns and sheds are full of junk . . . a cut glass salt cellar, a first rate screwdriver, a dear little jug from a child's teaset. It's rather like having one's own special bran pie."[33] With the purchase of the Old Rectory, Claude had inherited a mass of junk of the sort he loved, and it must have pleased him enormously to dig about in it. This did not deter him, however, from keeping on with his East Anglian paintings in holidays at Somerton. "I have now got four unfinished pictures here – two await next spring, and the other two are summer pictures – and three of them are really of one bit of one field. Considering that I can look for 360 degrees even standing on one spot I consider this pretty conservative. It is a nice field of course . . ."[34] He took a pride in this 'conservative' approach to his subjects, no doubt thinking of Cézanne's remark: "the motifs multiply, the same subject seen from a different angle offers subject for study of the most powerful interest and so varied that I think I could occupy myself for months without changing place, by turning now more to the right, now more to the left." Friends would often stay at Somerton. Euan Uglow in particular stayed for long periods and he and Claude went painting together, Claude striding off into the country with a great landscape strapped to his back. They painted a snowscape side by side when the snow was so thick that they had to leave the car and dig to find the road in order to get through to the house.

Between teaching and painting, Claude and Elsie had little time for the children. Reny took over the role of mother and ran the house. During the holidays Martin was usually out on the farm or amusing himself outside. Crispin's passion was fishing, but he was a less extrovert child and was often at odds with his parents. Claude sometimes accompanied him on his fishing trips, making watercolour paintings and occasionally small oils of the ponds and his son fishing. But Crispin was a worry to him and he found it difficult to handle him. Claude confessed to being "rather cross with myself as a father. I really must try and be a bit better at it" but the mixture of neglect, spoiling and disappointment at Crispin's lack of achievement in school did not help. "Crispin is in a difficult state and worries me . . . it takes the form of rebellion, destruction, aggression and endless playing everyone up. I'm not very good at dealing with him . . . What tiring creatures the little buggers can be and how one worries and loves them . . ."[35] Claude, so warm and generous to all his friends, was less successful in his very close relationships, possibly finding the emotional responsibility rather irksome and experiencing guilt at not fulfilling his emotional 'duties'. His mother, wife and son were all at times to represent a 'burden' to Claude, and as it were to spoil the fun. He was interested in people and genuinely fond of his fellow human beings, but shied away from emotional pressure. He himself needed affection and companionship, possibly to the detriment of his painting. Certainly his relationships with others, particularly other women, must have taken up a great deal of his time, but he may have protected himself from being too prodigal with his deeper feelings, saving them for his painting. His feelings, as one would expect, were very often triggered off by visual stimuli – looking at other paintings, looking at farmers working in familiar landscapes, looking at the sights and scenes he knew well.

The East Anglian landscape had interested Claude since staying at Rodwell before the war, and by the time he moved to Somerton, landscape painting was part of his stock-in-trade. The paintings seem to identify with England and show a pride in being unmistakably English. Claude also enjoyed the challenge of the flat East Anglian countryside. There was little foreground and it was often a case of making something out of nothing. He liked to understand the scene.

"I like to know this countryside, to have some idea of where a track goes, to be on terms with the people living in the farm and working in the field, because to do so makes one more at ease and literally in touch with the scene . . . I like the look of well farmed land where the hedges are trimmed back and the dense crop laps up to them or to within an inch or so of the macadam road. I like the seasonal changes, the rough plough of late autumn, the smoother and more granular plough of spring, the young greens, the yellowing crops, the blazing summer cornfields and the dry ochre stubble. I like especially that moment in late summer when the distant harvest machine – the autumnal cuckoo – is first to be heard, when the whole arc of visible land is yellow on yellow. Innumerable heads of corn hang in the heat. The stillness is full of small dry sounds, a continuous snapping and crackling, the skirmisher's musketry of Napier's Peninsular War."[36]

Claude also loved London, and despite being now the owner of a rather grand establishment in Suffolk, he remained basically a Londoner. Walking around London, as he had done all his life, was still able to give him a thrill. In the mid 1950s he experienced one of those rare moments of wonder after going to see the film *Camille*. "Coming out into Leicester Square I was astonished at the beauty of London that summer night. Perhaps it was the film. At any rate the scene in front of me was still magic, the heavy summer trees opposite faintly stirring and lit to a dull metallic green as they caught the various lights: through them a thready glitter of red and gold neon signs on the further cinemas . . . Above it all and saturating the scene a liquid dense and blue night sky with a full moon . . ."[37]

For a while the pattern of Claude's life seemed nicely settled. His teaching was rewarding and fulfilling, his painting respected, his work with the London Group interesting. He remained fairly hopeless about his financial affairs, despite the efforts of his old friend Valentine Ellis, who had long been his accountant. He seemed unable to keep up with his tax demands, although at the end of the 1950s Claude and Elsie were not badly off; their combined earnings amounting to over £1,000 per annum, with Elsie's income from Jamaica more than doubling that sum. Sales of paintings could of course never be counted upon, and Claude was not a prolific exhibitor. Valentine Ellis maintained a hilarious correspondence with Claude over his financial affairs, and was apt to receive missives in doggerel by way of apology for his shortcomings, often headed The Old Wrecktory, and signed by The Old Wreck. Some examples survive amidst his correspondence.

Dear Val, your letter is to hand,
I'll frame it by and by.
I read it, you will understand,
With feelings such that they demand
A suitable reply.

Your weak and feeble client and friend
(And Friend? Can that still be?)
Implores you never more to send
A letter starting with pretend
Demands for L S D.

It's true, it's true, I do, I do
Owe quite a lot of dough -
No doubt I owe a lot to you
And there's that bill still owing, too,
To M L S I know.

Tell me that fatal sum again
(I haven't got it here)
The drain, the drain - the pain, the pain
Is nigh to driving me insane -
I shan't survive, I fear . . .

Still what of that? I'll draw the cheque
And send it through the mails.
What if the effort breaks my neck?
What if my bank account's a wreck?
What if old Barclay fails?

The old old Rector will repay,
Draining his slender hoard.
So send the bill, and come what may,
Neither M, S nor Co shall say
They've not been paid by Claude.[38]

Another verse creation on the subject of finance has more of a snarl in it.

From the Old Old Rectory, Somerton, near Bury St. Edmunds,
Suffolk:
Dear Valentine (Chartered Account,
Of Valentine Ellis and Co)
Precisely I note the amount
Which-is-to-be-shared-by-that-despicable-Judas-Midgeley-and-that-contemptible-Philistine-Snelling-when-allelujah-allelujah-I-bravely-pay-what-I-OWE.
One hundred and sixty six pound
Is the sum - well, all but a bit.
May the Lord whose compassion abounds
Cherish-the-good-old-Rector's-Bank-Account-establish-it-in-the-Black-from-everlasting-to-everlasting-and-preserve-him-eternally-against-a-DEFICIT.
Here's a cheque in settlement - pray
Attend with professional care.
To the half bleeding nicker - O.K?
And-each-of-them-two-baskets-Mister-bleeding-so-and-so-Midgeley-and-sneery-leery-hoity-toity-Snelling-know-where-they-can-stuff-their-allelujah-allelujah-SHARE.
Enclosed you will also find
From the good old Rectoress,
Most properly sealed and signed,
Those-papers-you-refer-to-in-your-remarkable-rhymed-letter-of-even-date-delivered-recently-by-the-local-postman-at-our-well-known-Suffolk-ADDRESS.
And soon we hope you will come
To sojourn, and with bed and board -
When the blasted builders have done
It-would-give-the-good-old-Rectoress-the-greatest-pleasure-I-can-assure-you-to-which-of-course-you-must-add-the-satisfaction-and-pleasure-your-presence-would-give-to-that-possessor-of-a-set-of-chess-men-her-kind-and-saintly-husband-CLAUDE.[39]

NOTES

1 Auden, Wystan and Louis MacNiece, *Letters from Iceland*, Faber and Faber 1937.
2 Claude Rogers letters, collection Mr George Sweet.
3 Organ, Robert, letter to J Pery January 10 1993.
4 Sickert, Walter, Supplement to *The New Age*, April 7 1910.
5 Organ, Robert, op. cit.
6 Clutton-Brock, Alan, *Modern Artist* Vol 1 No 3, July 3 1955.
7 *The Times*, April 23 1954.

8 Bell, Quentin, introduction to catalogue of exhibition at the Hatton Gallery, University of Durham, 1955.
9, 10, 11 Claude Rogers Papers, Tate Gallery Archive.
12 Claude Rogers, Appendix III, Catalogue of exhibition '25 from 51', Sheffield City Art Galleries 1978.
13 Claude Rogers letters, collection Mrs Susan Jacobsen.
14 Townsend, William, *Journals*, Tate Gallery 1976.
15, 16, 17 Claude Rogers letters, collection Mrs Susan Jacobsen.
18, 19, 20 Claude Rogers Papers, Tate Gallery Archive.
21 Claude Rogers letters, collection Mrs Susan Jacobsen.
22 Wolfers, David, *The Tatler*, November 19 1958.
23 Wallis, Nevile, *The Observer*, November 1958.
24 Interview with Kenneth Gribble February 4 1993.
25, 26 Claude Rogers Papers, Tate Gallery Archive.
27 Claude Rogers letters, collection Mrs Susan Jacobsen.
28 Claude Rogers Papers, Tate Gallery Archive.
29, 30 Claude Rogers letters, collection Mrs Susan Jacobsen.
31 *The Studio* 148, July 30 1954.
32 *The Times*, April 23 1954.
33, 34 Claude Rogers letters, collection Mrs Susan Jacobsen.
35, 36 Claude Rogers Papers, Tate Gallery Archive.
37 Claude Rogers letters, collection Mrs Susan Jacobsen.
38, 39 Claude Rogers Papers, Tate Gallery Archive.

A halcyon time

The end of the 1950s and the beginning of the 1960s passed in a burst of glory for Claude. He was in his early fifties and his painting was going well. Although he was increasingly loaded with administrative work, he had a knack of deriving maximum enjoyment from meetings, often drawing, or sleeping, throughout. He told Kenneth Gribble that he had developed a good elbow and armlock for sleeping in meetings. He was increasingly respected as a teacher of art, in demand as a writer of testimonials for other artists and as an external examiner in other art schools. Even Robin Darwin had tried to tempt him over to teach at the Royal College of Art. Claude was co-opted by William Coldstream onto the National Council for Diplomas in Art and Design, which formulated new training and examination policies in the art schools.

In 1958 the National Advisory Council on Art Administration had been formed, with Coldstream as its Chairman. Its first report, issued in 1960, laid the foundations for a new era in art education, proposing the institution of the DipAD (Diploma of Art and Design) and the National Council for Diplomas in Art and Design (NCDAD) to administer it. The CNAA (Council for National Academic Awards) was formed in 1964 on principles which resembled its precursor the NCDAD. Coldstream would have preferred a four-year course for the DipAD, but this seemed unreasonable in 1960, and an acceptable compromise seemed to be a one-year Foundation Course, followed by three years for the Diploma. This plan was adopted by all art schools, and was maintained until the diploma course became a degree course. In 1970 a second Coldstream report proposed subdividing the Diploma into two categories, firstly a more flexible version of the three-year diploma, and secondly a four-year course with technological content related to the needs of industry.

Claude was appointed Chairman of the Fine Arts Panel of the NCDAD, which supervised the initial review of courses for the Award of the Diploma. His reviewing panels had the power to approve or withhold approval from any course which did not in their view meet the necessary requirements. Claude's wide knowledge of art was valued, and in 1955 he was co-opted onto the Arts Panel of the Arts Council of Great Britain, thus being involved in national patronage of the arts. As President of the London Group he was in touch with a great many people in the art world and aware of new young painters of talent. An ideal choice for advice on purchasing art, he served on the Calouste Gulbenkian Foundation's Advisory Committee for Painting, with Gowing, Coldstream, Philip James, William Scott, Hugh Scruton, Carel Weight, Peter Gimpel and Gabriel White. Their function was to nominate young painters for purchase of their art. He was also involved, via the London Group, in the birth of the International Association of the Plastic Arts (Association Internationale des Arts Plastiques).

The IAPA – or as it was later known, the IAA (dropping the ambiguous term plastic), was the brainchild of the then Director General of Unesco, who in 1951 set up a committee of enquiry into the possibility of creating an international association of artists. Unesco was already interested in promoting the visual arts, and had held an important exhibition in 1946, to which Claude had contributed. A conference of artists was convened in Venice in 1952, and Henry Moore and Graham Sutherland were asked by the British Council to represent the United Kingdom. A first General Assembly was planned in 1954, also in Venice, to establish how many countries were willing to take part; it was naturally hoped that many would take part in a spirit of cooperation to help heal the wounds of the war. With the help of the Arts Council under Philip James, Britain was included in the original membership, and leading art societies throughout the country were asked to contribute financially and by sending delegates to the meetings. The London Group put up money and Claude put forward Richard Carline and Morris Kestelman as its first representatives. Each country qualified as a member by being fully representative of the arts in its own country; if it was able to do this, a provisional national committee was set up, which could be accepted by the IAA as a National Committee, sending delegates to each of the large international conferences. These were held once every three years. In 1956 Philip James called a meeting for representatives of ten of the leading artists' associations in the United Kingdom asking them to set up a provisional national committee, and at this meeting it was agreed that membership should be open to all societies of practising painters, sculptors and engravers of professional standing, and individual artists of national standing. Many art institutions joined although the Royal Academy always refused to do so. In 1957 The United Kingdom National Committee was accepted into the body of Unesco, with Morris Kestelman as its chairman.

Claude took part in many of the international conferences – Venice in 1954, Dubrovnik in 1957, Vienna in 1960, New York in 1963 – which he enjoyed chiefly for the parties and the opportunities for sightseeing. He relished the more bizarre meetings with artists of other nationalities. A letter to Elsie from Dubrovnik gave an idea of his experiences. "The receptions at Dubrovnik were very well done and extremely entertaining. One really got to know the other delegates too. In order to facilitate things one wore a little plaque with our name written on it. Delegate approaches CR 'Mr Rogers are you paint or sculp?' 'Oh well matter of fact I paint. And ah - er - Mr Tchewvanvokavitchski, do YOU paint or sculp?' 'Oh. Me I am the paint. But I have the bad estomach. I am the sculp also - for the exercise.' "[1]

Claude played a major part in a conference held in London in 1965 on the professional training of the artist, preparing exhaustive questionnaires about art schools in all the member countries and analysing the answers. He was passionately committed to the teaching of art; although he believed that one could not teach a person to be an artist, he felt the study of art was as serious a form of study as any other university subject, and provided the best possible liberal education. He was not an ideal committee man, and as chairman of meetings would tend to let them ramble, being himself of a rambling disposition; but he was conscientious and committed.

In 1959 his services to the nation both as an artist and as a teacher were officially recognised, and he was awarded the OBE. This award caused him a mixture of pleasure and embarrassment. Perhaps there was some disappointment - Coldstream had been given a knighthood in 1956 - but there was also delight at the recognition, mixed with discomfort at his mother's extreme euphoria and insistence that every letter she wrote should carry the correct insignia. When, in April 1965, he was elected a Fellow of University College London, an accolade of which he was very proud, his mother sent the following letter: "So now you are Prof C M Rogers OBE FUC which of these ought to appear on an ordinary letter? Any case whatever you are my son, and I am only glad that the baby not 2 year old who screamed a night because he could not make the letters he had admired on a Railway platform, and smiled when his mummy said 'What a lovely A' persevered. Love darling Mother."[2] However, there is no doubt that he enjoyed being recognised as a figure in the artistic establishment of the day.

As president of the London Group, Claude was anxious to restore it to the commanding position among exhibiting societies that it had had before the war. This was a problem, which he summed up at one of the Group's special general meetings. "The art situation, as it has developed in the last two decades, has been most encouraging for artists as a whole. But the effect on the exhibiting societies has been bad. It has become easier for the young and talented painter to have a one-man show or to find a gallery interested in his work. Compared with 1939 there must be roughly four times the number of commercial galleries in London. It is easier to sell work, easier to start on a professional career . . . As a result the probationary period of the young artists has been pushed back. It now takes place in an art school, not, as formerly, in a grim period of years after leaving. The London Group was once the proving ground of the young artist. It is not quite so much now . . ."[3] Claude still considered the London Group to be "the only association of exhibiting artists worth a hoot"; he tried to update and modernise it, and he was instrumental in arranging the successful retrospective Jubilee Exhibition at the Tate in the summer of 1964. He summarised the show: "the consensus of informed opinion seems to have been that the exhibition contained a very high proportion indeed of serious work with a number of outstanding quality: that the exhibition helped to throw light on the course of painting in England during the last fifty years; and that the liberal outlook and unprejudiced approach of the Group continued to have value today."[4] This exhibition was Claude's swansong; after thirteen years as president he stepped down in 1965.

Claude was increasingly finding his individual voice as a painter. His 1954 exhibition at the Leicester Galleries had shown him developing his powers of observation and the scope of his creative imagination. It was followed in 1955 by a restrospective exhibition of his work which opened at the Hatton Gallery of King's College in the University of Durham, where Lawrence Gowing was Professor of Fine Art, and which then toured its sixty two pictures to Manchester, Bristol and Leicester. In 1960 he opened the new decade with a one-man exhibition at the Leicester Galleries, his last show there. He shared the galleries with Anne Dunn and Earl Haig, who remarked that "fifteen years ago we were almost as close together at the Camberwell School of Art. I was a student there and Rogers was my teacher." In this exhibition Claude showed 25 new paintings, at prices ranging from 90 guineas to 350 guineas: two portraits, a self-portrait, four still life paintings, along with landscapes, among them the first of a new series on the subject of burning stubble.

In the catalogue to this exhibition Claude wrote that "the landscapes in this exhibition were painted at Somerton, near Hartest, Suffolk. It is such an English countryside that the approach road has the identification number of B1066. In the later summer the combines are at work, leaving behind a trail of straw cut so short that it is often of little use. This is ploughed in as a fertiliser, but it is often burnt before the ploughing. I found the burning an astonishing and beautiful sight, and several pictures in the exhibition are the result of drawings done in the fields while this was going on".[5] The burning stubble paintings created a stir amongst the critics. Writing in *Apollo*, Horace Shipp exulted "We are back in the Open Air at the Leicester Gallery where alongside Earl Haig's rather heavy-handed abstracts of landscape and figure, and Anne Dunn's slighter evocations of natural forms, Claude Rogers has a series of fascinating variations on a theme of the burning of straw stubble after harvest. In his homeland in the Suffolk countryside he saw what he calls 'an astonishing and beautiful sight', made some drawings on the spot, and with these and his impressions created the scenes of the undulating fields, the tongues of flame licking the yellow earth, the swirling smoke meeting the wind at the top of the rise. The results are excellent. Rogers' normal landscape art can be movingly lovely, as witness the *Plough: into the Sun* in this exhibition. It can be banal as in the portrait of Lord Birkett. But in these pictures of a natural phenomenon which has stirred his imagination and given to his hand a subject spelling freedom of brushstroke and rhythmic composition, he has achieved something in the romantic yet literal English tradition where truth and beauty meet."[6]

In seizing on the subject of burning stubble Claude may have felt he had found a way in which he could free his brushstrokes, allowing a more expressionist handling of paint while not compromising with the truth of the subject or losing veracity. Claude was trying to move his work on, to experiment. Abstract expressionist work was being seen in London at that time, and this probably interested Claude. He was open to new ideas and acutely aware that new movements in art had to be fought for. Looking back historically, he had seen that "the generations of the 1880s and 1890s bore the brunt. Wyndham Lewis, Bomberg, Roberts, Nevinson and Epstein had really to fight for modern art and were scarred for life, saddled with a defensive hostility. The Bloomsbury cocoon defended a few. A few others like Ben Nicholson were fortunate enough to be able to stay singularly and warily aloof." Claude was against artists being in defensive positions. He looked at the new work with interest, and as a realist painter himself, he simply perceived the disposition of shapes within abstract work as an extreme form of realist painting. "Painters have always tried to convey an idea of reality by means of shape, whether this is entirely a reality of the mind or the reality of the visible world seen through their imagination."

He did not in fact see any great division between abstract and figurative art. But he knew that for him the outside world had to be the starting point. To some extent the subject dictated his handling of paint. Burning stubble as a subject invited gesture in the paintings – he could put the paint on in great swirls and smudges, while still maintaining a rigorous depiction of the shapes of the coils of fire. His perceptions were challenged. What did one actually see in the burning? What were the colours and shapes created? How could one give the flat plane of the picture the feeling of speed and heat and the insubstantiality of smoke with the landscape spread solidly underneath and receding into the distance? He did hundreds of drawings, looking for the characteristic shapes while avoiding too easy assumptions. He was forced to select shapes to represent the fire and smoke, and some of these, rolling across furrows and down hills, outlined in scarlet, are as solid as chariot wheels. In these paintings Claude also had the problem and the potential of incorporating time, movement and speed in the image; even human anxiety, the fear of burning, was a factor. He was again trying to paint the unpaintable – as in his seascapes, moving, intangible masses were represented in terms of their structure, often gaining a degree of solidity in the process. Sometimes he insisted too much, making an image too concrete for the subject, losing the element of surprise. But in most of the work there is a tension between the solidity of the painted shapes and the insubstantiality of the subject, and between the speed and fury of the subject and the deliberate slowness of creating the image, which gives the best of these pictures their dramatic power. If Claude insisted too heavily on his shapes, the paintings lost tension.

One critic picked up this loss of tension: "Mr Rogers' honesty and clarity of vision is of a sort which just robs the dramatic main theme of his collection – the burning of the stubble fields – of its ultimate edge of excitement. His handling of space, even when the values are as cleanly and sharply judged as they are in *Clover Field* or *Green Field, Hawkedon Church*, is curiously without depth and atmosphere, just as his even, shadowless light has a somewhat hygienic quality which avoids – except in the beautiful, rich autumn twilight of *Plough: into the Sun* – any suggestion of mystery. But a touch of these qualities would possibly have made the big *Wind Break*, with its great diagonal swing and spectacular vision of creeping flames, and coiling smoke, an even finer achievement than it is. Only in one picture does Mr Rogers attempt the somewhat easier, romantic drama of the fire at night; his best effects are seen in *Fire down-wind*, where the flames break in scarlet through a swirl of silver-grey smoke, and particularly in *Burning Field*, where in broad sunlight they snake in lines across a wide, gold slope of stubble."[7]

Alan Clutton-Brock, writing in *The Listener*, pondered on Claude's new subject. "For an artist who usually works slowly from nature, taking many sittings for a portrait and carefully guarding the subject of a still life from day to day, this might be thought an unpromising theme. Certainly it is not to be expected that this series should have the most characteristic features of his work, the gravity and composure, for example, of the other landscapes; but by way of compensation there are the brilliance and spirit of the handling, especially in the largest of the group, and many passages of rich and inventive colour. Moreover, this choice of an unusual subject is a natural reflection of a recent change, or rather shift, in the painter's style. He now paints a good deal more loosely than before, and with a new assurance; there is less modelling . . . and the colour is apt to be brighter and more resonant. The great merit of Rogers' painting is the breadth of the design, the amplitude and dignity which he gives to every form. The new freedom he has taken has not led to the loss of these qualities; on the contrary, the *Red Still Life*, though there is a marked simplification and even stylization of some of the forms, is one of the most impressive works he has ever painted, especially remarkable for the balance and serenity of the design. In the past the restraint which was needed to achieve such an effect was accompanied in some of the artist's work by a certain severity, even harshness, as if he had felt compelled to repress some natural exuberance. But in these new paintings, and particularly in the landscapes, there is certainly no repression; sweeping brushstrokes give the structure of the land and there is an uninhibited use of singing colour."[8]

Claude was not afraid of being experimental, of breaking out of his self-imposed gravitas, despite the fact that this was regretted by many admirers of his work. Keith Sutton writing in the *New Statesman* considered the *Red Still Life* the central picture of the exhibition. He ignored the painter's need to break new boundaries in his own work. Andrew Forge, an old friend and one of Claude's most perceptive critics, felt otherwise, and in a *Critics Broadcast* he averred "For years it has looked as though Rogers has rather wanted to suppress a lot of his own talent in the interest of a certain flat unyielding pictorial architecture. The drawing in his painting had become more and more rigidly attached to the edges of things, flatter, more static, his use of paint had become drier and less supple. But in the present pictures he seems to have burst clear of this self-imposed strait-jacket – the pictures breathe, they have space and a fast, free-moving rhythm."[9] Nevile Wallis, writing in the *Observer*, disagrees. "Claude Rogers' world at the Leicester Galleries is the clean, patterned sweep and spaciousness of the

East Anglian landscape, with an occasional portrait as searching as his own quizzical and piratic features. The London Group's president is most satisfying here in a partially abstracted table-piece, beautifully judged in tone; least happy when the burning stubble of the fields seduces him into a visionary sphere unsuited to a prose style."[10] Friends and colleagues took sides on his new painting. Hans Feibusch congratulated Claude, writing "You have achieved great freedom now, and it is based upon such solid experience, that in all this swirling flow of colour and shapes there is nothing uncontrolled or vague. To grasp the visual world so sharply and at the same time so imaginatively is a rare thing nowadays . . ."[11] Adrian Heath wrote "I have had very great pleasure from your wonderful exhibition; it's a pleasure too to write and tell you so; very few of the painters one has long admired seem to go on getting better. But you started remarkably and have consistently gone on consolidating and extending, a long story that brings to its contemplator happiness."[12]

Somerton was still a source of inspiration. Claude obtained intense pleasure from exploring the country around Somerton and looking for painting motifs; much of his pleasure can be sensed in a springtime letter to Susan Jacobsen. "I have involved myself in a spring landscape – everything growing madly . . . I practically see the ground disappear . . ." and "The fields look as though they had been ironed, not ploughed – velvety. I have been once or twice for a solitary walk down Rogers Lane. Yes, it is thus marked on a large map so I had to find it. It is a genuine, mud-bottomed, old fashioned lane of the sort I remember as a child – two ruts between banks and hedges. But it slopes downhill. The ruts are, at this time of the year, runnels of silver. Between them is a carpet of the greenest grass. The hedges are low cut. The green lane goes snaking away, the silvery water in the ruts dancing and gleaming in the most crisp and unexpected scimitar shapes . . ."[13] The battle to get the subject pinned down on the canvas could be arduous. And at the end of a Somerton summer he told her "I had a commission to paint a very large cornfield picture [this was *Cornfields at Somerton* painted between July 14 and September 30 1961 commissioned by Sir Dennis Proctor] and was rather relying on it. It was going fairly well too, but to paint it meant being there from 7.30 or 8 till about 10.30 when the light altered completely. It was a sunny sort of picture . . . lots of corn and a big branch cutting across the sky. Well, not only was it misty in the early morning – couldn't see a thing several days – but of course the corn got cut soon after. However, in anticipation of this I'd sweated away at it and got something I didn't altogether dislike for the nearer field.

However this was – or is – worked up out of all proportion to the rest and I can't get it right as a whole. Still I may – never know. But at the moment it doesn't look as though I shall be able to hand the picture over and that means no cheque which is very very sad indeed not to say grim."[14] Claude obviously finished the picture to his satisfaction the following week, signing it 'for Dennis Proctor' on the back, so presumably the essential cheque was forthcoming. But cheque or no, the painting would not have been handed over until it was fully resolved.

Claude was still trying to make his paintings look as 'real' as possible. Francis Hoyland remarked perceptively that "it is almost as if he wanted to achieve the impossible task of painting 'the thing itself' unmediated by perception. Cézanne shared this concern with holding a balance between percept and concept, but to him perception was an infinitely varied and shifting experience, whereas for Claude it was something that could be delineated in a set series of shapes that were susceptible to visual and manual measurement. Claude's interest in local colour was part of his interest in concepts – almost the verbally expressible concepts of things – whereas the tactics of his drawing remained, to a large extent, those of the Euston Road."[15] That Claude thought of painting almost as if he were making sculpture is borne out by John Wonnacott, who remembered Claude telling him that when painting a head he thought of it as a series of profiles, and that one should paint right to the edges of a thing. As a result his pictures are very strongly structured, and the objects within them as solid as models. Andrew Forge summed up his standpoint as a painter succinctly: "Representation is the *raison d'être* of his art. His subjects are not his picture's starting points but their goals. From first to last he pursues the reality of whatever it is in the outside world that made him want to paint."[16] Forge remarked on the relationship between Claude's drawing and his painting. The drawings are rigorous, each shape searched for and set down unequivocally, fixed and held still within its contour. The paint, which by the 1960s Claude was laying on in thicker slabs and layers, asserts the physicality of the shapes. As Forge says "It is there, it is there! he seems to be saying with each stroke of the brush, mashing in the paint. He uses it thickly and sometimes his insistence on the physical remaking of the subject leads him to astonishing effects as when the dense, opaque paint suddenly goes singing up into whites and pale blues as the form encounters the light, and one's eye expects to be able to penetrate and run round but finds one cannot. It is at such moments that the meaning of his style is clearest. The picture seems to be saying: It is here, it is here. Everything is here, flat on the surface."[17]

Throughout the 1950s and 1960s Susan Jacobsen was the recipient of many letters which show Claude's depth of interest in all facets of art history and his splendid descriptive powers. Their relationship was very close and Claude was unstinting in his desire to interest and amuse her in the letters. One letter describes a visit to the National Gallery ('Noshional Gillery' as his students maintained he pronounced it). "One of my pictures - a very early one - was damaged in the Euston Road show - at Brighton or somewhere - and Lucas of the National Gallery is going to repair it for the owners once the Insurance people give the OK. It's going to be rather a comic experience as at the moment he has, in that unpretentious little room, the *Virgin of the Rocks* nearly cleaned and the small Giorgione *Adoration of the Magi*. My word! You should see the *Virgin of the Rocks* now the muck has been removed. It is superb. Much less of a hole in the wall for one thing. The drawing is much clearer too, especially in the background. Rhuemann showed me some of the x-ray photographs. It seems that the initial lay in was done in a thin brown pigment, and that Leonardo manipulated this largely with his finger tips and the palm of his hand - stroking and rubbing the paint into place. It is rather eerie, looking at photographs of the edge of the canvas, to see the impressions of Leonardo's fingertips, as they left their mark when he lifted them from the tacky paint - clear and clean as a Scotland Yard record card."[18]

Another letter describes a visit to the Louvre where he copied a drawing of a *Rape of the Sabines* by Poussin. "This particular rape more or less showed you the different situations which faced a lusty young Roman in search of a mate. Some were having a frightful time of it. Not only was there the incumbrance of a kicking, yelling and hair-tearing girl arching back from brawny arms but worried Mama clung to his knees and bambinos rolled about his feet while conservative old Papa was doing his best to tear the toga from that Roman's back. Another chap was having quite a time wrestling daughter away from collapsed mum's embrace; and there were general chasings; and chaps passing floozies Rugby-football-wise to eager chaps on prancing horses. In the centre of the riot, however, *mirabile dictu*, a jolly and personable couple sauntered towards the left distance, he with one casual arm round a pneumatic haunch and the other hand waving airily at a distant hill crowned by an early version of a Blenheim Road villa, she pleased no doubt that she wouldn't have to marry boring old Scamander, and entranced by the virile and handsome personality of her very imminent ravisher, leaning cosily within his embrace, her head turned to catch his slightest intonation in the hubbub, and delighted that this hand had lifted her from the lucky dip. On the whole Poussin is not in the slightest sensuous . . . But in that chaste mythological never-never land of his there is staggering painting, marvellous design and . . . the most lovely colour."[19]

In 1963 J. Anthony Betts ARCA, Professor of Fine Art at the University of Reading, retired after a record twenty-nine years, and Claude was invited to apply for the post. After much thought, Claude accepted. The appointing committee had considered Harry Thubron, Lionel de Sausmarez and Philip Matthews for the job but hoped to attract Claude if possible. With his background and art teaching experience he was clearly a superb catch for Reading, and a particularly appropriate choice. Betts had run the school cleverly and efficiently, teaching all the time, building up a discipline of drawing and painting based on the example of Sickert and the Camden Town Group. This was an education that Claude himself had experienced and with which his own work was in harmony. He was, however, ambitious for expansion and development, and education was expanding at a great rate. Reading University was re-establishing itself and growing, and by the early '60s was moving into new buildings on a new site. Claude was able to take advantage of government money pouring into universities at that time. He was able to broaden the scope of the painting school to cover a wider range of artistic interests and introduce History of Art and Typography and Graphic Communication (the first course of its kind in the country) into the curriculum, as well as introducing in 1968 a postgraduate course leading to an MA, with Terry Frost in charge.

Reading School of Art was over 100 years old when Claude took on the Professorship. The idea for an art school had been proposed in 1858, but suitable premises became vacant only when the Reading Working Men's Club closed down in 1860. The original school opened with C R Havell, a local man, as Master, and 68 pupils - 20 in the Ladies' morning class and the rest in general evening classes. In 1870 the School of Art moved in with the newly founded School of Science to a shared building and a decade later united with the Oxford University Extension Centre to form a University Extension College. In 1902 this became a full University College teaching Letters (including Fine Art), Science and Agriculture.

As Professor, Claude was only the sixth incumbent. Morley Fletcher had taken over from C R Havell in 1897 and had introduced the technique of woodblock printing, which he had learned in Japan. His interest in printmaking and illustration was continued by W Seaby, a pupil of Morley Fletcher's who became the second Professor of Fine Art after W G Collingwood (first Professor 1905–11). At Seaby's invitation distinguished visitors came to the school including A S Hartrick, painter, printmaker and illustrator, and Walter Crane, painter, illustrator, writer and teacher. Seaby himself excelled in drawing animals and plants and the spacious premises around the school held cages of birds and animals for the students to draw. Roger Fry and Walter Sickert visited the school. Betts continued the printmaking and illustrative traditions, and was instrumental in appointing Robert Gibbings, the founder of the Golden Cockerel Press, as lecturer in Typography, Book Production and Engraving, and later William McCance, founder of the Gregynog Press, to a similar post.

Reading had a good record of promoting excellence in arts and crafts. It also had potential for development. The Professorship must have been irresistible to Claude (most of his friends were by now professors) and so must the full-time salary. Nevertheless he agonised over his decision. He was not a natural administrator, leaning towards creative chaos rather than streamlined efficiency. Also by this time the effects of diabetes made him tire suddenly and easily. Most of all, he loved London and the Slade with its familiar routine of teaching and spare time to paint. In April he wrote to William Townsend about his decision. "When they approached me I thought I'd better have a look (can't be many jobs coming along at my age, I thought; and we have to leave Taviton Street [London University repossessed the house] and Elsie's Gypsies are getting worse and worse). I must say the committee I saw were charming. The buildings were intriguing if odd (the original studios designed by Whistler and Pennell). A very good Prof's Studio (Betts has two desks in it and a lot of cupboards etc.) They said I could have a tutor-secretary (à la Ian) and, presently, make additions or alterations to staff . . . I spent an agonising three weeks dithering. In a way, it seems crazy leaving London, the Slade and all my friends there and I continue to have savage twinges. But I have felt over the past year or so that I wasn't contributing much to the Slade. It's very alive and the younger teachers are the important thing now. I shall miss Bill and you and the rest. Reading is near London, anyway, so I must try and get you all down and come up to town myself.

"It isn't a big school – about 80 students. The teaching is limited (only this last year has any abstract painting been done) – Sickerty. The syllabus and examination requirements are odd, beside being old-fashioned. Some of it will be easy enough to alter; but some of it wants careful examination to see what is there – what it actually means in terms of art education. The main thing that worries me is that (in common with all students irrespective of the subject they will ultimately read) the art student upon entry begins by working for a 'first examination for BA'. This he takes at the end of two terms and for it he must offer three subjects, two of which must be other than the subject he will read . . . In each case the syllabus is considerable. I cannot see that there can be much time for drawing and painting – nothing comparable to the time given in a pre-diploma course for instance – and such requirements must limit the kind of student it is possible to take. The University are proud of this arrangement of having equated Fine Art to other Arts subjects; and of an arrangement by which the student begins with a broad field of study. Its difficulties for the Fine Art student are apparent if one considers how much less advanced the school leaver is in art as compared with other disciplines . . .

"As you can imagine I have been giving considerable thought to the 'tutor-secretary'. The only real idea I have had is Tom Cross whom I like (which is a lot). He has, I gather, done a really good job in the Welsh Arts Council and I know he'd like a change. He knows art schools and has reasonable administrative experience. Don't know if he would like to do administrative work in an art school though . . ."[20] Tom Cross, a former pupil of Claude's at the Slade, was persuaded to accept the job; and armed with his administrative skills and those of the newly appointed Art Historian Peter Fitzgerald, Claude set about modifying and updating the School of Fine Art at Reading. He worked on much the same principles as those adopted by Coldstream at the Slade, encouraging a broader and more catholic approach to the visual arts. He inherited a complete staff – Harry Redman, Hugh Finney, Tom Barratt, Frank Ormerod the printmaker, and Christopher Lane and Norman Dillworth as sculptors. Without moving any of them, Claude introduced first visiting teachers and then permanent staff. He disregarded the qualifications deemed necessary for a university department; what mattered in the staff he appointed was that they were good artists. He combed the degree shows for promising young artists whom he thought would make good teachers. He was not afraid of taking on young and relatively untried tutors; both John Wonnacott and Ray Atkins were recruited as young men from Norwich School of Art. These two painters were to cover the figurative side of painting and to run the life room. Peter Kalkhof was put in charge of printmaking, and two part-time sculptors, Carol Hodgson and Louis Maurice were added to the sculpture department. Roger Cook and Rita Donagh were appointed to full-time jobs almost straight from their degree courses and while still in their early twenties. Claude surprised Rita Donagh by preferring her to several men also in the running for the job; unusually especially for that time Claude took female artists seriously.

Claude's admissions policy for students was equally informal; he disregarded any need for examination qualifications, but merely looked at the portfolio of work for signs of individual talent. Suzanne Monelle, a former student under Claude's professorship at Reading, recalled how he personally had picked her out 'from the bottom of the heap' and made her feel of value. To her, Claude was a father figure, fostering an ability he recognised; and it did not matter whether one was male or female, the only thing that counted was the ability to paint. Another former student, John Bangs (currently Principal Officer for Special Educational Needs with the National Union of Teachers), was a beneficiary of Claude's system and remembered his initial interview with Claude. "I came from a secondary modern school. Claude didn't care that I only had an E grade in A level art. He liked my work and, probably, that I was from a secondary modern school . . . I remember him saying that above all he wanted a social mix of students. He consciously chose people from a whole range of backgrounds; pre-dip, post-dip, grammar and secondary modern schools; and finishing schools . . . I don't think Claude put social mix before talent but it allowed him to make some quirky choices."[21]

Claude brought in visiting lecturers such as Richard Hamilton, Ralph Brown, George Fullard, Antony Green, Euan Uglow, Michael Andrews, Robin Denny, David Hockney, Prunella Clough and Frank Auerbach, whose visits encouraged a sub-expressionist tendency amongst the students. Joseph Beuys made several visits. The work of the permanent staff represented all facets of abstract and conceptual art, as well as figuration. There was no overarching school style. Claude's policy was to provide variety and to force students to be aware of different ideologies in art. The keynote was a striving for originality. As John Bangs put it, "Claude's strength and also his main weakness was that he expected everyone to be an original, fully-fledged modern artist, even if they had just joined the department at the age of nineteen. This left each year with some casualties . . . and a lot of students non-skilled. We never had a consistent technical training. On the other hand, his expectation really kicked everyone into following their own path, with each student encouraging each other rather than following a single art school style."[22]

Claude treasured the fact that Reading was a small intimate University at the time he went there; it was "a halcyon time for higher education, with wide-ranging government plans for expansion." The

Art School's place within the wider context of the University served to dampen art student preciousness and brought in a wide range of ideas from other departments. Reading during the 1960s seemed to the students a unique hive of ideas, providing the best possible liberal education as a preparation for life.

Claude spent three or four days a week at Reading. He was regularly in the studios talking to the students, and he also painted in his own room. He never in fact acquired living quarters in Reading, he and Elsie and the family maintaining their house in London. He would drive to Reading in his old Jaguar. Luckily by this time he had passed his driving test, having only learned to drive at the same time as Crispin. An early driving test report, preserved among his papers, records that he failed because he did not, among other things, "take suitable precautions before starting the engine, take correct and prompt action on all signals by traffic signs, regulate speed to suit varying road and traffic conditions or make proper use of accelerator or gears"! Even after passing his test he was something of a danger on the road.

Claude installed a sofa-bed in his room and he roosted there during term-time, breakfasting at the Café Olé nearby and dining either with colleagues or picnicking in his studio. Ian Tregarthen Jenkin remembered visiting Claude at Reading and prowling around the studios in the evening, collecting plates and forks and cups from the students' still life arrangements on which to eat an improvised evening meal. This mode of life was strictly against the University rules and the Bursar tried in vain to stop it, but Claude remained deaf to his rebukes. A bit of excitement was generated when word got around that Professor Hodges was sleeping in the University. Professor Hodges was an aged and distinguished professor of aesthetics, married, with a house in Reading. The university staff were very worried until they ascertained that the culprit was Professor Rogers.

Claude's salary on his appointment at Reading was £4,000 per annum, which represented a considerable increase on his Slade salary. Most of the administrative burden was taken off his shoulders by Tom Cross. He also had a full time secretary. He was able, and expected, to paint in his room at Reading. It was important that he should be seen to do so by the students. He was in fact one of the last of the old working professors.

Time was of no consequence to Claude. Living as he did in his room, the hours stretched well into the night. He would spend a whole morning drafting a letter, and the letters would go through copious drafts, filling the day nicely. Tom Cross and Peter Fitzgerald acted as a pair of guardian angels, making sure he went to the right meetings, extracting letters from the 'Thursday file' where incoming mail was buried, and making sure they were answered. Neither of them would allow him to drive his Jaguar if they were in it, and they often chauffeured him to meetings. On a previous occasion he had failed to negotiate a bend in his Jaguar and had driven straight into a house where some people were eating lunch. Needless to say they had been 'terribly nice' about it – people were always 'terribly nice' in Claude's stories.

A major event at Reading was Claude's delivery of a lecture on the Euston Road School of Drawing and Painting. This was given on March 6th 1969 at the request of Peter Fitzgerald, and was clearly going to be something of importance. Claude found lecturing nerve-racking and often had to take valium beforehand; he found it difficult to organise his material and no amount of persuasion from Fitzgerald could induce him to produce a written draft beforehand, although he agreed to try and edit his notes down to one hour. His inside knowledge of the subject was vast and a lecture on the Euston Road was certain to be a historical event. The word got around London and many distinguished people came to Reading, packing the small lecture theatre. The lecture not only overran the time but also the emergency tape provided to record it, lasting for three and a half hours. Nobody, however, left the room. The audience was held spellbound as he relived his personal memories of the years before the war. Most of the lecture survives on tape as a very fresh and personal account of the Euston Road days. He saw the events of that time very much in terms of personalities; there is no wrestling with abstract ideas or ideologies.

Claude's introduction of new staff who taught with a Conceptual or Pop orientation caused a rift within the department which broadly divided into sides: abstract and figurative. Abstract and Conceptual painting, which had swept into Britain from America, had become the fashionable avant-garde, and was quickly seized on by students in the art schools. Claude, eager that Reading should be in the forefront of art education, felt that his department should encompass all the new ideas. New tutors would make sure the students had the 'latest' in art education. Claude probably did not envisage that this would cause a schism within the department or generate anger. He himself had been perfectly comfortable all his life with non-figurative painting – close friends such as Victor Pasmore and his brother-in-law Merlyn Evans were abstract painters – and he had not in the past felt this to be a threat to his own work. It is possible that he became conscious of the marginalisation of figurative painters during the 1960s, aware that "poor deserving artists were losing their perishing good names." In the face of the rather bullying stance adopted by abstract painters, it seems he came to believe that figurative painting, with its more factual approach, was the province of lesser mortals and that abstract painters, operating in the more rarified atmosphere of pure ideas, held the ideological high ground. Coldstream seems to have shared this view and was well known for leaning over backwards to accommodate the latest fad and taking it seriously. Both he and Claude may have given some credence to ideas of Platonic 'essences' and psychological theories about intrinsically valuable visual forms lost in human race-memory. They may have pondered again on the idea of 'synaesthesia' and of all art aspiring to music, which is necessarily abstract. Claude, curiously enough, appears to have made no comments about this in his writings. In his painting he knew that he could 'only' work from nature. It is a common human characteristic to discount what one can do well. Claude may have felt that his own way of working within a tradition of painting did not break new ground and therefore did not carry much weight. As a natural conciliator perhaps he had difficulty arguing the cause of painting from nature. In the face of disagreement within his department, he seems to have taken the line of least resistance. By the end of the 1960s staff and students throughout the country were having meetings to declare life painting a waste of time and space, and Reading was no exception. John Wonnacott and Ray Atkins had been appointed by Claude to teach life painting and to stand for the perceptual attitude to art. At Reading they never had a good fixed life room as they had at Norwich School of Art, but were kept on the move from room to room, although Claude always found the money for models. However, the pressure on Claude to abandon life painting was severe, and he finally let it, and them, go.

The students were aware of a division amongst the staff, with the abstract lobby gaining the upper hand. The small group of students who worked in the life room with Ray Atkins and John Wonnacott were seen as reactionaries. One former student, Dulcie Foo Fat, remembered that those years were not very comfortable for students interested in figurative painting, and recalls the disdain which was heaped upon one poor girl who wanted to make William Blake the subject of an extended essay.

Claude believed passionately in Terry Frost as a fine painter and supported his ideas on painting. Frost was not in favour of slow, measured painting in front of the motif; his own work was concerned with reinventing sensory experience in paint. He rejected the Euston

Road methods of painting, the painstaking acquisition of hand-eye coordination, seeing them as "away from life, reality, away from the spiritual, there is no magic, no connection with the 'spirit', no poetry, just dull academic 'rightness'." Above all he felt it dangerous for teachers to dominate their pupils, and he felt the figurative painters tried to do so, incurring the risk of arresting their students' artistic development. The department of Fine Art at Reading adopted a policy of 'self-determination' in the teaching of art, with students given maximum freedom to experiment, to develop their own ideas, to reinvent the wheel. There was very little specialised content in the teaching – it was done by osmosis, by the exchange of ideas, and by comparing notes with other students. Originality was at a premium. Naturally this suited some students more than others. Some worked; some did no work at all. There remain some who definitely regretted the absence of compulsory objective drawing during their art school years. Thirty years later, the debate on the best way of teaching art is still open.

There is no doubt, however, that Claude's Professorship at Reading raised the profile of the Art School and made it one of the more exciting in Britain. Claude's friends from all over the country visited it, and their visits proved a rich mixture for the students. Claude inaugurated a Senior Common Room Dining Club which held lunches once or twice a term. Terry Frost remembered one at which Coldstream and Claude, both nearing retirement, agreed they would reopen the Euston Road School with the same pupils, now sufficiently wealthy to afford the fees, and the same models. The thought of these wrinkled old females had them really excited.

The late sixties were a time of general upheaval in the universities and in Claude's view the disturbances had a lasting influence on art education, reinforcing the popular suspicion that the art student is a radical and disruptive being. He was forced to cope with the upheaval in the standards and expectations of students while assessing other degree shows. His friend Stanislav Frenkiel remembered on one occasion, when examining with Claude at a London College of Education, being confronted by a young woman who announced "I regard you two old men as has-beens and I don't think you are fit to examine me. You belong to a different generation and a lost world, and it is as if I were to be examined by dinosaurs." Frenkiel was ready to explode but Claude defused the situation by drawling in reply: "My dear young woman, WE don't want to examine YOU. You ASKED to be examined. If you don't want us, please tell your teachers and we won't examine you. You can go out of this room and never come here again." After frenzied consultations outside, the student re-entered with an abject apology.[23]

Kenneth Gribble remembered Claude telling him of an occasion when he was examining with Robert Medley and a group of other tutors. The tutors were invited into a studio which was empty but for a row of chairs, on which they were asked to sit. The lights were switched off and when switched on again, a naked man stood there. The lights were switched off and on, and each time the naked man was revealed in a more provocative stance. Robert Medley became seriously excited, and in order to placate him the student was given a first-class degree.[24]

If Claude's benevolent professorship at Reading established the art school as a leader amongst British art schools, it had a less positive effect on his painting. He was 56 when he took on the job, and his age, combined with diabetes, made him tire easily. His sudden lapses into sleep could be embarrassing; it was sometimes difficult to explain to a nervous student being interviewed that the professor was sound asleep because he was diabetic. Terry Frost recalled going with Claude on a visit to Rowneys the paint manufacturers, and being very embarrassed at the splendid lunch laid on for them to hear Claude snoring loudly. He was forced to engage the company's attention while Claude slept unselfconsciously in the middle of the assembled directors.[25]

The travelling-and-camping schedule at Reading began to take a toll on Claude's health. He also suffered Bell's Palsy in 1967. Apart from one or two portrait commissions (Professor Blackett was painted in Claude's room at Reading) not much painting was done. By 1968 he began to worry about this. He was forced to decline from showing with the London Group because he was saving his few paintings for a suggested one-man show which did not in fact materialise. He wrote to Andrew Forge about the problem. "The trouble is that in these two years I have only completed about five paintings I would care to show . . . I really need a sabbatical . . . I've been teaching without a break since the war, three and four days a week and could do with a sabbatical however short . . . I have a place to paint at Reading but the work I try and do there is even slower than usual. There are too many distractions and interruptions."[26]

It was not merely the distractions and interruptions. Claude was forced to question the ideological base of his own work in the light of the new ideas being explored in his own art school. At the Euston Road and at the Slade he had been surrounded by other like-minded painters. At Reading his work was out on a limb. He probably came to view it as rather old-fashioned and certainly Elsie often remarked that their work in those days seemed boring. But he was enough of an artist to look for a way out of the *impasse* he felt himself to be in. In 1969 he thought he had found it. He went on a flight to Athens with Peter Fitzgerald and the sight of the Alps from above, with the wing of the aeroplane extended over deep space, moved and excited him. For the next six years he painted a series of aerial views, done from drawings made inside the aeroplanes. The subject must have appealed to him as a way of putting together flatter, more abstract shapes – a last bid, as it were, for abstraction. He had been interested in the visual aspect of flight when he was taken up in a plane during the war, but the sudden excitement of seeing wingtips against space as a possible motif for painting came years later. Once bitten, he became so obsessed with these aerial images that he found himself a way of flying more frequently. He judged an amateur painting competition in Reading and quixotically gave the prize to a man whose abstract painting struck him as unusual amongst a lot of dull, competent work. It transpired that the prizewinner was a pilot flying regularly to Copenhagen, and Claude flew with him whenever he liked on provision that he never left the airport precincts. He flew as much as possible, drawing and making notes for paintings: "Perfect flight. Little cloud even at 26,000. Drew hard over Alps again but perhaps 2 seats further back than last time so not the same view . . .

"Breaking Cloud: red of wing still apparent through the streaming overcase though misty. The aluminium parts of the wing . . . almost invisible – same tonality as vapour but some diff, in colour. Huge shapes of cumulus heads and glimpses of blue and confused; big movements; higher cumulus heads silvery: below darker (but not v.d.) edge of wing b. against it and in part defined by an ochre line. Scale of cloud (against wing) big. Saw a little to my side so that plane spar often cast a dense shadow . . . the changes of angle in a wing v. important."[27]

Claude painted over thirty large aeroplane paintings and in them experimented with the placing of wing against void, or cloud over distant land, working in a range of shapes and colours he had hardly used previously. In most cases the design of the painting is satisfying and the colour is often beautiful – *Zeider Zee* exploits a wonderful mid-blue – but one tends to miss the intricate lines and worked, gnarled paint that the persistent pattern of observation/correction, observation/correction produced in his work. In these airy paintings the paint surface is as flat as the canvas. They look modern but sometimes bland. It is possible that Claude's desire to move with the times in his work forced him into a larger scale which he found difficult to handle, and he was most successful in smaller pictures such as *Flying into the Alps*. But these paintings are always heroic attempts. In them Claude was trying to incorporate, not only indications of speed and movement, but also weight above lightness and the anti-gravitational anxiety of being airborne. He was again trying to paint the unpaintable.

The aeroplane pictures sparked off another series of paintings done from a high vantage point, the *City at Night* group, which he painted from the attic of his Highgate house. These paintings of the city lights receding into distance have similar maze-like designs and flattened shapes, and Claude used a beautiful range of violet blue-blacks against yellows and browns. The suggestion of great distances creates a tension with the flatness of the canvas and they are dramatic and powerful. With these works Claude came as near to abstraction as he could without sacrificing the intensely observed qualities characteristic of his art.

NOTES

1 Claude Rogers letters, collection Mr Crispin Rogers.
2 Claude Rogers Papers, Tate Gallery Archive.
3 Claude Rogers, Minutes of Special General Meeting of the London Group, November 5 1961.
4 Claude Rogers Papers, Tate Gallery Archive.
5 Claude Rogers, Introduction to catalogue of exhibition.
6 Shipp, Horace, *Apollo*, April 1960.
7 *The Times*, March 7 1960.
8 Clutton-Brock, Alan, *The Listener*, March 17 1960.
9 Forge, Andrew, *The Critics Broadcast*, March 13 1960.
10 Wallis, Nevile, *The Observer*, March 1960.
11, 12 Claude Rogers Papers, Tate Gallery Archive.
13, 14 Claude Rogers letters, collection Mrs Susan Jacobsen.
15 Hoyland, Francis, letter to J Pery December 12 1992.
16, 17 Forge, Andrew, *The Studio*, January 1958.
18, 19 Claude Rogers letters, collection Mrs Susan Jacobsen.
20 Claude Rogers Papers, Tate Gallery Archive.
21, 22 Bangs, John, letter to J Pery August 13 1992.
23 Interview with Stanislav Frenkiel, March 11 1992.
24 Interview with Kenneth Gribble, February 4 1993.
25 Interview with Terry Frost and Tom Cross, March 19 1992.
26, 27 Claude Rogers Papers, Tate Gallery Archive.

The end game

The halcyon years were coming to an end. In March 1970 Elsie had a stroke. She was then 61 years of age. The stroke felled her in the bathroom of the Highgate house, and she was wedged in there, unable to move or speak, until an ambulance crew managed to extract her and get her to University College Hospital. Claude was completely shattered. He had treated Elsie somewhat cavalierly all his life, and his relationships with other women were generally known to her, although rarely discussed. He now rallied to her side and was with her all day every day, partly in the belief that constant attention would restore speech and movement and partly in an attempt to expiate his sense of guilt. He forgot Reading and simply did not appear there for weeks. He shunned his female friends, and remained all day in the hospital. Elsie later wrote "my husband showed me great devotion and he was with me from between ten or eleven in the morning until I was settled down to sleep, that is except when he went out to snatch a hasty meal. I remember that he made me laugh a lot during those first weeks, what about I do not know, but shared laughter is a form of communication. He also played a game with me when I was able to nod and shake my head; when I was brought into hospital I could neither move nor speak."[1] Claude was determined to bring her back to full possession of her faculties, and his efforts were eventually repaid. One day when he was watering the flowers in her room, talking as usual all the time, he said to himself "Oh drat these flowers, what are they called?" and he heard from behind him a hoarse whisper "Hydrangea". It was the first word Elsie managed to utter. Later, after she was moved to a hospital in Wimbledon, she clearly had something to say, and after trying and trying she finally managed to blurt out "Claude, you smell. You need a bath."

Claude's devotion inspired Elsie to fight back and she rallied well; in June Claude was able to write to his colleague Frank Bowling in New York "As to Elsie, that gal really has got guts. When you were over here she was absolutely flat out, unable to move or talk and now and it is really very little time, she is walking about without a stick most of the time and talking quite a lot, if slowly, and even beginning to move her right hand."[2] Six years later, in 1976, Claude was still marvelling at her courage. In a letter to George Sweet he wrote "the Few sisters are incredible in their guts, Margerie pulling herself up by her shoelaces after Merlyn's death and Elsie refusing to be put down by her stroke and doing her left-handed collage and now driving. I take off my dutch cap to them."[3]

Elsie's right arm and leg never fully recovered, and she was forced to train herself to write with her left hand. She could no longer paint, but she took to making large and elegant collage pictures. Claude helped her with them, placing the cut shapes for her on the background while Elsie lay in bed directing operations. Examples of these collages are in the Tate collection. Inevitably Elsie had to retire from her job at Gipsy Hill Training College, handing over the headship of the department to her colleague Stanislav Frenkiel. She was now at home all the time, and Claude was needed. Elsie's predicament and his own ill-health made retirement for him seem sensible; he retired from Reading as Professor Emeritus early in 1972.

While attending to Elsie in hospital, Claude had made drawings in hospital, of her and the nurses who looked after her. These drawings bore fruit in one small painting, *The Paraplegic*, now in the Tate. It shows Elsie attempting to walk down a hospital corridor, supported by two nurses. Her mouth is slightly open, she is clearly anxious and unsteady, and the nurses are carefully and patiently taking her weight. Their bent legs, rendered in the picture in strips of flat black paint, are beautifully observed, and the colours are fresh and true. Claude's desire to face the facts of his personal disaster with an unprejudiced eye has resulted in one of his best paintings - prosaic and accurately recorded, yet tender and humane. He has dealt with intractable material in terms of subject, composition and colour, to create a small masterpiece. When he himself was in hospital, he pondered on this choice of subject. "To my friends, on the whole it is a bit eccentric - and to some . . . horrific, this interest of mine in hospital life as a scene to be observed and painted. It isn't (on my part) an interest in human misery though there is enough of that too. I am interested I suppose in the behaviour of my ward companions. I see them in bed, seated at table, in groups (especially the nurses who naturally group themselves in the course of the ward routines). But there is a content, overtones, the tenderness of these young girls with young and old and especially the lost old men. And some of these in their irrationality are a marvel and neither tragic nor comic nor sentimental and the nurses deal with them with simplicity too."[4]

Claude and Elsie's life was enlivened by Crispin's marriage in December 1971 to a Danish girl, Kirsten Loubjerg Hansen. Crispin and Kirsten lived in Denmark for about two years, and Claude and Elsie visited them there. Claude was very productive, bringing home a crop of small paintings from this visit. In 1974 a grandson, Timothy, was born.

Claude at first welcomed his retirement. He had for years been longing for more time to paint, and he relished his new freedom. He described it in a letter to his friend Kenneth Gribble: "It was an extraordinary satisfaction to get into a rhythm again, to wake up day after day, and to know that however horrific the present state of the canvas on your easel happened to be, you would presently be off, after breakfast, to face up to it. One went into the room, had a good look, and then began squeezing out paint. Suddenly the light seemed to be getting bad, and to one's surprise, it was already 2.30 or 4 o'clock."[5]

Elsie bought Claude a studio in Tasker Road (2 Mall Studios), a big room with a gallery/bedroom and bathroom and a small kitchen and garden at the back. Claude spent much of the day there painting, and his productivity greatly increased. He continued work on his series of aeroplane pictures, interspersing these with Suffolk landscapes or foreign townscapes. He visited his friend Rosemary Pearce, who worked for the British Council in Athens, in 1969, 1971 and 1972, and kept sporadic notes on the work he did while in Greece. "I have done 3 paintings so far – tiny. They are v. slight of course but – here – look as though they've caught something of the bright light and clarity. However, remembering those little paintings I brought back from Aix-en-Provence in '38, how gay they looked in Aix and how grey when I unpacked them back in England, I begin to wonder."[6] Another note testified to Claude's methods of working and his need to 'switch off brain' in order to let the painting develop. "Made some real progress – I think – with my painting. Not what I thought would happen exactly – well it never is that – and had a pretty low opinion of it . . . But saw next day that something had happened – I had just concentrated on drawing in colour and line and let every idea go hang – something unexpected, so that suddenly, city, mountains and sky and for the first time, really seemed to me to be of a single thought (may be wrong of course)".[7]

It is probably impossible for painters to grasp the complex relationships within themselves between intellect and intuition – the right mixture to produce their best work is perhaps only hit on instinctively and cannot be expressed in words. Claude clearly puzzled over this, and never quite managed to handle himself optimally in order to produce consistently top quality work; sometimes he did, sometimes he did not, and it seems he was never quite sure why.

Claude channelled his efforts into working for a major retrospective exhibition. This was organised by Peter Fitzgerald at Reading, and opened at the Whitechapel Gallery in April 1973. The exhibition, which toured to six different cities, contained 128 paintings and drawings, dating from 1928 to the early months of 1973, and showed all the stages in Claude's development as a painter, from the Euston Road paintings, the street scenes of Chiswick influenced by Sickert, the Bonnard-like landscapes of the 1930s, the post-war 'transitional' paintings leading on to the firmly-designed, flattened work of the 1950s, as well as the later series of stubble burning, aeroplane views and hospital paintings. Andrew Forge, in his introduction to the exhibition catalogue, pointed out that throughout Claude's work there was "a characteristic reaching out for shape", which became the cardinal unit in his picture-making and that the flattening of forms within a clearly defined contour freed him to use pure, local colour symbolic of the object described (eg pink flesh, blue uniform) rather than passages of colour altering with the fall of light. Forge asked himself if Claude's academic approach to painting and drawing placed him in some sort of anachronistic backwater, but concluded that "the painter working from observation seems to remain in some kind of eternal present."

Marina Vaizey, reviewing the show in the *Financial Times*, picked up the question of Claude's position in contemporary art. "Much of the most intellectually stimulating new art has abandoned the conventional uses of paint on a surface, and correspondingly, much new painting seems sterile and dull. Every once in a while, a resounding exhibition comes along though to reaffirm my spectator's faith in the power of that old-fashioned paint on canvas, and such an exhibition is the present retrospective of Claude Rogers . . . Rogers has painted what he knows, from people to landscape to those eerie views that aeroplanes rush over. Scenes of sombre restraint, like *Bloomsbury under Snow* have a still, sparkling immediacy; he gets at the feel of things, animate and inanimate, and his consistent development, his sturdy skill, his robust sensitivity, show what still can be done with pencil and paper, brush, paint and canvas. His colours are often surprisingly vivid, and rewardingly subtle, textures and impasto varied according to need of image rather than theory."[8] Tim Hilton reviewed the show in *The Studio*, remarking that "the dignity which comes strongly out of Claude Rogers' retrospective has a lot to do with a non-tricky, unswervable dedication to making paintings . . . their frankness (and modesty) shows a fine type of artistic veracity."[9] And John Russell, writing in the *Sunday Times*, noted that "to catch a one-man show by Claude Rogers in London you would have had to be here at the right month in 1940, 1947, 1954 or 1960: not a hope, otherwise. It was known only to his friends, and to his grateful and affectionate students, that he was one of the best painters in England."[10]

Claude experienced the expected mixture of emotions at seeing a retrospective show of his own work ranging over 45 years. He wrote to George Sweet "I am so pleased at your reaction to the show – delighted you seem to like it. I'm not dissatisfied with the way the new paintings look . . . To me the other paintings – well, all the paintings – have the nostalgia of old battlefields, where the tactics were not perhaps very original and the solution often owed more to chance and luck than to design. Looking at them I often wonder how they came out like that."[11]

The exhibition attracted a lot of attention, and was a critical success. After it was over, Claude came down to earth with a bump. He found himself once again without an income of his own, and complained to Susan Jacobsen. "It was a bloody summer and autumn. To begin with my show, which I quite liked and which got good (or ish) reviews but really didn't sell, only two (good sales but nothing in cash) so that without pension or teaching, I got really down. I know I wasn't nearly as badly off as you or some others because Elsie has a little coming in, but it's hateful having nothing myself . . ."[12] He continued to do a lot of painting, however, and Fischer Fine Art took him on their books, giving him one-man shows in 1975 and 1978. It was the first time he had had a dealer since the Leicester Galleries closed, and sales from the gallery relieved some of his financial worries. Also a new patron came into his life in the shape of Priscilla Dugdale, wife of Sir William Dugdale. The Dugdales had seen Claude's retrospective and had bought a *Landscape with Combine Harvester* from Fischer's gallery. Lady Dugdale, who had herself trained as a painter, met Claude by chance at another exhibition, recognised him and introduced herself. They were to become friends, and Claude stayed with them at Blyth Hall, near Birmingham, several times, working on a portrait of Sir William and indulging their mutual passion for football. The portrait of Sir William, however, was nipped in the bud by Claude's sudden visit to hospital in 1976, and, although eventually started, it was never finished.

In the autumn of 1976 Claude was due to go into University College Hospital for a routine check up, and he wrote to Priscilla Dugdale: "Dear Cylla, I'm so sorry but the UCH has written to say that there is a bed awaiting me on Wednesday 6th October, the very day that I am supposed to start on the painting of Bill. As beds are not all that easy to come by and I want to get the thing over, I shall have to go in I'm afraid. What a bore. Well, I shall take some drawing materials and let's hope I get a picture out of it."[13] While he was in hospital he suffered a small coronary. When his brother and sister-in-law went to visit him they found he had telephoned all his girlfriends and that there were always several at his bedside. Claude enjoyed the attention and told Susan Jacobsen "I really am remarkably well and damnedly lucky beyond belief. Who else would have chosen to have whatever sort of coronary I have had on the way down to the cardiac dept of UCH to have a routine test?"

Claude remained in hospital for a while. Hospital life once again wrapped him within its own fascinating world, and when he was allowed home he confided in a letter to Priscilla Dugdale "It's odd being back. Both going in and coming out I seem to experience the kind of dislocation I am told happens on a long flight into another climate. Apart from time (and summer time) there is hospital time - each day stretches out endlessly, but stuffed with incident - not boring. It's a pretty awful confession, I suppose, but in some way Hospital suited me. I was a participant willy-nilly - a 'patient' under 'treatment', temperature, pulse, blood pressure etc recorded regularly throughout the day. My left wrist was held out, my mouth gaped as the nurse hove in sight and everything happened without the necessity of my right hand ceasing work even for a moment . . . I was truly 'participating'. But I could also draw to my heart's content. With a constantly shifting scene, varying in tempo hour by hour - nurses, patients, doctors, students - singly, gathered in groups, active, passive - an endless stimulus to draw. Of course it's nuts but when they told me they were letting me go home . . . I almost felt as I felt once in Florence when I realised three days only were left and I still wanted to see this that and the other at least one more time. Anyway, when today I looked through the hospital drawings I have brought back with me I find there were at least fifty, and some pastels."[14] This letter is reminiscent of his letters to Elsie from Southport Hospital during the war. In both cases he enjoyed having his life taken over for him, relieving him of the responsibility of day-to-day decision-making. Claude enjoyed being mothered.

During this stay in hospital Claude's physical weakness in no way detracted from his mental agility, and he was at his most observant. Not only did he draw and write copiously, but he also kept diary notes about hospital life. "There are moments when, after a silence of long-lasting length a ward comes to life as though a claxon has sounded battle station. The deck clatters and scrapes with hurrying and purpose. Nurses zigzag across and across with the hairline precision of gun teams at the Royal Tournament. Wrists shake down the mercury. Arms extend with unconcious grace to hang up a new flagon on the drip gallows. Heads cock at those strange upsy-down fob watches on which 12 is south, 6 is north. The puff of the blood-pressure bulb is heard."[15]

Probably his medical background enabled him to take an intelligent enjoyment in the scene.

As UCH was directly opposite the Slade it was not difficult for Claude's friends and colleagues to visit him, and they kept him amused. A new friend, the singer Esther Salaman, came regularly, bringing "a delicious air of enjoyment and life when she arrives". Victor Pasmore came, complaining that whenever he saw Claude he always had a leg in the air. Claude was delighted to see him. "Victor came one evening having been to d'Offays's. He brought a breath of air and life into the ward. Somehow without in fact being particularly noisy, he is always surrounded by gusty sounds. He lurches in like a seaman because of his hip: and in appearance and demeanour much reminds me of Captain Hook's appearances when on the pirate ship in *Peter Pan*, the floor seems to rise and fall, green lightning flickers and the air is full of 'belays' and other truisms. What a pleasure it is to be with him."[16]

In the autumn of 1976 Coldstream had an exhibition and Claude expressed some relief that he was unable to see it. "I'm sure it's good but I feel my work is drifting steadily away from the once common (more or less) line and coward that I am, I don't in my present wobbly state want to feel the impact of his immense personality – especially as there is so much I admire and like about his work."[17]

In December 1976 Claude was back in hospital, mainly out of concern about 'a foot that goes dead'. He wrote to Priscilla Dugdale; "I have gone back to UCH, partly because I want my feet mended. Diabetics are susceptible to circulation troubles and it now seems that a small operation will greatly improve my comfort and their mobility. (I dare say a more radical solution would be to replace them with small tank tracks, noisy and bad for the carpet, but admirable out of doors eg for landscape painting). Actually I came in with a second baby heart disturbance – nothing really but I thought it sensible to go and they agreed . . . I am here over Christmas . . . I can't believe a hospital Christmas will have altered much since I used to help Keith, my medical brother, decorate wards at St. Mary's Paddington . . . There has been a great rallying round the Rogers movement, so that not only is Elsie assured of plenty of company, parties, and good times, but she will be ferried here, so that this extraordinary and affectionate old couple will be constantly reunited. We are agreed that we will undoubtedly benefit from the enforced holiday in our long and cherished companionship – forty years, no less, this coming year. It must be some sort of wedding – can't imagine what . . . Of course the other great thing about being here is that I have been able to make more drawings. While at home I started four small hospital paintings from the drawings I had done but as so often happens in my experience found that vital information had been left out. The return here has therefore been a godsend in a way (I am in the same ward and sister put me in the same bed!) and I have been drawing much of the time."[18]

Claude was still in hospital for his 70th birthday on January 24th. Susan Jacobsen took him a bottle of claret and found him painting the dome of University College in snow, surrounded by a most unhygienic mess of paint and turps. He had also turned again to his notes for a book on the Euston Road School, and she helped him with the manuscript.

He kept in touch with Priscilla Dugdale by letter, advising her on her painting and sending her oil pastels and brushes: "Over the years I have accumulated a large collection of brushes, mainly I suppose because I have always treated them well, wiping them and washing them in soap and water . . . as an automatic and rather enjoyable chore. As a result I still have brushes that date from the Slade, one or two given me by Tonks from the art materials left in Sargent's studio when he died, which he told Tonks to distribute to the Slade students of that time. There is a lovely large square sable I treasure which comes from this source. I also have some very long-handled brushes . . . that belonged to Sickert. These brushes are marvellous to use when starting on a biggish painting. Some of my older brushes have worn to my hand over the years, so that, for instance, a large filbert shaped brush has one side almost worn to a straight edge and is used by me instinctively for some crafty arty touches – about as near to the 'secrets of the old masters' as I am ever likely to get."[19] He also admonished Priscilla Dugdale to draw when she was in hospital, writing;

"There are wonderful subjects late at night when the nurses are studying or doing paper work and most of the lights are out. And a subject I'm set on; of a fairly comatose elderly patient watched in a dull way by his loving dull and blank wife. The patient and visitors; I want to do drawings without much thought except as best I can for accuracy, and see what happens . . . My own experience has been that literally ANYTHING is worth drawing provided you have a curiosity about the way it looks and get really absorbed in trying to get it right . . . While I have been here I have been in one of the big wards; and while, by day and night, that offers endless subjects . . . it can be hell at night, rather like a jungle, with strange animal cries . . . Bill Coldstream was in to see me the other day and we had great fun devising a new system of art training. On entry each student spent a term strapped into a bed in the hospital. They were required to draw anything they chose to draw within their field of view. Of course, a number simply could not take it – possibly they burst into tears and broke their pencils. They were then discharged – 'cured' of art, as it were. Those who did interesting drawings, however, became 'out patients' on a three year course. There were various wicked refinements. Once Bill and I set one another going we build up and up, until laughing is painful . . . I should be going home for good this weekend but they haven't made up their mind yet. I'm anxious to be home on my birthday, having absurd superstitions that if I paint on New Year's Day and my birthday, it will be a Good Year . . ."[20]

Unfortunately Claude did not get home until after his birthday. No sooner did he return home than he contracted shingles. He wrote to Kenneth Gribble "Obviously the Lord God has forgotten that I am a nice, little Jewish boy, and thinks I am a beastly Egyptian. Can't you advise the Old Boy that he has made a mistake?"[21] Claude had begun work on two portraits of Dr. Anna Frenkiel, and she was able to dress the sores for him before sittings. He also worked on the portrait of Dr. Questel, the Canadian biochemist, which he had begun on November 27 1976. He managed to overcome some of the pain caused by the shingles when working on this portrait. He noted in his diary "30 × 28 is proving a good size. The lifted head makes the omission of the hands good, since with them, there would have been a tendency to a double focus." On February 27 he finished the portrait. "With about an hour to spare this morning I decided that I could not usefully do more unless I really tried to push the arms very much further and that was impossible and probably undesirable. Anyway, I decided to call it a day and we signed it together. I am pleased at this custom of mine, reserving it on the whole for paintings I've enjoyed and others who have been helpful – Tawney, Haldane, Blackett eg – and for more 'official' portraits where I've felt the people who commission would like the signature of the subject."[22] The following day he worked on one of his two portraits of Esther Salaman. "Yesterday afternoon had a couple of hours on Esther in the full elation of being able to hand over the Questel portrait despite the long train of frustrations that dogged the painting of it. In those two hours with Esther, heaven help me, I aged her painted face by ten years at least."[23] He kept Priscilla Dugdale informed about the progress of this picture. "A painting I very much want to bring to a good conclusion, of the singer Esther Salaman . . . has suddenly taken a turn for the worse, blast it. Esther is wearing a dress (which looks modern) belonging to Yvonne Guilbert (Lautrec's model) – a marvellous delicate lace over a deep sage green underskirt which shows through the cream of the lace as a pattern. She sits well, sometimes learning songs by playing tapes . . ."[24]

Fischer Fine Art planned a new exhibition of Claude's painting for January 1978, and Claude began to work with the show in mind. He managed to paint a number of landscapes at Somerton, and took great pleasure in being in Suffolk again. "The corn is all gone but the mere sight of pale golden meadows streaked with the silver-sided stubble rows . . . interspersed with plough gave me a lift. And the smells. And here it is quiet . . . My legs are not good, not painful or anything but such slowcoaches and running out of muscle . . . alas! I see little chance of marching into the crackling corn again with all my clobber and setting up and staying down a canvas *en face du motif*."[25] Some of the landscapes were done from drawings, as were the series of hospital paintings. In some of the work his handling of the paint changed, becoming thicker and greasier, as if insistently dragged and ground on to the canvas. Both *A Sleeping Patient with his Visitor* and the *Landscape with Stormy Sky*, in which the flat areas of colour shriek rather than sing, have this greasy unattractive look, which nevertheless emphasises the uncompromising nature of the pictures. Other paintings of the same time, such as the *Three Nurses*, are handled with flat matt areas of paint.

Fischer's men collected the paintings for exhibition in January 1978 and Claude contemplated giving a party in his empty studio to celebrate the difference between this birthday and the previous one in hospital, but decided against it, remarking that "a painting room is as private as a bathroom, and generates the same warm, intimate smells, even though they revolve round turps and oil rather than soaps and unguents". The private view at Fischer's went well, and he sat at a table at one end of the gallery while people came up and talked to him. His legs were still not good. "It isn't that my legs hurt, it's just that they don't yet damn feel like legs, if you can imagine it. Cooked asparagus, yes, but much as I adore that, it's no substitute for really up-and-coming leggy LEGS."[26]

During 1978 Claude began work on a portrait of Jean Flood, Principal of Newnham College, Cambridge. Apparently he did not find her an easy subject as the drawings done during four or five sittings did not satisfy him. Finally he decided he must get on and requested a double sitting. Jean Flood wrote "he turned up late and somewhat flustered. He had put the canvas on the roof of his car and without noticing it, it had blown off somewhere en route. He had no hope of retrieving it – at least not in usable condition – so he drew furiously for something like four hours that day. I must have positioned myself badly for by early evening when we finally broke off I was in excruciating pain in my neck and right shoulder. Next day the doctor prescribed morphine which made me frightfully ill. I went into the Evelyn where I underwent a protracted series of tests and the diagnosis was cancer of the spine. This was a false alarm but it took me months to recover and meanwhile Claude died."[27]

Claude himself was very ill; in July 1978 he was back in UCH. Coldstream popped in most days from the Slade to see him, and Claude was still planning new pictures. "Today I told him about wanting to do another patient and visitor painting, not as last time from drawings with elements of 'making up' (which I dislike) in it, but getting a real hospital bed and a man in it, and a woman sitting alongside." Later in the year he was moved to Westminster Hospital to see if something could be done about his legs. His former pupil, Francis Hoyland visited him there, and a doctor friend of Claude's who was also there said he was worried about his 'furry feet'. Hoyland immediately had a vision of Claude as a hobbit which seemed entirely appropriate; but the real meaning of this remark was more tragic. The doctors were considering whether to amputate Claude's feet. They decided against it, and after a long spell in hospital Claude was sent home. Coldstream arranged for the nurse who attended him at home to be paid out of an artist's benevolent fund. Claude was still working spasmodically on the Euston Road manuscript and would ask Susan Jacobsen over to Highgate to help him with it. She recalled that "he still believed he would recover but he was afraid and though he insisted on my reading the 'book' and working on a new first chapter, he really wanted me to hold his hand. I did both. Nobody seemed to mind . . . One day he made me clean a picture that was going a few days later to an exhibition of Hampstead painters at Arkwright Road. It was an early landscape from a window in Taviton Street. He died before the show opened."[28]

Claude died on February 18 1979, with London blanketed by a huge snowfall. He was 72 years old. Elsie was concerned that the Greek amulet against the evil eye that he always wore on a chain around his neck was not on his body when he died. It had probably been removed by a nurse in Westminster Hospital.

There is some evidence that during the last years of his life Claude was returning to his Jewish roots, although his interest was a historical rather than a religious one. His funeral was organised on the principle of 'the way you come in the way you go out' and was therefore a Jewish one, held at Golders Green Crematorium. Many of his friends were surprised to find that Claude was Jewish. They knew that he was not religious, painting having throughout his life taken the place of religious belief. Claude saw this as quite natural, for painting inevitably expressed the valid beliefs of the period. "It has always been connected with universal beliefs such as religion because it is itself religious in kind. When no formulated belief exists to which painting can be tied the painter falls back on his affectionate eye to give it significance."[29]

Claude's funeral was a sad but also a celebratory affair. It seemed that half the art teachers in England were there. William Coldstream gave a wonderful address, tracing Claude's history from the Barrowgate Road days in an amusing way. Afterwards, a great crowd congregated at Claude's studio for a farewell party organised by Crispin, with gastronomic advice from Euan Uglow. Many had benefitted from his generosity and affectionate concern, and it was unlikely that they would come across another with Claude's combination of qualities - kindness and interest in other people, personal humility, genuine human warmth and above all a passionate and enthusiastic dedication to painting.

With Claude's death a link in the chain of British figurative painting was broken. His contribution to British painting, still little acknowledged, was considerable. He believed in the value of tradition, and the insights that an understanding of the history of art can give a painter - insights which can act as a springboard for a painter's pursuit of his own subject. He believed that his job as a painter was to give an unfalsified record of his own interests and experience, and that his expression of these experiences in paint might, in some way, add to and enlighten other human experience. He firmly supported Adrian Stokes' view that "art is the mirror of life, just because the creative process mirrors and concentrates the character common to all the processes of living, namely the identification of inner states with the organisation of the outside world."[30] He felt that a painter creates work out of the material given to him during his lifetime, and that this act of creation is an act of faith and hope for the future. It was therefore important not to cheat on the experience and put forward a false picture. Throughout his life Claude was concerned to give as true and unsentimental a rendering of his subjects as possible. He was straightforward, plain-speaking, but passionate in his love of the visible world and of painting it. His work has a heroic and hard-won integrity. This is his legacy to future generations.

NOTES

1, 2 Claude Rogers Papers, Tate Gallery Archive.
3 Claude Rogers letters, collection Mr George Sweet.
4 Claude Rogers diaries, collection Mr Crispin Rogers.
5 Claude Rogers Papers, Tate Gallery Archive.

6, 7 Claude Rogers letters, collection Mr Crispin Rogers.
8 Vaizey, Marina, *The Financial Times*, April 18 1973.
9 Hilton, Tim, *The Studio* 185, June 3 1971.
10 Russell, John, *The Sunday Times*, April 8 1973.
11 Claude Rogers letters, collection Mr George Sweet.
12 Claude Rogers letters, collection Mrs Susan Jacobsen.
13, 14 Claude Rogers letters, collection Lady Dugdale.
15, 16 Claude Rogers diaries, collection Mr Crispin Rogers.
17 Claude Rogers letters, collection Mrs Susan Jacobsen.
18, 19, 20 Claude Rogers letters, collection Lady Dugdale.
21 Claude Rogers letters, collection Mr Kenneth Gribble.
22, 23 Claude Rogers diaries, op. cit.
24 Claude Rogers letters, collection Lady Dugdale.
25 Claude Rogers letters, collection Mrs Susan Jacobsen.
26 Claude Rogers letters, collection Lady Dugdale.
27 Letter from Dr Jean Flood to Mr Christopher Pemberton, January 10 1992.
28 Interview with Mrs Susan Jacobsen, September 20 1991.
29 Claude Rogers Papers, Tate Gallery Archive.
30 Stokes, Adrian, *Colour and Form*, Faber and Faber, 1937.

LIST OF ILLUSTRATIONS

The artist's pictures are in oil and are in private collections, unless otherwise indicated. Picture measurements are in inches, height before width.

Colour

Between pages 160 and 161

LIST OF ILLUSTRATIONS

Black & white

Between pages 64 and 65

Between pages 128 and 129

INDEX

INDEX

INDEX